GROVE PRESS MODERN DRAMATISTS

Grove Press Modern Dramatists
Series Editors: *Bruce King* and *Adele King*

Published titles

Further titles in preparation

GROVE PRESS MODERN DRAMATISTS

NEW BRITISH POLITICAL DRAMATISTS

John Bull
Lecturer in English
University of Sheffield

Grove Press, Inc., New York

First published in 1984 by
Higher and Further Education Division
MACMILLAN PUBLISHERS LTD
London and Basingstoke

First Grove Press Hardcover Edition 1984
First Printing 1984
ISBN: 0-394-54242-8

First Evergreen Edition 1984
First Printing 1984
ISBN: 0-394-62309-6

Printed in Great Britain

GROVE PRESS, INC., 196 West Houston Street,
New York, NY 10014

5 4 3 2 1

Contents

List of Plates

1. *Christie in Love* by Howard Brenton, Royal Court Theatre Upstairs, 1970. © Donald Cooper.
2. *Measure for Measure* by Howard Brenton and William Shakespeare, Northcott Theatre, Exeter, 1972. © Nicholas Toyne, Topsham, Devon.
3. *The Churchill Play* by Howard Brenton, Nottingham Playhouse, 1972. © Nottingham Playhouse.
4. *The Romans in Britain* by Howard Brenton, National Theatre (Olivier), 1980. © Donald Cooper.
5. *The Genius* by Howard Brenton, Royal Court Theatre, 1983. © Donald Cooper.
6. *Brassneck* by Howard Brenton and David Hare, Nottingham Playhouse, 1973. © Nottingham Playhouse.
7. *Teeth 'n' Smiles* by David Hare, Royal Court Theatre, 1975. © Donald Cooper.
8. *Fanshen* by David Hare, Crucible Theatre, Sheffield, 1975. Reproduced by kind permission of Joint Stock.
9. *Licking Hitler* by David Hare, BBC TV, 1977. © BBC.

10. *Saigon: Year of the Cat* by David Hare, Thames TV, 1983. © Thames TV.
11. *Comedians* by Trevor Griffiths, Old Vic, 1975. © Donald Cooper.
12. *Comedians*, Old Vic, 1975. © Donald Cooper.
13. *Through the Night* by Trevor Griffiths, BBC TV, 1975. © BBC.
14. *Oi! for England* by Trevor Griffiths, Central TV, April 1982. © Central Independent Television.
15. *Destiny* by David Edgar, BBC TV, December 1977. © BBC.
16. *The Jail Diary of Albie Sachs* by David Edgar, RSC Warehouse, 1978. © Donald Cooper.
17. *Mary Barnes* by David Edgar, Royal Court Theatre, 1978. © Donald Cooper.

Acknowledgements

In general terms I am grateful to an entire generation of writers and theatre workers. And, in particular, I should like to record my thanks to Howard Brenton, not least for his willingness to discuss at length the problems faced by the modern political theatre; the University of Sheffield for the research-grant which made the writing of this book possible; the staff of the University of Sheffield Library; Carole Ebsworth for her consistently penetrating analysis of my text; Philip Roberts; Anne Monaghan, by way of apology for the article that just kept growing, and which she never received; Carol Gillespie for typing the manuscript; the Sheffield students who have worked with me on many of the plays discussed; and F. Ido for constant encouragement.

Editors' Preface

The *Grove Press Modern Dramatists* is an international series of introductions to major and significant nineteenth and twentieth century dramatists, movements and new forms of drama in Europe, Great Britain, America and new nations such as Nigeria and Trinidad. Besides new studies of great and influential dramatists of the past, the series includes volumes on contemporary authors, recent trends in the theatre and on many dramatists, such as writers of farce, who have created theatre 'classics' while being neglected by literary criticism. The volumes in the series devoted to individual dramatists include a biography, a survey of the plays, and detailed analysis of the most significant plays, along with discussion, where relevant, of the political, social, historical and theatrical context. The authors of the volumes, who are involved with theatre as playwrights, directors, actors, teachers and critics, are concerned with the plays as theatre and discuss such matters as performance, character interpretation and staging, along with themes and contexts.

BRUCE KING

ADELE KING

1968–83: A History

1968

Jan — Tet offensive by Viet Cong.

Feb — Following mass exodus into Britain of expelled Kenyan Asians, Bill restricting entry passed.

Mar — Mass demonstration in support of Viet Cong outside American Embassy, in Grosvenor Square.

Lyndon Johnson decides not to restand as US President.

Apr — Assassination of Martin Luther King.

Enoch Powell's 'rivers of blood' speech.

Race Relations Bill receives the Royal Assent.

Rudi Dutschke shot during demonstration in West Berlin.

May — Student demonstrations and occupations in France, later accompanied by general strike and factory-occupations. France briefly brought to a halt.

Strikes and demonstrations in universities and colleges throughout Western Europe.

June   Assassination of Robert Kennedy.

Aug   Unemployment at 560,731.

Mayor Daley's troops riot outside Democratic Convention in Chicago.

Russian troops invade Czechoslovakia.

Oct   Prime Minister Harold Wilson and Ian Smith in talks about Rhodesia on HMS *Fearless*.

Queen's plans to visit Argentina cancelled as a result of continuing dispute over sovereignty of the Falkland Islands.

Nov   Richard Nixon elected US President.

1969

Apr   Bernadette Devlin elected MP for Mid-Ulster.

May   100,000 workers on strike on May Day against proposed but subsequently abandoned proposals on trade-union 'reform'.

Aug   British troops into Northern Ireland.

Oct   Nationwide moratorium demonstrations in US against continuation of Vietnam War.

1970

Jan   End of Nigerian Civil War.

Mar   Three 'weathermen' terrorists blown up by own bomb in New York.

Apr   US troops into Cambodia.

May   Six students killed by State Troopers at Jackson State and Kent State Universities, in aftermath of anti-war demonstrations.

June   Successful mass campaign against projected South African cricket-tour of England.

Wilson's Labour government defeated by

Conservatives and Edward Heath becomes Prime Minister.

Sep   Popular Front for the Liberation of Palestine hijacks three aircraft in Europe.

Salvador Allende of Chile becomes the first elected president of a Marxist government.

Oct   Pierre Laporte, Quebec Minister of Labour, kidnapped and killed by 'Quebec Liberation Front'.

Dec   Bread riots in Poland, followed by resignation of Communist Party Secretary Gomulka.

1971

Jan   Nationwide demonstrations against Industrial Relations Bill.

'Angry Brigade' bomb house of Secretary of State for Employment, Robert Carr.

Feb   Collapse of Rolls-Royce Ltd.

June   Education Minister, Margaret Thatcher, ends free milk in schools.

'Work-in' at Upper Clyde Shipyard.

Aug   Introduction of internment without trial in Northern Ireland.

Industrial Relations Bill receives the Royal Assent.

1972

Jan   Unemployment over 1 million.

Strike of Britain's 280,000 miners, resulting in electricity-cuts.

13 people killed in 'Bloody Sunday' Massacre at Londonderry, Northern Ireland.

Feb   British Embassy burnt down in Dublin.

Miners' strike ends in victory for miners.

	IRA bomb kills seven people at Parachute Officers' Mess at Aldershot.
Mar	British government introduces direct rule for Northern Ireland.
June	The Watergate break-in.
	The 'Pentonville Five' imprisoned for defying the Industrial Relations Bill, but subsequently released after trade-union agitation.
July	Major bombing-campaign by IRA in Belfast, followed by British Army's 'Operation Motorman' against 'no-go' areas.
Aug	Idi Amin of Uganda announces expulsion of Ugandan Asians.
Sep	Eleven Israeli athletes killed by pro-Palestinian terrorists at Munich Olympics.
Dec	Longest criminal trial in British history ends in ten-year sentences for eight members of the 'Angry Brigade'.

1973

Jan	Britain joins EEC.
Mar	IRA bombs at the Old Bailey in London.
Sep	President Allende removed and killed after military coup in Chile.
Dec	Government declares 'state of emergency' during second miners' strike. Introduction of the 'three-day week' to conserve energy-supplies.

1974

| Feb | Heath calls General Election over the 'state of emergency', and loses to the Labour Party, which forms a 'minority' government under Wilson. |

Apr   End of Fascist rule in Portugal.
May–Dec   IRA bomb-campaign in England, culminating
           in the death of twenty-one people in Birming-
           ham explosion.
July   The Colonels' 'Junta' ousted in Greece.
Aug   Nixon resigns in aftermath of Watergate
           cover-up.
Oct   General Election produces working majority
           for Labour Party under Wilson.
Nov   General Franco dies in Spain.
           Revolutionary government takes power in
           Angola.

1975
Feb   Heath defeated by Margaret Thatcher for
           leadership of Conservative Party.
Apr   Communist victory in Vietnam and Cam-
           bodia.
May   Trial of Baader–Meinhof terrorists in Stutt-
           gart, West Germany.
           Referendum on Britain's continuing member-
           ship of the EEC results in a majority in favour.
July   Wilson introduces strict £6 per week limit on
           wage-rises.

1976
Feb–June   IRA bomb-campaign in England.
Mar   Wilson resigns as Prime Minister and is
           replaced by James Callaghan.
June   Soweto massacre in South Africa.
Aug   Riots at Notting Hill Festival in London.
Sep   Chairman Mao dies.
Oct   'Gang of Four' arrested in China.

1977

Jan Charter 77, on human rights, published by Czech dissidents.

Mar Formation of Lib–Lab Pact.

June Mass picketing of Grunwick film-processing plant, in support of low-paid workers, chiefly immigrants.

Sep Steve Biko dies in detention in South Africa.

Nov Strike by fire-brigade workers. Army mans fire-services.

1978

Mar Aldo Moro, ex-Prime Minister of Italy, abducted and killed by 'Red Brigade'.

May Liberals announce withdrawal from Lib–Lab Pact at end of parliamentary session.

Oct Labour Party Conference rejects all policies of wage-restraint.

Dec Vietnamese troops invade Kampuchea.

1979

Jan Co-ordinated strikes by British Public Service workers results in the 'Winter of Discontent'. $1\frac{1}{2}$ million public-service workers on twenty-four hour strike.

Feb Shah of Iran deposed.

Apr Near nuclear disaster at Three Mile Island, Pennsylvania.
Blair Peach dies in demonstration against the National Front in London.

May General Election results in Conservative victory, Margaret Thatcher becoming the first woman prime minister.

Aug Lord Mountbatten killed by the IRA.

Nov	Decision taken by Conservative government to deploy 'Cruise' missiles in Britain.
Dec	Zimbabwe National Front agrees to accept arrangements for cease-fire in Rhodesian war.
	Russian troops invade Afghanistan.

1980

Jan–Mar	Strike of British Steel workers.
Apr	Independence for Zimbabwe.
	Iranian Embassy siege in London.
May	Trade-union Day of Action against government's economic and industrial-relations policies.
July	US boycotts Moscow Olympics in protest against Russian invasion of Afghanistan.
Aug	Unemployment tops 2 million for first time since 1935.
	Formation of the independent trade-union, Solidarity, in Poland, in the aftermath of the Gdansk shipyard strikes.
Sep	Labour Party Conference votes for unilateral nuclear disarmament.
Oct	Callaghan resigns as Labour leader.
Nov	Ronald Reagan elected as US President.
	Michael Foot elected as leader of the Labour Party.

1981

Mar	Social Democratic Party formed in Britain, under the leadership of the 'Gang of Four', right-wing ex-Labour Party MPs.
Apr	Riots in Brixton, South London.
	Hunger strikes by IRA 'H' Block prisoners in Maze Prison, near Belfast. One of the strikers,

	Bobby Sands, elected MP for Fermanagh and South Tyrone.
May	Bobby Sands dies.
July	Urban riots in Toxteth and Moss Side, followed by so-called 'copy-cat' riots on a smaller scale in other English cities.
Oct	British Nationality Bill receives the Royal Assent.
Dec	Imposition of martial law in Poland. Unemployment reaches 3 million.

1982

Apr	Argentinian invasion of Falkland Islands. British task-force removes the invaders to the accompaniment of a great deal of populist jingoism in Britain.
June	Israel invades Lebanon.
Sep	Israeli-inspired massacre in Lebanese refugee-camps. Labour Party Conference votes to expel members of Militant Tendency.

1983

June	Thatcher wins re-election with continuation of monetarist programme. Foot resigns as leader of the Labour Party.
Sep	Neil Kinnock elected as leader of the Labour Party.
Oct	Over 200 members of US and French 'peace-keeping' force in Beirut killed by pro-Palestinian terrorists in bomb attack. Continuing protests against nuclear weapons in Britain, principally at the Women's Peace Camp at Greenham Common airforce base,

culminate in the largest ever anti-nuclear demonstration in London. Huge demonstrations also in West Germany, Italy, Austria, Sweden and Spain.

Marplan survey reports a majority of British people opposed to deployment of Cruise and Pershing missiles.

US troops invade Grenada.

In first general election for ten years, the Radical Party successful in Argentina.

Nov   First Cruise missiles arrive at Greenham Common.

US 'peace-keeping' troops in Lebanon in virtual war with Syria.

Reagan remains firm in his intent to stand for re-election as US President.

What does not change/is the will to change

For Carole

1
1968 and All That: Agit-Prop or 'Avant-Garde'

There's a war being waged right now, right here this
minute for control over people's perception of the last
twenty years. History is being rewritten.
(Peter Flannery, *Our Friends in the North*, 1982)

In the late 1960s a number of quite startling changes
occurred in British theatre, changes which for the first time
challenged the very basis of theatrical organisation, and
heralded the beginning of the most consistently exciting
decade of drama of the entire century. From the bruised
dreams of the sixties counter-culture, a new generation of
writers emerged, frequently and violently in disagreement
about the forms and aims of the new drama, but in
agreement on one thing, the desire to create a drama that
would stand in the vanguard of political and social change.
From the outset, the predominant tone was of provocative
confrontation, aimed as much at the values of the 'alternative' society as of the establishment it opposed. Their plays
reflected a profound disquiet about the current state of the

1

nation, and, although these playwrights occupied a variety of political positions, their political ideals were well to the left of the Labour Party and indeed quite outside the terms of reference of conventional Parliamentary 'democracy'.

Like the previous dramatic revival of 1956–60, the new drama developed as a part of what can easily be seen as a period of cultural crisis; but, unlike it, the challenge to mainstream theatre was far more widespread, far more sustained. Where the major new writing of 1956–60 had been largely contained by two London theatres, the Royal Court and the Theatre Royal (Stratford East), the work of such writers as Howard Brenton, David Hare, Snoo Wilson, Trevor Griffiths, Heathcote Williams and David Edgar was rapidly disseminated the length and breadth of the country. In part, this was because of the potential immediacy of the new drama – able to present at very short notice an enactment of a particular situation to an identifiable audience – and in part because of its mobility – no longer reliant on conventional theatrical venues, elaborate and costly sets, detailed itineraries, and settled companies.

Many of the new companies emerged from specific political activity, as did many of the playwrights. Agit-Prop's first production, *The Little Artist* (1968), was a response to the student occupation of Hornsey Art College, whilst David Edgar's early work stemmed from his involvement with student politics at Bradford in the same year. More often than not, the political intent of avowedly agit-prop groups to play to working-class audiences notwithstanding, writers, cast and audience would be drawn from an amalgam of university and college students and an increasingly defined mass of disaffected 'counter-culturists'. Traditional arenas were passed over in favour of the new 'arts labs', community centres, working-men's clubs, university and college studios; anywhere which

facilitated a readily accessible and, above all, cheap performance, outside what were regarded as the institutions of
official cultural excellence. The abolition of theatre-
censorship in 1968, in itself a product of the struggles of the
previous generation of writers – and in particular, in their
very different ways, of Bond and Orton – as well as the
general shift in the cultural climate, helped facilitate this
unorganised mobility, as did the enormous expansion in the
number of groups of young writers and actors working
together to supply the demand.

This was not the only difference, however. With the
exception of Arden, the new writers of the 1956–60
generation, and in particular Wesker and Osborne, offered
no real threat to the traditional format of the well-made
play. Their political protest was contained within existing
theatrical models. Their characters may have proclaimed a
refreshingly abrasive form of radicalism at the audience –
although Osborne's increasingly less so – but they did so in
plays which were remarkably unthreatening in format.

The class of '68 was a very different proposition, and
their debate, within a self-consciously *avant-garde*
framework, about the nature and aims of theatre will
occupy much space in what follows. This has implications
both for the kinds of drama produced, and for the way in
which the writers I shall be considering may be defined as
political.

The roots of the problem lay initially in the attempt to
separate a new political theatre from the mainstream, but
the confusions became more intense during the seventies as
the new drama was, according to your point of view,
increasingly taken over by the mainstream, or, by its
intrusion into the repertoires of the National Theatre, the
Royal Shakespeare Company, the provincial theatres, and
even to some extent the West End, itself able to subvert the

expectations of that mainstream. Jonathan Hammond is not untypical in his dismissal of the political nature of the new drama: 'Fringe theatre belongs to an "alternative" culture rather than to a revolutionary culture; it is directed towards the elitist intellectual, with some specialised information, rather than the working-class fighting capitalism and bureaucracy.'[1]

Such a view would find ready agreement with many of the writers in the period under review, and yet it offers a rather limiting and problematic definition of what might be meant by 'political'. As we shall see, a central dilemma of the new drama was that it flourished not in spite of a central contradiction, but because of it. Alain Touraine's assessment of the events in France in 1968 – 'the encounter between a revolutionary movement and a non-revolutionary situation'[2] – can equally be applied to the plays that were to a considerable extent prompted by the events of that year. The tension between the *avant-garde* stance of much of the drama and the realities of political life did much to produce the blend of optimistic fervour and cynical pessimism that is, in essence, the political sub-text of so many of the plays. If they offer what is seen by critics as confusion, they are at the very least reflecting what has proved to be a very confused situation. But none of the writers I shall be discussing is unaware of the problems, and heated debate continues to the present day.

It is not my intention to offer anything like a complete coverage of the work of all these new writers. Rather I have chosen to write about just four – Howard Brenton, David Hare, Trevor Griffiths and David Edgar. This narrowing of the field will allow a better coverage of what are for me the most important playwrights of their generation, and will in addition go some way to demonstrating the different strategies available in political theatre. Of the playwrights omitted my chief regret is that there is insufficient space to give the work of John McGrath its due credit. Because so much of his best work has been performed in Scotland – raising different though related issues – and because my overall commitment has been to the plays in performance, the omission was in the end inevitable. Of the generation that preceded them, consideration should ideally also have been given to Arden – who with Margaretta D'Arcy has been almost alone in tackling the problems in Ireland head-on – and to Bond. Fortunately they have received attention elsewhere in this series. However, it is worth noting in passing that mention of Bond points to a key distinction. Whereas Bond's work has become increasingly located within a more broadly European tradition, the work of the writers I shall be considering has remained to a peculiar and important extent British in its perspectives. I want to start with some explanation of why this should be.

Broadly, the 1956–60 revival can be associated with the reaction of a young radical intelligentsia to the post-Suez years of Tory rule, the Macmillan years of prosperity, and with the beginnings of a non-affiliated Left, the activities of which are best seen in the early period of CND and the 'Committee of 100'. After the collapse of CND as a unifying left grouping, as a result of its failure to develop other than as an umbrella pressure-group, and more specifically after Gaitskell's betrayal of the Labour Party's commitment to unilateral disarmament, there had been little radical cohesion until the Wilson election campaign of 1964. Fired with recent memories of the Kennedy Administration, and with the 'white heat of technology' issuing from his very nostrils, Wilson had seemed to offer to the majority of left activists the last chance, within a broadly Parliamentary framework, of instituting a full programme of socialist change as initiated by the 1945 administration.

However, the failure of the Wilson government to pay even lip-service to radical reform, let alone socialist change, slowly brought about a redefinition of political struggle on the left. As early as 1965, the first of the new generation of agit-prop theatre groups, CAST, was formed in response to its members' disillusionment with the government. At this time they were alone; by 1978, there were 'at least 18 full-time subsidised socialist groups, in addition to perhaps as many unsubsidised or local groups who propagate revolutionary socialist ideas'.[3]

The terms of this redefinition are conveniently summarised in *The New Left May Day Manifesto* of 1967, edited by Stuart Hall, Edward Thompson and Raymond Williams, three men whose early work on working-class history and culture coincides with that of the Arden–Wesker generation, and whose influence was to continue to be felt in the work of the new playwrights. Its importance derives from its articulation of a non-controversial rejection of the parliamentary road to socialism.

The years of radical campaigning, from Suez through Aldermaston to the early sixties, made connections that still hold, groups that still function. . . . And it seemed, for a time, that all this effort was coming together, into a new move forward. While the Tory illusion disintegrated, the Labour Party, under the leadership of Harold Wilson, caught up for a while, the sense of movement, the practical urgency of a change of direction. . . . After those years of shared effort, we are all, who worked for the Labour Party, in a new situation. For the sense of failure – a new kind of failure, in apparent victory – is implacably there, in every part of the Left.[4]

The importance of this 'sense of failure' must not be

overlooked, and it is mirrored in many of the plays considered in this book. The years 1945 and 1964 are frequently invoked in what was to become a central preoccupation of the new drama, a critical exploration of English radical history. Griffiths is unusual in that he has extended the re-examination back to the 1920s and the General Strike (*All Good Men*, 1974), and beyond that to the more properly Marxist beginnings of the British Labour movement (*Occupations*, 1971, and *Absolute Beginners*, 1974), though McGrath has attempted a similar course in his Scottish plays (most notably in *The Game's a Bogey*, 1974).

Generally the preoccupation has been with post-war England. Hare's *The Great Exhibition* traces the decline of a Labour MP newly elected in the Wilson years, and *Plenty* takes us from the 1939–45 war, through the Festival of Britain and Suez, stopping in 1962, showing the hopes for the imminent Labour Administration as already undermined. Brenton and Hare's *Brassneck* charts the rise of the corrupt Bagley family from 1945 to the last years of the sixties, whilst Edgar's *Destiny* opens in a newly independent India in 1947, and concludes with an election campaign in the mid seventies. The first new play in the Barbican complex, Peter Flannery's *Our Friends in the North*, makes the point well. Owing much to the thematic structure of *Brassneck*, it serves almost as an anthology play. It opens with the Wilson campaign, then weaves a complicated thread through local and national government wheeler-dealing, police corruption, the pornography trade, the last years of imperialism in Rhodesia, and the failure of the Labour Party to effect change, culminating in the guns and bombs of the urban guerrilla. What all these plays have in common is a presentation of public life as a spectacle of corruption producing cynicism and despair in the individual who attempts to confront it. They share with the *Manifesto* an uncompromising rejection of the parliamentary system as one well able 'to absorb or deflect new kinds of demands', and the sense of a need for the formation of an extra-parliamentary movement, though they are rarely able to articulate what form it might take. 'What we must build beyond this is a new kind of movement, which is defined by the fact that it cannot defeat it by electoral action alone.'[5]

There is, however, another way of expressing the importance of the period 1945–63. It is not just the immediate historical period from which a playwright might naturally draw his material. It is precisely the lifetime of the playwrights concerned, all of whom were born at the beginning of the period and reached the possibility of direct political activity at about the time Wilson was peddling his wares. So, it is to be expected, from the first generation of writers to have been brought up in the wake of the post-1945 socialist programme, and in particular with the hope offered by the Welfare State and the Education Act – promising, but not properly delivering, a society in which social and medical care, and higher education, would be available to all – that the experience was necessarily a personally felt one. Not that we are here dealing with the real rejects of the system. All four of the playwrights in this book, and virtually all of their fellows, were university-educated, the intended elite on which Wilson's new social democratic society would be founded. And it was to this generation above all, the young radical intelligentsia, rather than the organised Labour movement, that *The New Left May Day Manifesto* was addressing itself.

What is now most interesting about the *Manifesto* – which was signed by just one playwright, Wesker – is how moderate it appears in its demands, how temperate in its

8

language. Even as it was published, it had been outflanked by the street rhetoric of the new New Left, and certainly as the barricades went up in Paris one year later, on the night of 10 May, it had become little more than an historical curiosity. Already opposition to the American presence in Vietnam – the specific catalyst to the student revolt in France that dates from 22 March at Nanterre – was unifying the non-affiliated Left in a manner that far exceeded the heady days of CND, both in numbers and in militancy; and, furthermore, the Russian invasion of Czechoslovakia was about finally to remove what small vestiges of credibility remained after 1956, and Hungary, for the Communist Party as a left alternative in Britain. However, the very ordinariness, the typicality of the *Manifesto*, should alert us to the dangers of placing an undue importance on the strictly *political* significance of 1968 in shaping the new drama. It was primarily the experience of the immediate past and its lessons of failure and compromise – and beyond that the rediscovery of an earlier socialist history, about which Edward Thompson and Raymond Williams had done most to reopen debate – that shaped the political consciousness of the new playwrights. Contemporary events elsewhere were to provide the cutting edge.

Now, none of this is to deny the importance of the events of 1968, but rather to suggest a need for a redefinition of that importance. When Catherine Itzen proclaims, in a manner that is typical of the reductionist logic of many recent critics, 'rarely can one year be singled out as an isolated turning point, but in the case of 1968 so many events coincided on a global scale that it clearly marked the end of an era in an historically unprecedented fashion, and the beginning of a period of equally unprecedented con-sciousness and activism',[6] it is difficult to believe that she is prefacing a book on British drama. The evidence is simply not there to sustain the claim. For the playwrights were rarely interested in the 'global scale' – certainly not in the years immediately following – and a closer look at her particular globe produces a very different picture. The Tet offensive may have signalled the end of the American adventure in Vietnam, but meanwhile, in the States, Mayor Daley's police were cracking skulls outside the Democratic Convention in Chicago; Nixon was getting himself elected with something to spare, and the Chicago conspiracy trials and Watergate were waiting in the wings. In Europe, as in America, militant adventurism was rapidly dwindling into individual acts of terrorism, with the revolution moving from the streets to the attic and the cellar. At home, Bloody Sunday and the escalation of armed conflict in Northern Ireland was around the corner, and the decade ended with the re-election of a Conservative administration. The 'swinging sixties' went out with more than a suspicion of a whimper. The new drama was more a product of this despair than the 'unprecedented political consciousness and activism' that Itzen conjures up.

The globe needs to be broken down. It is on France that attention should be focused – in part because of its geographical proximity, but principally because of the very nature of the events in 1968. What happened there that spring is historically without precedent – the creation of a potentially revolutionary situation within the context of a stable and securely affluent society. It was a situation that was fermented and stage-managed not by the traditional organs of political conflict – the unions and political organisations of the working-class – but by a young, radical and alienated intelligentsia. A movement that started in a university in the suburbs of Paris was briefly to bring France to a standstill, and to threaten even the Gaullist regime, as serious attempts were made to construct a revolutionary counter-society that would bypass the machinery of the modern state. There was, in reality, never the remotest possibility that anything like a genuinely revolutionary movement would be created on a mass scale. Although tentative moves were made towards the formation of an alliance between the students and the workers, the 'revolution' remained to the end what it had always been, the property of a political *avant-garde* as suspicious of the organisations of labour as they were of those of government. Specifically, it was the determination of the French Communist Party, and the Communist union, the Confédération Générale du Travail, to deal with the Government along the traditional lines of increased money and decreased working hours, together with the power-seeking prevarications of Mitterand's Socialist Alliance, the Fédération de la Gauche Démocratique et Socialiste, that ruled out the possibility of real political change; but the debacle was no accident.

The struggle began over a number of specific university-oriented issues, and, although the occupations spread rapidly from educational to industrial sites, the link between the two areas was never properly made. Nor could it be, for there was at heart a fundamental split. The traditional organised Left still thought and acted in accordance with a vitiated version of Marxist analysis, based on the primacy of class-struggle – a struggle which in France as in England had become institutionalised into little more than an annual squabble about pay-rises. The revolutionary *avant-garde* had already moved beyond this position, and were increasingly to do so as events developed and they discovered just how far their critique could be pushed. They sought nothing less than a redefinition of political struggle as it affected the individual in his everyday life. Factional dispute was, as always, rife, but the dominant analysis, and that which found its way most forcibly back across the Channel, was that of the Situationists, whose earlier strategic penetrations – in particular at Strasbourg University in 1966[7] – were in effect a preview for the events of 1968.

> They developed a theory based on an exhaustive theory of the conditions of life inherent in overdeveloped capitalism – the forced consumption of commodities produced in abundance, the reduction of life to a spectacle, the stupefactions of urbanism and ideology, the hegemony of the bureaucrats, the alienation of labour. These theorists sought to break the stranglehold of modern life through the abolition of the class society, of the commodity production system and of wage labour, and through the transcendence of art and culture by their absorption into everyday life.[8]

This extension into a total cultural context of what had become an ever-narrowing sense of political struggle is crucial, and helps to explain both the dynamism of the May movement and the inability of the traditional Left to come to terms with it. The Situationists saw the conventional apprehension of political struggle as an essential part of the process of fragmentation and alienation which it ought to have been opposing. A negotiation about terms and conditions did nothing to alter the fundamental relationships of people in society. Furthermore, to posit a division between work and leisure activity was to fail to realise that they are both a part of the same spectacle of consumption. As a Situationist tract put it,

don't say	*say instead*
work	forced labour
art	how much does it cost?[9]

David Edgar summarises the distinction well: 'Revolutionary politics was seen as being much less about the organisation of the working class at the point of production, and much more about the disruption of bourgeois ideology at the point of consumption.'[10] The posters and graffiti that covered Paris were rarely direct calls to political action. They were imaginative confrontations to the entire machinery of state, calling upon the individual to smash through the screen of public life. 'Take your desires as your reality', 'under the cobble-stones is the beach': no political programme is advanced, indeed the suggestion was always that programmes of any sort were to be opposed. Sylvia Harvey:

> These aggressive but non-programmatic slogans reflect both the strengths and the weaknesses of the May movement: both its searching for a more adequate and more radical analysis of the reality of daily life under technocratic capitalism, and its idealistic, often anarchistic, utopianism.[11]

Viewed in this way, it is not difficult to start conceiving of the May revolt as a piece of extended street theatre – a street theatre which invited participants to play out their contradictions in the world, and which denies any distinction between art and reality. When the French National Theatre, the Odéon, was occupied, the costume-store was immediately looted, and for several weeks the occupation was guarded by figures in chain mail. And, if the debates inside provided more prosaic fare than was customary, certainly meetings at the Sorbonne were rarely far from the theatrical as rival factions sought to gain control of the communications system. That summer the Cannes Film Festival was disrupted by demonstrators, and everywhere

13

there was evidence of political warfare on a specifically cultural front.

It is this sense that Howard Brenton reacted to the events.

> May 1968 was crucial. It was a great watershed and directly affected me. A lot of the ideas in *Magnificence* came straight out of the writing of that time in Paris, and the idea of official life being like a screen. . . . May 68 disinherited my generation in two ways. First it destroyed any remaining affection for official culture. The situationists showed how all of them, the dead greats, are corpses on our backs – Goethe, Beethoven – how gigantic the fraud is. But it also, secondly, destroyed the notions of personal freedom, anarchist political action. And it failed. It was defeated. A generation dreaming of a beautiful utopia was kicked – kicked awake and not dead. I've got to believe not kicked dead. May 68 gave me a desperation I still have.[12]

The terms of reference here are entirely cultural, the values of the establishment set against those of the counter-culture. The emphasis is removed from the traditonal left arena of class-conflict and mass struggle, and placed instead on the 'consumption of values', both of the establishment and of the 'alternative society'. For Brenton, the significance of France in 1968 was not that it heralded a new revolutionary dawn – indeed quite the reverse. A new generation of young radicals were 'kicked awake', made to see behind the broken screen of the grotesque spectacle that is public life.

As Brenton indicates, it was in *Magnificence* (1973) that he gave fullest articulation to his experiences of 1968. The play marked a distinct break in his writing, moving him for the first time directly into a consideration of contemporary political life. However, it is a consideration that leaves completely out of account conventional left politics. The play centres on the smashed dreams of the alternative culture, concentrating in particular on the figure of Jed, the romantic terrorist figure. Although the play ends with Jed dead as a result of a pathetic bombing of a pathetic Cabinet minister, condemned by his more orthodoxly active friend, Will, for the senselessness of his violence, it is Jed's rhetoric, his Situationist-inspired analysis, which gives the play its strength. Seeing it in 1973, there was the sense that Brenton was being pulled in two directions at once. Cliff attacks Jed for his lack of participation in the larger struggle: 'There's only one way, time was you knew it, Jed. Work, corny work, with and for the people. Politicizing them and learning from them, everyone of them. . . . You know you are, right now there. . . . A nothing. Zero. A crank with a tin box of bangs.'

Jed responds with what is one of the most vivid speeches of the play:

Went to see a terrible film once. Carpet-baggers. With Carole Baker. Right load of old tat, going on up there on the big silver screen. Boring, glossy tat, untouchable being on the silver screen. And there was this drunk in the front row. With a bottle of ruby wine. And did he take exception to the film, he roared and screamed. Miss Baker above all came in for abuse. Something about her got right up his nose. So far up, that he was moved to chuck his bottle of ruby wine right through Miss Baker's left tit. The left tit moved on in an instant, of course. But for the rest of the film, there was that bottle shaped hole. Clung. One blemish on the screen. But somehow you couldn't watch the film from then. And so thinks. . . .

(*With a bow.*) The poor bomber. Bomb 'em. Again and again. Right through their silver screen. Disrupt the spectacle. The obscene parade, bring it to a halt! Scatter the dolly girls, let advertisements bleed. . . . Bomb 'em, again and again! Murderous display. An entertainment for the oppressed, so they may dance a little, take a little warmth from the sight, eh? (*He laughs.*) Go down into the mire eh? Embrace the butcher eh? Think on't.

What is interesting about this speech is that it occurs in a play first performed some five years after 1968, in a context which calls its terms of reference into question, however accurately it describes Brenton's dramatic techniques in the earlier plays. 'Petrol Bombs through the proscenium arch', as he depicted it. In *Fruit*, written in response to Heath's electoral success with the Conservative Party in 1970, there is nothing to qualify the argument of the bomber, and the play ends, after a long account of class struggle as the basis of political change, with a petrol bomb thrown against the wings of the stage.

This rejection of the primacy of class-struggle as the basis of revolutionary change was exemplified most obviously in the work of Portable Theatre, founded jointly by David Hare and Tony Bicat in 1968, and soon joined by Brenton. It was for Portable that *Fruit* was written. Their format was simple, a small 'mobile group equipped to carry a handful of harsh, explosive shows to England's campuses, post-68 Arts Labs, and even theatres, in a calculated series of three monthly cycles'.[13] The shows were done on a shoe-string and were, as the name suggests, readily 'portable'. They eschewed both the naturalistic tradition of social drama which had dominated left-wing theatre since the mid fifties, and the dialectical Brechtian model, in favour of a series of assault courses in which the audience was frequently as much the target as the ostensible subject-matter. The dominant image was of an England in the final decadent stages of decline, and on the eve of cataclysmic, but undefined, change, 'of tightly knit social institutions in extreme decay'.[14] Although many of the plays included prophetic, usually terrifying, visions of the immediate future, the stress was always less on any discussion of change than on the presentation, almost the celebration, of the decay. The plays were bizarre, surreal manifestations of late-sixties sub-culture, and their aim was to disturb, to shock. The vision of 1984 articulated by the fanatical and outmoded villain, Hepple, at the end of *Revenge* (1969) – the play that Brenton had on at the Royal Court's Theatre Upstairs at the time of his first commission for Portable – is typical:

Funny. My dreams of a criminal England, it's all come true with the 1980s. The casino towns, the brothel villages, the cities red with blood and pleasure. Public life the turn of a card, the fall of a dice. The whole country on the fiddle, the gamble, the open snatch, the bit on the side. From Lands End to John O'Groats, the whole of England's one giant pinball table. The ball running wild, Glasgow, Birmingham, Leeds, Coventry, London, Brighton, wonderful. (II xii)

Now, political theatre as thus conceived is clearly very different from that as understood by agit-prop groups such as CAST, Agit-Prop (later Red Ladder), or 7:84; and this difference is crucial, helping to explain how Brenton could finish up writing for a National Theatre that John McGrath, of 7:84, has said he 'would run about twenty-five miles from', were he to be offered a commission.[15] From the outset, Brenton's work was more concerned with theatrical potential than with the minutiae of political debate. Indeed, it was just this tension which split Brighton Combination, the group that Brenton was working with before he joined Portable.

> There was this idea that theatre should be communicative work, socially and politically active. There was the idea of very aggressive theatrical experiment. And there was always that tension in the Combination – which has been resolved now that they are at Deptford – between theatre and community work. They really are a socially active group now, not a theatre. I went the theatre way.[16]

The distinction between the traditional Marxist analysis based on class struggle – the basic model for all agit-prop theatre in this period – and the French Situationist-influenced attack on the spectacle of consumption is in practice not a simple one. Styles and techniques were there to be begged and borrowed in the subsequent years, but it did mean from the beginning that there was a conscious attempt to reach two theoretically different kinds of audience. Brenton is clear on this distinction:

> We have a very bad record with working class audiences – we've hardly played to any. Our weapon has always been a middle-class, middle-brow weapon really. But we used to have a percentage of what we called Agro dates. The Carnegie Hall, Warrington springs to mind as an example. You knew from the start you were doomed. All you could hope to do was spread the maximum bad vibrations amongst the audience.[17]

In contrast, David Edgar with General Will, and John

McGrath with 7:84, consciously turned away from both traditional and alternative theatrical venues, seeking audiences within the working class whose history and struggles form the substance of their plays. In the case of Edgar, this was initially almost more by accident than design, although he has subsequently worked more deliberately in this direction; but for McGrath the decision was quite carefully taken. McGrath admits to an excitement at the potential of the large subsidised theatres, but sees this as irrelevant to the audiences he wishes to reach. 'Well really, I just don't know about National Theatre audiences. . . . I'd rather have a bad night in Bootle. You get more from it if somebody's going to come up at the end and say, do you know what's happening in Bootle?'[18]

But the starting-point for both Edgar and McGrath is much the same as for Brenton and Hare. Edgar's political activity began with his involvement with the student movement of the late-sixties, and he describes himself as 'a child of my time – specifically that vague 1968-ish axis and the failure of the 1964 Labour Government. . . . I was on the political end of the counter-culture, strongly influenced by IS [International Socialists] with whom I have always had a close affinity.'[19] His early work has close affinities with that of Portable – Brenton, in particular, was an important influence during his period as resident writer at Bradford, whilst Edgar was working as a journalist there – but he has moved steadily towards the general position held by McGrath, as a result of his subsequent political maturing. Edgar has said perceptively, 'I think I got into left-wing politics on a kind of rhetorical level',[20] although he is now generally recognised as a playwright for whom research is a basic tool.

McGrath's involvement with the events of 1968 provides a useful point of comparison. He was already well estab-

19

lished as a writer, principally for film and television – his work on the first episodes of BBC TV's *Z Cars* meant that he had played a crucial role in the development of television naturalism – and had had in addition a modest stage success with *Events While Guarding the Bofors Gun* (1966), a play based on his experience as a National Service man, and comparable in theme and in the conventionality of its format to Wesker's *Chips with Everything*. In April 1968 he started work on a new play, *Random Happenings in the Hebrides*, the first of what was to be a series of plays dealing with political strife in Scotland. The action of *Random Happenings* was to begin in 1964, and was to be largely concerned with the interaction between spontaneous and unorganised left activity, and the attempts of a newly elected Scottish Labour MP to work for change within the parliamentary system. Although the play makes no overt reference to the French Spring, it reflects a debate engendered by McGrath's own experiences.

I started to write ... and in May 68 things started happening in Paris. And I went over and spent some time there. ... And the importance of the thinking around that whole time, the excitement of that whole complex set of attitudes to life which that para-revolutionary situation threw up was incredible – the thinking about ordinary life, the freshness of approach, the urgency and the beauty of the ideas was amazing. *But* what didn't happen was the organisation. ... In the middle of all that, you have this absolute contradiction. I came back and left the play, actually for about six months to a year, and then I finished it. But it was changed by that whole experience. Apparently it had nothing to do with Paris and people throwing stones at CRS [Compagnie Républicaine de Sécurité – the riot police], but that experience went into it. That conflict.[21]

The contradiction that McGrath describes between the excitement of spontaneity and the need for organisation is central not only to what obviously became a very personal play, but also to the entire debate about the nature of political theatre post-'68. As *Random Happenings* took its final form, the conflict assumed major thematic importance. Although the format of the play remains close to the naturalism of McGrath's first work – developing well the theme of enmeshed sexual relationships of the small island community as an image both of social reality and of its disintegration – the play raises questions that its naturalism will now allow it to solve. The dilemma of the MP, Jimmy, is one that links him with the McGrath who had experienced the contradictions of Paris at precisely the same time that he was discovering the problems of the Scottish political struggle. The new strand in the work, which is well indicated in the sub-title of the play, *The Social Democrat and the Stormy Sea*, was to be increasingly developed by McGrath in later plays. It is a move towards a qualified form of agit-prop theatre which has taken him progressively further and further away from the large theatre venues which Brenton and Hare have found increasingly attractive. Not that *Random Happenings* quite makes the jump, in the way that such plays as *The Cheviot, the Stag, and the Black, Black Oil* (1973) were to do. But it raises the questions. The suggestion is that it is certainly too late to effect meaningful change on the tiny island, and that individual acts are to be regarded with a sense of ambiguity; they are probably too little, too late. However, the urge towards using the play as a means of discussing the day-to-day business of political change is strong. Jimmy finally abandons official channels in a desperate adventure to keep the fishing vessels on which the island community depends. It is, as he realises, a futile and romantic act, and anyway doomed as the fleet has sailed while he has been busy talking about action. The duality of spontaneity and organisation which McGrath had witnessed at first hand in the French struggle is given a strong dramatic impact.

> JIMMY: *We're* romantics. (*Indicating the men.*) *They* are the ones who should be – (*He makes a violent gesture of revolution.*)
>
> CATRIONA: Come on, Jimmy. You did what you could, I suppose.
>
> JIMMY: Did I?

The ending of the play is ambiguous only in terms of its naturalistic format. It appears to raise conventional questions for an audience about the correctness of Jimmy's behaviour, in the manner of Ibsen's social dramas. But the division that Jimmy makes between the 'romantics' and the 'men' is a clear one, and reinforces the way in which McGrath has moved away from a presentation of failure within the system as a focal point, to the suggestion of the need for organisation outside of it. Jimmy's is a personal failure, but it is a failure that is there to be learned from, a starting-point for future activity. In this sense, the play is not self-enclosed.

Subsequently, McGrath's plays would move further away from the idea of history as tragic failure, and concentrate on its potential for political education. He went on to form 7:84, a socialist theatre group committed to taking political theatre to non-theatrical venues and, at least in intent, to non-theatrical audiences. Coincidentally, the company's first production, *Trees in the Wind*, was

22

performed at the 1971 Edinburgh Festival, alongside Portable's most provocatively outrageous offerings, *Lay-By*, Chris Wilkinson's *Plays for Rubber Go-Go Girls* and Snoo Wilson's *Blow Job*. The contrast could not have been more extreme, and yet both groups regarded themselves as practitioners of political theatre. While McGrath's play was a densely layered account of political change, rehearsals for which were supported by a huge list of required reading, Portable offered a studied assault on international sensibilities. Their three productions were bizarre pantomimes of excess, stylistically confusing, and drawing freely from the pornographic detritus of mass culture. Inasmuch as there was any consistency of political analysis, what was offered was a disturbing series of visions of nihilistic disintegration, aimed as much at the counter-culturists of the Festival as at the establishment. Alongside the Portable offerings, *Trees in the Wind*, one of McGrath's most notable achievements, appeared almost untheatrical.

The previous year, the Royal Court had played host to about twenty of the new groups, under the 'Come Together' banner. Its borrowing of the Beatles' title was a good indication of what was on offer. Interestingly, although the kind of political theatre about to be undertaken by 7:84 was represented by the pioneering CAST, virtually all the other pieces were avowedly *avant-garde*. Portable was represented by Brenton's *Christie in Love*, and there was also a revival of Heathcote Williams's *AC/DC*, whilst much of the Festival consisted of essentially performance-art shows. This is scarcely surprising. Although agit-prop was to develop throughout the seventies in parallel with, and frequently borrowing from, the *avant-garde*, its political programme and its attempt to locate new audiences were taking it progressively away from theatres such as the Court and all that it represented.

23

As McGrath has since expressed it, very strongly but not unfairly, 'the audience has changed very little in the theatre, the social requirements remain constant, the values remain firmly those of acceptability to a metropolitan middle-class audience, with an eye to similar acceptability on the international cultural market'.[22]

What must be stressed, however, is that none of those working in the *avant-garde* would have initially disagreed with McGrath's remarks. Their assault on such audiences was simply another version of the same statement. The difference is that the *avant-garde* not only stayed with the theatres but, according to your perspective, to a large extent came to dominate their output or were dominated by them. It is important to stress that we are here talking largely about the subsidised London and provincial theatres, and not the commercial venues, which have shown the same indifference to the new drama as they did to the early plays of Osborne and Wesker.

In 1973 a forty-minute film written by Brenton and directed by Tony Bicat was first shown at the Almost Free Theatre. *Skin Flicker*, like several of Brenton's plays of this period, including *Magnificence* and the televised *Saliva Milk-Shake* (1975), reflected the growth of urban terrorism from the activities of the First of May Group and the Angry Brigade of the late sixties. Echoing specifically the Laporte kidnapping in Canada, the film is concerned with a group of young terrorists who abduct a cabinet minister – incidentally murdering his wife and child – first torturing him and then killing him. Surrounded by the police, one of the group kills his comrades, then himself. Their acts have been filmed by a porno-movie maker, and it is revealed that the whole episode has been incorporated into a film as a part of an anti-terrorist training-programme.

The ironies are acute and deliberate. The use of the

24

porno-movie maker, and the title of the film, are commentaries not only on the obscenity of the acts, but also on the vicarious expectations of an audience more interested in the spectacle than in the possibility of real political change. The muddled and inhuman acts of the terrorists are transmuted into a 'snuff movie' which in turn becomes a part of the educational apparatus of the enemy that they wish to destroy. This sense of a film within a film within a film raises quite consciously questions about the role of a radical drama set in a non-radical theatrical context which are crucial, but the upholders of the agit-prop tradition would go further, seeing in the obsession with individual terrorism an image of the inability of the *avant-garde* to come to terms with the harsh realities of mass political change.

It is apparent that this division of political theatre into two distinct camps is no historical accident. Although they share the common ground of disillusionment with, and removal from, Labour Party politics of the sixties, and the 'revolutionary' experience of 1968, there is at heart an ideological separation. The *avant-garde* occupied the territory of a counter-culture intent on bypassing the discourse of orthodox political debate, whilst the agit-prop groups remained essentially a part of activist class struggle, working usually, though not exclusively, under the umbrella of a particular left grouping. However, it would be misleading to suggest that, in practice, the division has been absolute. The relationship has been mutually symbiotic, the *avant-garde* being increasingly infused with a didactic seriousness as the seventies advanced, and the agit-prop groupings readily borrowing techniques from fringe and alternative theatre.

Certainly, as the confidence of the counter-culture waned in the early years of the decade, and as the manifestations of optimistic festival gave way to individual despair and the tactics of the urban guerrilla, much of the momentum of the fringe was dissipated. Influenced by the greater availability of Arts Council money, and with the achievement of Equity minimum rates for actors in all fields, the sponsored theatres offered a seductive welcome in from the cold. At the same time, the surprise electoral victory of the Conservative Party in 1970, and the stepping-up of industrial confrontation with the miners' strike, and the 'three-day week' which led to the downfall of the Heath government, led many young radicals to rethink the philosophy of the new New Left. David Edgar, looking back on this period in 1978, is in no doubt that the steady increase in agit-prop theatre at the expense of the fringe can be directly attributed to a new wave of working-class militancy.

It is clear that the growth of a more class-orientated theatrical strategy was not merely an internal development. . . . Some groups, indeed, are aware in retrospect of missing the boat, and remaining in the counter-cultural tradition long after it had become clear that reports of the death of working class militancy had been much exaggerated.[23]

But again, the growth has not been a steady one. As the decade developed, the contrast with the brief period of prosperity of the sixties became more apparent. A diet of economic retrenchment, of industrial uncertainty and of rising unemployment, has made the more optimistic postures of much agit-prop theatre look somewhat foolish. Just how many times can the banner of revolution be unfurled after the presentation of yet another factory-closure, yet another kick in the teeth for workers' solidarity? David Edgar again, in 1979:

> I was fed up with seeing agitprop shows that were messy, and also I was increasingly thinking that the politics you could get across were very crude, whereas the world about us was getting more complicated. . . . I do like agitprop, and I'm very fond of my agitprop plays. . . . There may again be a period when agitprop will have more relevance than I believe it does now. But I don't think I'll every go back to it, because the sort of subjects I want to deal with now won't take it.[24]

Such a response sums up well the way in which, towards the end of the period under review, the two traditions have again become enmeshed. In a decade in which Edward Bond has expressed a desire to move beyond 'question plays' to the provision of answers, in which Brenton has spoken of his desire to write a Utopian play in answer to his *Churchill Play*, and Edgar has moved into a theatre that 'eschews tub thumping at the same time as I was going round the country tub thumping',[25] the new political drama has evidently undergone many changes. That is fundamentally what this book is about.

2
Howard Brenton:
Portable Theatre and
the Fringe

You don't write to convert. More – to stir things up. For
people to make what they wish of it. When it comes to
agit-prop, I like the agit; the prop I'm very bad at. I'm not
wise enough. Yet.

(Howard Brenton, in *TQ*, v, no. 17, 1975)

Of all the new playwrights, Howard Brenton is the one to
have been most embraced by the subsidised theatre, and
yet it is an embrace full of paradox. His work has been
consistently successful at the box-office, but it has been
greeted with a degree of critical abuse that has only
intensified as it has become increasingly well known. His
ambiguous acceptance by the theatrical establishment has
allowed him to utilise the facilities of the large theatres in a
move towards a reformulation of 'epic theatre', but he has
never ceased to question the point of the exercise.

His first London production was in 1969, and by 1974 he
had already been commissioned to write the first new play
for the National Theatre (*Weapons of Happiness*, 1976) – a

commission turned down by Osborne. More recently, the RSC has performed *Sore Throats* (1979) and *Thirteenth Night* (1980); and the National has staged his adaptations of Brecht's *Galileo* (1981) and Buchner's *Danton's Death* (1981), as well as *The Romans in Britain*, a play which played to packed houses in the context of an unprecedented torrent of media abuse and the unsuccessful prosecution of the Director under the Sexual Offences Act. Brenton's foothold is secure, but his ability to offend remains undiminished.

The paradox derives from the unique position that Brenton has come to occupy. More than any of the writers in this book, his roots were firmly in the fringe, and more than any of them he has brought the shock tactics of the fringe into mainstream theatre. Brenton stressed this sense of deliberate confrontation when talking about the opening of *Weapons of Happiness*:

David [Hare, the director] and I regard ourselves and our cast and our production team as an armoured charabanc full of people parked within the National walls – we've brought our own concept in with us because we want consciously to use the National facilities to show off our work to its best advantage.

(*The Times*, 10 Aug 1976)

In addition, although Brenton now writes largely for the subsidised theatre, he still occasionally revisits fringe territory. *A Short, Sharp Shock for the Government*, written with Tony Howard in 1980, was a savage lampoon on the new Conservative administration, complete with the bloody ghosts of Airey Neave and Lord Mountbatten; perfectly in keeping with earlier fringe activity, and very much a companion-piece to *Fruit*, written ten years earlier

29

to 'celebrate' Edward Heath's election victory. For much of the theatrical establishment, Brenton remains what he has always been, the wolf within the gates. To look at his early work is to look at the attractions and the problems of the post-'68 fringe.

Brenton was nine when he wrote his first play, about the Harris Tweed character in the *Eagle* comic. It was an interesting first choice of material, for not only do versions of the absurdly bumbling English eccentric 'gentleman' reoccur frequently in his early work as caricatures of the establishment – in the part of 'Major Bertram Buggery . . . Head Warden, Queen Elizabeth Home for Orphaned Little Bleeders', in *The Education of Skinny Spew* (1969), or in that of Brigadier Badge, who announces to the audience in *Hitler Dances* (1972), 'I know I am a parody of myself . . . but back here in 1942, there *is* a war going on' – but it foreshadows his use of comic-book heroes, as with Greg and Phil's argument in *Gum and Goo* (1968).

> PHIL: If Superman did crush Dr Death the RED SKULL
>   would have revenge, 'cos of his invincibly evil brain.
> GREG: Rubber Man would crush the Red Skull anyday
>   . . . Then Captain America would sweep in with his
>   mighty shield of freedom and ZAP all in sight. ZAP!
>   Be great to be a super hero.
> PHIL: Be great to be a super villain.

Most of Brenton's early plays were concerned with children. In them he presented a simplified, scaled-down world in which the children are not portrayed as embryonically rational creatures in an innocent world, but as disturbingly frank examples of the aggressive animality that surrounds them in the grown-up society. Their playgrounds are urban battlefields of blood and sex, and their behaviour denies the premises of all liberal educational theory. Whilst with Brighton Combination – where he also worked on an adaptation of Rabelais's *Gargantua* – Brenton wrote *Gum and Goo* for a teachers' conference. The piece is based loosely on the children's games that figure so often in his work, and culminates in the two boys pushing the girl down a hole after she has been foiled in her attempt to go off to play 'Dracula' games with a 'dirty old man' – 'We play biting lovely ladies' necks an' crosses through your heart.'

The news from the front was no better in the two short plays he wrote for Chris Parr for the 1969 Bradford Festival. *The Education of Skinny Spew* traces the young-ster's development from the womb, through the killing of his parents in an attempt to rid himself of the tyranny of the old – 'And I'll kill all the other Mums and Dads. No more fathers, beating up their kids! No more mothers, screech-ing! All over the age of ten, I'll kill off too. And the world will be all PLAY. And everyone will pee in the sea, whenever they want' – to his institutionalisation and enforced 'education' at the orphanage – 'An' they all got me. The dogs. The coppers. And Major Buggery an' the Matron. An' the old queen on the by-pass. An' they all got me, 'cos they couldn't let me grow. What I was. The Mums and the Dads could not let me grow.' *Heads* is concerned with the dilemma of an adolescent girl who, unable to choose between 'beautiful body' and 'beautiful brain' in her two men, cuts off the two heads, and ends the play still dissatisfied. Not that the parental figures have anything to give the children. They offer either brutality or at best an inability to cope. The policeman in *Gum and Goo* prefig-ures the Inspector in *Christie in Love* in his arrest of the child-molester, seeing no connection between law-enforcement and morality: 'You're a catch, sonny boy.

31

We've not had a child fingerer down the station for weeks. It'll be drinks all round on the Inspector tonight.'

The vision of society presented is bleak, but these early plays do not depend on any depth of characterisation or profundity of insight for their success. Everything is stripped down to bare essentials, whilst still leaving the protagonists with an almost poetically released rhetoric in which to articulate their thoughts. What is most exciting about them is the stylistic combination of the games routines with a loose thematic concern with education. What Brenton does is to make self-evident the impulses behind such activity: the terrible simplicity of 'Cowboys and Indians', for instance – a game which is ended in *Gum and Goo* with the Indian Maid left to perish down the hole; or of 'War Games' – 'My Dad says Hitler was the biggest bad man who ever lived. And Winston Churchill stood on the cliffs of Dover in his battle-dress and he made this speech 'bout filling up the hole with the English dead. Then Winston Churchill took out this great big gun and he SMASHED Adolf Hitler.' This use of children's games is to be found often in the later plays – with Bobby in *Epsom Downs*, for example – but it is put to most terrifying effect in *Hitler Dances*, where a group of children playing at World War Two on a bomb-site dig up a German soldier thirty years after and start to discover the violent games for real.

> I saw children in Eindhoven, which was flattened twice in the war . . . a bomb-site with children playing on it . . . and there the idea was lodged in my mind, because it was like children playing on this heap of rubble – history. And the idea of a German soldier coming out of the ground became meaningful.   (*TQ*, v, no. 17)

That the children conjure with the meaningless names of 'great men' of history as they would with those of their comic-book heroes is a part of the point Brenton wishes to make. Their absurd mythologising is a simplistic version of the essentially comic-book view of history through which most of their grown-up counterparts attempt to view the modern world. The two plays that Brenton produced for the 1970 Bradford Festival continue this process of demythologising, a constant theme in his work from the book on Hitler written as a child to *The Churchill Play* (1974). *Wesley* was performed in a Methodist Church, and offers an extremely ambiguous account of the founding father, while *Scott of the Antarctic, or What God Didn't See* – performed in Bradford Ice-Rink, with skates and loud-hailers – was an uncompromising debunking of an explorer who is sent off by God after the King of England has complained that the Pole has been left white on his political map dominated by the pink of the British Empire. This interest in unconventional auditoria was to have continued with a version of *Moby Dick* to be produced in Bradford Corporation Swimming-Baths, but this came to nothing. Meanwhile Brenton had become involved with the company that was to prove so important in his move towards becoming a political writer.

In the late summer of 1969 Brenton went to the Arts Lab in London's Drury Lane to see an adaptation of Kafka's *Amerika* by the newly formed Portable Theatre. Since he was the only person to do so, the performance was cancelled and 'we went to the pub'. From this first meeting with Tony Bicat and, more importantly, David Hare came a commission to write a play about 'evil', *Christie in Love*. 'My wife Jane and I were living in a rotting basement flat in Notting Hill. I realised that this in fact was Christie and Evans' area. The caff where he picked up one of the girls was just around the corner. So I thought up the central idea of the play' (*P & P*, Feb 1972).

The set for the show was provocatively non-naturalistic, a single pen made of rusty chicken-wire, six feet by ten, full of 'torn and screwed up pages of a popular newspaper', which served as Christie's garden and front-room, a police-station, an executioner's shed and a lime-pit. 'It's not a setting in a conventional sense. I don't want it to be *like* a garden or a room. It's theatrical machine, a thing you'd only see in a show. It's a trap, a flypaper for the attention of the spectators to stick on' (Brenton's note in *Plays for the Poor Theatre*). The dirtiness of the set – 'the pen is a filthy sight' – was as important as the use of the popular newspaper; it embodied the ambiguity of the audience's interest in such a case – 'The General Public is a dirty animal', the Inspector tells the Constable in the first scene. The audience was seated all around and as close as possible to the pen. It was an image that stuck in Brenton's mind. In 1975, an 'environmental set' was created for his reworking of *The Churchill Play*, *Government Property*, in Denmark, where the audience was seated all around the barbed-wire perimeter of the concentration camp, within which there was a great vat of mud. The intention was the same in both instances, to prevent the spectators from distancing themselves from the action, to force them to respond directly rather than as through the safe and private perusal of the newspaper or television account.

The audience entered to a repeated tape giving the bare outlines of Christie's life, the names of his victims, and the date of his execution, all producing the expectancy of a documentary approach, before the Constable, who has been digging in the paper-pit all the while, launches into a dead-pan recitation of crude limericks. Again the intention is to alter the audience's perception. The limericks were delivered straight-on, preferably finding individuals to focus on, forcing them to experience the disparity between the grubby and, by their delivery, unfunny verses, and the enormity of Christie's acts, whilst at the same time establishing the connections in terms of popular obsessions. Before Christie makes his first appearance, the policemen are displayed not as reliable arbiters of social norms, but as vulgar and obsessed representatives of public propriety. They are not real policemen, and their language is a strange mixture of 'music-hall' patter and class-based morality.

INSPECTOR: The bones of English Ladies. That's what he's been burying down there, somewhere. Burying English Ladies in his garden. We're going to do him for that!
CONSTABLE: We're going to do him for that Sir!
INSPECTOR: I've heard of some nasty things in my life. But burying English Ladies in your own backyard just about takes the candle. Dig 'em up!

The phrase 'English Ladies' is as carefully misplaced as the entirely inappropriate 'takes the candle' with relation to murder. The effect is to make the 'discovery' of Christie the more chilling. 'The artifice of the garden and the "stage" nature of the policemen's parts are intended to throw the Christie part into relief. With Christie I tried to write a fully fledged naturalistic part.' The effect on stage is much like that described by Tony in *How Beautiful with Badges* (1972): 'It's like going up to a cut-out Kodak girl, outside a chemist. An' touching her cardboard flattie titties. And to your dismay . . . a real hand comes out and grabs you. And real lips move on the photograph, saying "You touched me." ' The metaphor is a telling one, and it expresses well the sudden jumps out of comic flatness which Brenton handles so well, sudden jumps that immediately change the whole terms of reference.

Even when the Inspector starts to question Christie, his interest centres not on the fact of murder but on the juicy details of Reggy's sexual practices; it is, it is intimated, all that an audience will be really interested in . 'Our pathologists conclude the women were getting cold. You had 'em dead, didn't you?' And then, pushing a glass phial of semen under the murderer's nose, he announces, 'Medical Science tells us there are millions of little Reginalds in that tube', a quasi-technical remark that soon gives way to, 'The dead tarts, Reg. They're full of your stuff. Science knows you fucked them all.' The play offers no solutions of any kind, save to suggest that, in a society in which the Inspector and Constable stand as moral analysts, there is an honesty of intent about Christie.

> Everything Christie did seemed obvious to me. . . . It seemed to me to be the search of a lover. . . . The policemen attempt all sorts of explanations – they try to find a meaning to the crimes. But none of these explanations work – there is *no* solution. The play should give an audience a sense of moral vertigo. (*P & P*, Feb 1972)

Popular comedy, newspaper reports, establishment minds, science – all serve to stress the distancing of human understanding. They do not reveal the source of Christie's inhumanity, but reinforce his humanity. He is the only human thing in the play. The audience is invited to see that society, and not man, is looking down the wrong end of the telescope. The real 'horror' of Christie is his normality, something with which the Inspector cannot deal: 'Why can't a mass murderer be just a bit diabolical? Why can't a pervert like you, already in the annals of nastiness, have fangs or something. Roll your eyes around. Sprout horns. Go on Reg, let's have a real bit of horror!'

Revenge, a play that had started as a comic version of *King Lear*, with the king as a failed gangster who has given away his territory to three ungrateful daughters, can be seen as a companion-piece to *Christie*, and it is not surprising that Hare should have offered him a commission on the strength of it. The would-be master crook, Hepple, newly out of prison, sets out to avenge himself on his adversary, Assistant Commissioner Macleish, a man who is as obsessed with his pursuit, as one of the predestined elect, of moral order, as Hepple is with that of criminal chaos. They are the two sides of the same coin – and are played by the same actor – and both end the play as dead and disappointed ghosts, the confusions of the real world rendering their notions of good and evil absurd. The villains who form the 'Adam Hepple Super Gang' are shambolically incapable, and Macleish's moral vigilante squad is peopled with ineffectual two-dimensional coppers. Hepple is eventually caught by a 'line of cut-out police-men'. Too late, Macleish realises his mistake: 'It's the 1980s now. Rapes every night. No citizen abroad after dark. The coppers armed. Gangs roaming the street at will, burning down police stations. The country's gone to the devil. You lived before your time, Adam.' As with *Christie*, no solutions are offered; criminal and policemen are both a part of a redundant game.

The England that Brenton's characters inhabit is an urban one, a pin-table map with the major cities flashing in multi-coloured lights. Occasional trips are made to a rural world: Jed's in *Magnificence* (1973) to blow up Alice and his rose-garden, or the criminal's comic pastoral retreat in *Revenge*, where Bung's dreams of marrying a milkmaid and settling down in a chocolate-box cottage are quickly destroyed by Hepple:

> I hate the country. Listen to the bleeding birds twittering. Shut up, can't you . . . And bleeding cows and bleeding sheep and bleeding bulls after sticking their horns in your arse. It's not my natural habitat and it's not yours, mate. We belong to the streets and pubs and back doors, and Leicester Square and the Elephant and Castle.

In *How Beautiful with Badges* – commissioned by Open Space and performed during the 1972 Camden Festival – the two Hell's Angels, Gut the Buzzard and Child Molester, sit cramming themselves with pills and alcohol 'in the countryside, brain cells going down like flies'; in the sky they see 'a million LP covers', and become alarmed at the mooing of a cow, and at the clouds passing over the sun – 'I wish they wouldn't do that.' Their ultimate fantasy is a countryside turned into a concrete playground.

> There is an argument for concreting over the old Isle O'Wight. Putting it all on there. Nature. In buildings. Yeh, you'd have a building like a chest o' drawers. A cow in each drawer. And the rest o' the country, be freeways. Like L.A. With jungle for scenery. The odd dead tiger on the tarmac. Ridden down by some wild clown. Tyre marks through his stripes. Fucking Paradise. L.A. Reckon we'll ever see it, Molester? L.A. Clover leaf intersections. Eight lanes an' speeding. The concrete rollercoaster. The country of the righteous. No clouds to bug you there, my old Molester.

This fantasy is opposed in the play by Tony's ideological analysis, as Maoist boy-scout, of the same landscape:

this in't no country. Few miles south o' Reigate, River
Mole. Sloping banks. Clumps o' woods. Folksy styles. Ye
Olde Oaks. Your odd swan, your odd moo cow in the
meadow. Nature? It's all got up by the bourgeoisie.
Camouflage. No fishing no boating. Keep out trespassers
will be prosecuted. Barb wire round the blue-bells.

On the one hand the urban jungle, and on the other the
territorial imperatives of commuter country. It is a clash
which assumes ever-greater importance for Brenton.

In *Lay-By*, the collaborative effort by Brenton, Brian
Clark, Trevor Griffiths, Hare, Steven Poliakoff, Hugh
Stoddart and Snoo Wilson, the countryside serves as a
location for pornographic photography, a convenient hin-
terland through which runs the motorway that links the
cities. The play was 'based on a case of wrongful conviction
for rape, and it raised a lot of – not so much issues as the
landscape of the people up the M1. And it seemed like this
extraordinary suppurating artery up England' (*TQ*, v, no.
17). The lay-by is not a stopping-off point for picnics, but a
setting for violence, a collecting-post for the refuse of the
city. In the field with his two 'models', the pornographer
complains that the idyllic pose is ruined by the 'fucking
great silage tower stuck in the middle foreground', to which
Joy replies, 'I don't like the countryside. It's not . . .
natural. It's not indoors.' What is involved here is more
than the irony of the objection to the intrusion of a silage
tower into a 'dirty' photo. The notion of what is natural is
turned upside down – 'All this green in the city, it's not
natural', says Rot in *Revenge*. What unites liberal reformer
and committed revolutionary is a belief in change based on
an optimistic view of human potential. In Brenton's plays
of the 'Portable' period, what is elsewhere regarded as
deviance from the norm is seen *as* the norm. It is natural for

children to fight and claw like the grown-up beasts that they will become, and it is unnatural to regard the modern, and therefore urban, world as anything other than a stage for crime and social disorder. The argument of the hospital attendant at the end of *Lay-By*, washing down the corpses of the three main characters prior to mashing them up to make jam, is not answered by his companion's plaintive, 'We're not animals.'

> So they put these perfectly normal mice in this cage see? And they leave them. Just feed 'em and leave 'em. And they multiply and die and multiply and some more die. And the number grows. And grows. And there isn't enough room any more. They can't turn round. Take proper exercise. Tripping over each other's shit. And then it starts to fall apart. Anarchy, chaos. Total irreversible breakdown. Nothing. Void. The whole thing.

For Portable, the politics arose from the drama. Inasmuch as they had a political platform, it was a consistent vision of nihilistic disintegration, relying heavily on 'uncool' dramatic shock tactics. In *Lay-By*, the pornographer has the girls posing for his camera, and the 'rape' is enacted on stage. As a result, bookings on the conventional circuit became more and more difficult, and the fringe audiences became, as Brenton realised, too sophisticated. He began to feel increasingly that 'the fringe was a historical thing . . . it was becoming "arty" ' (*TQ*, v, no. 17). Furthermore, the cultural climate was changing. The unexpected victory of the Conservative Party under Edward Heath in 1970 was a salutory corrective to the dreams of an alternative society, in which it was thought change could be effected by by-passing the system. Committed agit-prop groups were forced into considering the issues that arose from industrial

unrest – culminating in the miners' strike and the three-day
week – and to leave behind them the heady rhetoric of
alternative strategies.

> Utopian generosity becomes paranoia as the world
> closes in. Naive gentleness goes to the wall, and Man-
> son's murderousness replaces it. . . . The truth is that
> there is only one society – that you can't escape the world
> you live in. Reality is remorseless. No one can leave. If
> you're going to change the world, well there's only one
> set of tools, and they're bloody and stained but realistic. I
> mean communist tools.   (*TQ*, v, no. 17)

There is an irony in Brenton's words of 1975, for he more
than anyone had been intent on pricking the bubble of
'naive gentleness', but they point to the essential weakness
of Portable's political stance. None of their characters has
any involvement with political ideology; they are pre-
political animals, passive embodiments of the decay that
they inhabit.

In *Fruit*, written for Portable as a reaction to the General
Election result of 1970, Brenton moved for the first time
into the world of political strife, although it is a political
world still seen in essentially negative terms; 'a really great
burst of nihilism', Brenton said of *Fruit* and of the last act of
Lay-By, 'is one of the most beautiful things that you can see
on a stage' (*P & P*, Feb 1972). *Fruit* is concerned with the
attempt of a degenerate thalidomide victim – 'I am a living
symbol of your excess. A weed in your paradise. A bad
dream of the Capitalist market' – to blackmail a new Tory
Prime Minister by threatening to reveal that he is a
homosexual; hence the title. The plot fails because the
Prime Minister resists in the firm knowledge that the public
do not care, and the play ends with a Welsh Syndicalist MP

lecturing Paul on the central importance of the class struggle ('I end the play with a man saying the right thing for the wrong reasons' – *P & P*, Feb 1972) – an analysis which gives way to despair. 'If I didn't have a firm theoretical grasp, I think I'd kill myself at Christmas time . . . On the other hand, while we're waiting for the Thames to run red, and all that, we can get on.' The MP then demonstrates how to make a petrol bomb, and the final image of the play is it exploding against the wall of the theatre – 'God knows how we're going to get away with that', as Brenton's stage direction concludes.

The most excitingly sustained vision of decay was to come later, in Brenton and Hare's collaboration on *Brassneck* (1973) for Richard Eyre at the Nottingham Playhouse. The action is moved directly onto the political arena. The play traces events between the formation of the new Labour Party government of 1945, through disillusionment and the property speculation of the sixties. It is set in a Midlands town, and follows the activities of a family of capitalist profiteers, profiteers whose ironic toast as the play ends is to 'the death of capitalism', last days which are to be spent in their marketing the ultimate consumer commodity, Chinese heroin: 'a product for our times, the perfect product, totally artificial, man-made, creating its own market, if there's a glut the demand goes up, if there's a famine the demand goes up, an endless spiral of need and profit' (III. ii). Just as in *Revenge*, police and criminals are united in a common and mutually dependent fantasy, so in *Brassneck* the decline and fall is celebrated by those who will continue to sell picture postcards to the eager crowds as the last brick of civilisation falls.

Tom Browne, already ex-Communist Party and moving through the gross-roots of the Labour Party as the play opens, is vehement that this time things will really change, but as he speaks he is already learning to play golf prior to entering the Masonic Lodge and, ultimately, becoming public-relations man for the Bagley family.

> I want to get into public life. Set myself to work. . . . I used to think I would spend the whole of my life in draughty halls, pamphleteering, be a crank with a megaphone at the factory gate . . . that's what happened to my father – romantic – died cursing his friends for minor misinterpretations of the exact meaning of revolution – that mustn't happen to us, Harry. If that happens to us, God help England. And working people.

What the play will show happening to 'us' is of course far worse, trade-union militant and seedy speculator united with the local Tory establishment in a dance of death. Given the resources of what was at the time the most exciting repertory theatre in the country, Brenton and Hare dispensed with conventional scenery in favour of a complicated collage of back-projected slides and, although the technical problems were not always overcome, created for the first time a version of the 'epic' model that was to increasingly preoccupy Brenton as he moved towards his formulation of the play on the grand scale.

Brassneck is remarkable for its size and its range, for its breakdown of narrative continuity, its refusal to fill in gaps, and for the conjunction of public events with private history – most gloriously handled in the Bagley wedding on Coronation Day 1953. It rejects the psychological explanations of conventional social drama. The changes in Tom Browne, for instance, are not proved but simply shown. 'The theatre is a dirty place. It's not a place for a rational analysis of a society – it's there to bait our obsessions, ideas and public figures' (*P & P*, Feb 1972). The truth was to be

43

found in the Poulson trial, in an assumed audience consensus about modern England. 'There is a screen called public life which is reported on the telly and in the newspapers. This version of public life is a spectacle, it operates within its own laws.' What *Brassneck* and *Fruit* attempt is a subversion of the spectacle – in *Fruit* events on stage are actually monitored through the TV screen; but, as Brenton had already discovered, a move towards the conventional theatre brings a whole series of new factors into the game, specifically a rigid establishment with its own perspective on the parade.

Immediately before *Brassneck* Brenton had been involved with two traumatic productions, the first of which was to cause him to rethink his strategy towards the theatrical establishment, and the second the break-up of Portable, thus cutting off his most obvious link with his past. Jane Howell had invited Brenton to bring a play to the Northcott Theatre, Exeter, and in September 1972 his version of *Measure for Measure*, directed by Bill Gaskill, opened to the accompaniment of board-room furore. What Brenton had done was to take the basic structure of Shakespeare's play and transpose it onto a version of contemporary Britain, in which Angelo became a racialist, modelled quite clearly on Enoch Powell, and then postulate on the possible events that might follow in an era of moral right-wing backlash. Claudio became a black rockstar involved in blue movies, and the Duke an ineffectual ex-public-school Macmillan figure at sea in the new world of grammar-school meritocracy.

The play is not subtle, nor was it intended to be. It opens with the Duke relinquishing power during a test match at Lord's. The score-board reads, 'West Indies 598 for 3 declared, England 32 for 6', and as the scene develops wickets tumble steadily. Angelo's first words after the

Duke's departure hammer home the point: 'I want a Home
Office Report on that black power bowler. On my desk,
first thing in the morning. We'll put an end to spectacles of
national disgrace. . . . There will be a sense of purpose,
there will be law in the country, there will be order.' He
embarks on an anti-pornography campaign: 'The coppers
have just done the Roxy Cinema . . . came right through the
silver screen, at a steamy moment. Coppers' boots, right
through Ingrid's lovely whatnot.' Mrs Overdone complains
– and is entreated for mercy by Claudio's Salvation Army
sister. Brenton deliberately renders Angelo's 'seduction'
by Isabella comically absurd. His speech of anguish, direct
from Shakespeare, is delivered in the lavatory, 'clutching
the pipe to the water tank', and when she leaves his
agonising is rapidly deflated: 'In my heart the strong and
swelling evil of my conception. . . . The risk! The fool-
hardiness! . . . I . . . could make her wear things.' Again,
there is no interest on Brenton's part in Angelo as an
individual; he is shown in the most unfair way possible, a
supreme example of the two faces of right-wing puritanism.
The Duke's bed-switch, filmed by a porno-movie maker,
goes awry when Angelo reveals that he had known about
the plot all along, and the play ends with the new ruler even
more securely in power.

ANGELO: I offer this view of history. It is a paradox. The
old order, unchecked, will bring forth a new and
harsher form of itself. Call me cynical if you will, but I
welcome that. . . . Therefore I will proceed to fashion
the England of my dreams. And you will learn that
where power has rested, there it *shall* rest. For a
thousand years.   (II. xv)

The production was very successful in terms of audience

response, but this was not where the problems lay. Its political simplicity offended simply because of its simplicity. It left nothing to hide behind. 'I knew Exeter was a High Tory Town and . . . the board of the Exeter theatre are Powellites, they're right-wing Tories, and that underlay all of it. It's as simple as that. And they said, "Why should these people come down here and piss all over our theatre? And piss well, what's more?" ' The pressure forced changes in the script; the lawyer retained by the Northcott's board claimed that Powell could sue for up to £40,000, and the specific identifications were removed.

> It taught me something, that your enemies know what they're doing, they're not bumbling old fools. They never once attacked on an artistic front, which we could have fought. . . . It was the first big theatre that I'd ever written for. I felt I put my head in the door and they had it off by the neck, without any trouble, and that was a terrible lesson.   (*Gambit*, vi, no. 23)

Whilst *Measure for Measure* was simmering, Brenton had been working with Tony Bicat, Brian Clarke, David Edgar, Francis Fuchs, David Hare and Snoo Wilson on the Portable show *England's Ireland*. Never happy about working in collaboration, Brenton felt this was the only way he could tackle the most pressing political issue of the moment. 'As an English writer I was completely incapable of writing about Ireland, and that's why I joined the group' (*TQ*, v, no. 17). *Measure for Measure* and *England's Ireland* represent a complete change of direction, a desire to grapple directly with the politics of now. As he has found himself writing for the public theatre, the feeling of a need to talk in positive terms about political change has hardened. Just as Angelo's speech invited constructive disagreement, so the tableau of the 'Troubles' in *England's Ireland* leaves problems unresolved. It did not seek to provide answers, rather to reframe the questions. And, furthermore, it did so in the context of a theatre and a society that found itself unable to debate the issues: 'the one thing that united Labour and Tory at Westminster through the sixties was a desire to forget about Ulster completely' (I). The words of James Connolly's ghost provide the context:

> Set about the organisation of the socialist republic or your efforts will be in vain, and England will rule you forever. . . . The enemy is not the naked cross of the Protestant religion. Our foe is not the Shankill worker but the landlords and sweating capitalists of Ireland and England. Forge links. This is a class struggle.

What is most impressive about the play is not its political stance, but its employment of a succession of differing theatrical styles, frequently overlapping, to demonstrate the confusion beneath the rhetoric.

In one of the most disturbing episodes, Sean O'Christie, an uninvolved musician, is picked up and tortured by English soldiers. Throughout, the parallel with the Passion is made, culminating in something 'like a very bad, crude passion play'.

> I said I did not want my hair cut. As I played in a group. My hair was growing to my shoulder. The doctor said the rash went up to the top of my head, and the hair would have to come off for the proper treatment. A soldier shaved my head with scissors and razor. It did not hurt at the time. Other soldiers and RUC men watched and jeered. . . . I was painted from head to knees with a white

lotion. All body hair had been removed, including pubic hair. I was naked all this time, and very cold. (*The* BARBER *takes off the cape. His body is flaky with dried lotion. They dress him in a big suit of army fatigues.*) And Herod with his men of war set him at nought and mocked him, and arrayed him in a gorgeous robe, and sent him again to Pilate.

The mixture of stark documentation and allegory works to shattering effect. The audience experiences O'Christie's conversion, not to the passive martyr but to a revolutionary, as a member of the Provisional IRA.

Much of the material came from eye-witness reports – of the Civil Rights march on Londonderry, for example, or the accounts of wives whose husbands have been taken – and this is mixed with sinisterly comic routines: the soldier dressed as the Yellow Card telling the others 'when to fire'; members of the English Parliament discussing Ireland during a wine-tasting, an event that is concluded by Roy Jenkins vomiting into a bucket and informing his colleagues, 'The essence of civilisation is to make sure that when one is sick the white wine comes up with the fish.' To be writing about Ireland at all, when only Arden and D'Arcy remained unsilent, was remarkable enough, but to do so in such a theatrically provocative way was more than all but a handful of venues could tolerate. It was only performed a few times, and this effective censorship killed off the show and with it Portable, for which it was the final financial crisis. The fringe had become

not dangerous anymore. . . . It had to be dangerous, it had to be a gut operation or else it was no good. And so we began to get big shows out . . . *Lay-By* . . . and then *England's Ireland.* But on both these occasions we were

> forced back down underground. We couldn't get into big
> spaces; they wouldn't have us. Particularly with *Eng-
> land's Ireland*. 50-odd theatres refused to take it. Many
> lied directly, we knew they'd lied.   (*Gambit*, VI, no. 23)

From now on, Brenton would tackle the problem direct,
writing big shows for big stages. He has remained aware of
the inherent dangers, but 'if socialist work doesn't dominate the arts, something else will'. The immediate culmination of the decision was his most important play to date,
The Churchill Play.

Brenton had first considered the problem of revolutionary terrorism in *Magnificence*, at the Royal Court
(1973). The play marks a transition in his work, and as such
is not a total success. 'The trouble was, it was half-and-half,
you see . . . half a fringe play and half a big formal theatre
play,' (*TQ*, V, no. 17). More than anything else it helped
him make the jump, and certainly the sense of the play
moving towards the conclusion that is suddenly not what
the writer wants is strong. The first scene was a perfect
example of the naturalistic Court house-style. A group of
young people take over a house as a squat. They daub
slogans over the walls, to be seen only by themselves, and
argue about tactics. The debate is as internalised as the
room in which it is set, and it is dramatically halted when a
tramp, genuinely homeless, gets up from beneath the pile
of newspapers where he has been all the while asleep. The
police and bailiff arrive, and the play moves into its
secondary political phase, the advocacy of direct violent
action against the ruling class by Jed. In the final scene Jed
goes, armed with gelignite, to the Home Counties garden of
Alice, an ex-Cabinet minister, intent on a symbolic act of
destruction: 'To get it real. And get it real to you. And get
at you Mr English Public Man, with oh yeh the spectacle,

the splendour of you magnificently ablaze for the delight
and encouragement of all your enemies.' He rejects Alice's
protestations of civilised humanism and blows them both
up.

Thus far *Magnificence* sounds very much like a Portable
production, with its roots firmly in late-sixties alternative
strategies – 'One of the problems about *Magnificence* was
that there was a huge personal element in it and that it was
written about people exactly my age whose minds bear
similar shapes to mine and my friends' (*Gambit*, VI, no. 23).
However, belatedly Brenton attempts to argue against the
position occupied by Jed, the character who has dominated
the action. 'There were ideas in the play which were just not
getting a voice and in fact these were the ideas I believed in.
So I wrote an epilogue. I had this man come forward and
say exactly what I felt about it. It's a very puny ending.' The
play ends with Cliff alone, addressing the audience: 'The
waste of your anger. Not the murder, murder is common
enough. Not the violence, violence is everyday. What I
can't forgive you Jed, my dear, dead friend, is the waste.'
What was beginning to preoccupy Brenton was no longer
the immediacy of the 'weapons of happiness', but how you
survived a political struggle that by its very nature would be
long and hard. It was a hard-won rediscovery of the politics
rejected by his early work, and it is not until *The Churchill
Play* that he was ready to attempt the analysis. 'It takes a
long time and it's boring, but if you're going to do anything,
we know what to do politically. You know what political
life is like. If you're going to do it, don't destroy yourself.'

The immediate instigation for *The Churchill Play* came,
in 1974, from Richard Eyre, who suggested, after the
success of *Brassneck*, that Brenton might like to mark the
centenary of Churchill's birth. The play was written very

quickly at Eyre's house in Nottingham, but it is a part of a sequence that it would be useful first to establish. Brenton had been commissioned by the BBC in 1972 to write a radio-play. The script he turned in was about a political concentration camp, and it was prompted by a desire to write about two things: 'it was in part an attempt to write about Ireland, and it was written in the shadow of the Industrial unrest of that year, the miners' strike, the three-day week, and the very strong possibility of anti-Trade Union legislation'. The prisoners arrive and set about building the camp, and there is an 'incident' with the Irish militant, Convery, an incident that is only reported by Reese in *The Churchill Play* but which is still of key importance. An army operational tape is made of a prisoner, based upon a deposition to a priest by a Republican prisoner about his interrogation, but here edited into an innocuous press-release, and the play ends with the camp beginning to fall to pieces. The BBC, in line with their policy of not broadcasting any sensitive Irish material, refused point-blank to record the play, and Brenton incorporated strands of it into the Nottingham commission, including the role of Colonel Ball, which has figured in all versions. After *The Churchill Play*, he produced a film-script, *Rampage*, an adaptation of *Government Property*, which was paid for in advance by United Artists but never made. Then in 1975 Jane Howell took an adapted version of *Government Property* to Denmark. Brenton doubled its length, adding a shower scene and showing the men working. It was very successful but the company was unable to get bookings in England. Finally, in 1978, a revised version of *The Churchill Play* opened at the Other Place, Stratford, the most important change being a toughening of the final violent set-piece. It is important to establish this chronology, if only to demonstrate the importance of the camp-motif, versions of which have appeared over seven years of what is as yet a short writing-career.

In *The Churchill Play* Brenton succeeds for the first time in achieving the synthesis of general analysis and particular location. The events in the play are both dramatically convincing and well able to bear the weight of the larger significance that is Brenton's main concern. The play opens with one of Brenton's most stunning theatrical tricks. '*A dim light. Above a huge stained glass window of medieval knights in prayer. Below, candles round a huge catafalque, which is draped with the Union Jack. At each corner a* SERVICEMAN *stands guard, head lowered in mourning.*' The scene is Westminster Palace Hall, January 1965, and the coffin contains the body of Winston Churchill, lying in state. The mood is immediately shattered when the men start talking amongst themselves. 'So dead a' night. 'Lone wiv 'im. Wha's left of 'im. What's left a' England. An' outside the General Public. Queuin'. Dead a' night, fer the mornin'.' But this careful desecration does not prepare the audience for the two shocks, out of naturalism and back into it, which follow in quick succession. The guards argue, then stop as they hear a noise from the coffin, finally stepping back in terror as the Great Man rises from his box to address them. 'Don't worry. On m'way to Bladon Churchyard. English graveyard. Sod. Eh? Eh? English elms. Larch. Oak. Eh? Choc-box last resting-place for the old man. Bloody sentimentality. Dogpiss on my grave, more like.' The voice and the image are perfect – '*the Churchill actor must assume an exact replica*' – but, as he accepts a light from the Sailor, military commands are heard off-stage, full lighting goes up on a cobbled-together set, and we learn that we have simply been watching a rehearsal for a play.

52

Howard Brenton: Portable Theatre and the Fringe

The presentation of reality as play is central. As the act develops Brenton gradually 'educates' the audience into a realisation that the actors are political prisoners preparing an entertainment for a Parliamentary Committee 'somewhere in England, in 1984'. Information about the situation leading to the construction of the camps is gradually released, as the tension leading to direct and calculated violence is built up. That the camp is named after Churchill makes the link between the local narrative and the wider historical context; it is logical that the camp should be so named, for Brenton attempts to establish an inevitable development between the political values symbolised by Churchill and the present, barely futuristic, situation. The roots are to be found more specifically, as they were with *Government Property*, in the army's occupation of Ireland and in the industrial troubles of 1972 – as is made clear by the Sergeant:

> Ten years down Ulster then English streets. Then the late seventies and the laws against industrial unrest. Soldier boy at the picket line, working men 'is own kind comin' at 'im yellin' Scab Scab. I went down a mine, a corporal then, in the strike o' nineteen eighty. The miners o' that pit tried t'kill us, y'know that? Only time I've ever been in Wales. Women spit very 'ard. At Corporals anyway. The British Army's got politicised, y'see.

The Sergeant's position is opposed by that of Captain Thompson, the prison doctor in charge of recreational activities. He is another version of the liberal academic, Martin, in *The Saliva Milk-Shake*, caught up in a political world not of his making, but one which resists from both sides his attempts to make it more humane. The prisoners

53

are suspicious of his help with their play – 'all they want . . . to humiliate us . . . make us look daft' – and his colonel is only too aware of the subversive potential of their 'Churchill nonsense':

> You're quite a big young man, Thompson. But there's a little worm in you. But . . . Water it down, cut it about. Put a few patriotic remarks . . . About England . . . In it. That is an order. Winston Churchill saved this country from one thousand years of barbarism. So no disrespect to the memory of that great man.

Brenton uses Thompson's wife to establish the connection. Throughout the play she pleads with him to become a real doctor, and to accept Mummy's money towards a nice house in the Home Counties. 'It's not bad, what I want, is it? It's no disgrace. A house, with a garden, in the south of England. Decent. Mild. Safe. Away from this . . . Rural slum. Slum landscape, slum fen . . . barbed wire.' There is no place in this vision of the modern world for his agonising position; 'the pleasant roads in southern suburbs are as much a part of the wire in Long Kesh as the wire itself' (*TQ*, v, no. 17). Thompson has no reply to the blunt honesty of the Sergeant: 'Look at it from the soldier's point of view, Sir. 'E wants what 'e wants bad. Do you want what you want, bad? I mean you must do . . . Less you're a real . . . Liar, I mean a real self deceiver, eh? I mean, really washed up?' He ends the play having his pathetic offer of help in the break-out rejected as absurd.

That his offer of medical aid should be rejected is both inevitable and ironic, for it is the culmination of the imagery of disease which dominates the play. Throughout, the Churchill actor talks of the Great Man as a steadily rotting corpse, and an identification with the state of the nation is always apparent.

> Of my father's syphilis. The tender secret my family has cherished, the terrible fact. Lord Randolph Churchill, brilliant meteor of his day, the man they said would run the English Twentieth Century. . . . Died of that filthy disease. . . . I came home from India, to a quiet sitting-room. Out of the window the English countryside and warm gentle rain. . . . I cannot express, even to myself, the obscenity of what the disease had done to him. It had . . . scraped his brain. . . . I have feared his disease all my life. . . . My Father's disease, visited upon me, as the Bible says, generation upon generation.

Earlier Joby makes the connection directly to Peter Reese: 'Schubert, t' composer, died of the clap, y'know' . . . Inflames the brain. Makes artist think a weird an' wonderful tunes an' shapes. Inflation does 'same for a country. Weird an' wonderful, till backbone rots.' Humane cures are no longer an issue; Thompson's response to his wife's appeal to him to return to research on heart diseases is to refer to himself as the 'English leper'. When the drunken Labour peer asks the Sergeant about recreation before the entertainment, he replies, 'What do you do with a slobbering, rabid dog? Don't let it go round infecting us all, do you Sir? Y' take it out and shoot it, don't you Sir? Like we did in Ireland.'

And immediately before this, Morn has made his own analogy: 'You and the English Army . . . You tear the skin back, eh? Rip the flesh. And you go on, through the epidermic wall, deep into the body, to put your hand on an internal organ, liver, kidney, heart. . . . To squeeze. I speak of the body politic. . . . The English Army taking over

England.' Thompson's final lesson in the impossibility of combining the roles of doctor and prison-guard comes when he discusses the latest Ministry of Defence project, the white box. 'You are tied in a white room. The eye cannot focus. . . . And in the end you become a white, three-D void. Of course, there are drugs. And surgery.' The word he is finally forced to apply is 'butchery'. What is continually stressed is that the fine distinctions no longer matter. 'We are all caught up in some vast conspiracy of obedience', says Morn. 'Who is responsible? None of us, all of us.' Thompson's last words in the play come too late for him: 'House, lawn, plants under the roof. All built on this. Mud, these men. I am a doctor.'

The impossibility of belief in a middle course is reinforced by what we learn of the prisoners. Joby ''it a po-liceman' when covering a picket-line as a journalist; Peter Reese committed an act of 'petty vandalism'; Furry left 'back door open' for some union lads 't' pop in'. The offences are trivial and the punishment, unlimited imprisonment, brutality and a strong chance of being 'dumped', as George Lamacraft is for fooling about, out of all proportion. Of the others, only Jimmy Umpleby, of the 'neo-Luddites, Leeds Chapter', a character in the mould of Jed in *Magnificence* – who has succeeded in doing what the Angry Brigade failed to do, blow up the Post Office Tower – would fit into anything like a criminal role; and Jimmy is continually mocked by the others for his frivolous violence. 'Post Office Tower, oh yes', says Ted. 'And they put it up again and clamped down on you. You were the last . . . Farts of the age of Aquarius.'

Only Mike McCullough, and the Convery who does not appear, can be thought of as possessing a political brain, and of representing a real threat to the establishment. Until late in the play, Mike refuses to be drawn into their arguments – though significantly it is his single-word suggestion 'Breakout' that concludes the second act – but, when the escape attempt occurs, he is the organiser and it is to his words that all pay heed. Once Jimmy has ruined their slender chances by firing off a gun – 'What else is there for us, you see? Go out, on fire. Wi' a gesture' – Mike immediately halts the attempt. He rejects Jimmy's world of political gestures, as surely as he does Joby's passive role: 'We're like the plague. They'll not let us out of 'ere' – a continuation of the imagery of disease prompted by the Civil Servant's description of them as 'cancer cells'. Mike is a 'portrait of an activist', and what is important for him is the continuation of the struggle, rejecting in the process the fatalistic notion of terminal disease and Jimmy's romantic brand of revolutionary suicide. His last speech to his mates offers both despair and minimal hope. 'And we go out that door, and they cut us down . . . Nowhere to break out to, is there. They'll concrete the whole world over any moment now. And what we do? (*A slight pause. Smiles*.) Survive. In the cracks. Either side of the wire. Be alive.' Freedom may, as Joby argues, have gone, but the struggle will continue for Mike in an England that has become one vast concreted Camp Churchill. 'The camp is Hell, and amongst other things the play says, "This isn't so bad is it, it's not Belsen?" '

Ambiguity about the possibility of political action is shown most clearly in the 'play within a play' that the prisoners present – a device owing something to the mechanicals' entertainment for their superiors in *Midsummer Night's Dream*, and to the *Marat–Sade*. The 'play' is a remarkable piece of writing, moving rapidly between opposing styles, and gradually revealing beneath its surface comedy the raw nerves of dissent that take us naturally into the attempted break-out. In part its function is simply to

57

offend, 'to take the piss out of a great Englishman', the statesman who helped to carve up the modern world and the archetypal figure of an establishment whose ideology has provided the bricks of the camp. The 'play' is concerned to demythologise but also to demonstrate the failure of the socialist programme in post-war years, defeated by, amongst other things, the ability of the old order to infiltrate and to subvert. The figure of Tom Browne in *Brassneck* is one that might be invoked again in this context.

After a slightly altered reprise of the opening of the play, the prisoners take the two audiences, that of the Parliamentary Commission and that in the theatre, 'back through history'. A series of slides depicting English history from Churchill's funeral back to the Fire of London in 1940 are flashed onto the screen, and thereafter the 'play' is concerned with the war. We have already seen a rehearsal of an abandoned scene, the hilarious depiction of the Yalta Conference, with Roosevelt, Stalin and Churchill sat in a tin-bath with Peter Reese as a bar of soap representing Truth 'easily lost at bottom', and now the prisoners attempt to show the other side of the story. The famous incident at Peckham, for instance, when someone is supposed to have shouted to Churchill, 'We can take it. Give it 'em back.' is altered to, 'We can take it. But we just might give it back to you one day.' The entertainment is an act of defiance and also the cover for a greater, the attempted breakout, but its positioning in the play results in a deliberately problematic lesson. The 'play' is in the end only a sop and can be stopped at any time – recent parallels with actual and attempted censorship on the stage and television are obvious – and the specific end is unsuccessful. Beneath the comedy Brenton has important things to say, but one of the most important would seem to be that by implication the theatre audience are as likely to identify with the members of the Parliamentary Commission as the prisoners, so that any hopes for the play being heeded are expressed in necessarily ambivalent terms. 'Who is responsible? None of us. All of us.'

The Churchill Play expresses eloquently, then, not only a metaphor of the nation as one vast policed camp rotting away, but also the contradictions inherent in arguing against the inevitability of this vision to an audience about whose political allegiance there is considerable reason to doubt, and with no clear sense of how to proceed. Brenton felt at the time that his dilemma was felt by many contemporary writers: 'In a way I think we're all a bit like Chekhov. He didn't *know* what was only a few years away, but he felt it in his bones . . . it's as if he knew the Russian Revolution was almost there' (*Guardian*, 9 May 1974).

3
David Hare: The State of the Nation

To me it would be sad if a whole generation's lives were shaped by the fact that a belief in change had fallen temporarily out of fashion.

(David Hare, 'A Lecture', published with *Licking Hitler*)

In a recent *Sunday Times*, a feature on David Hare and Christopher Hampton was accompanied by a photograph described wrongly as being of the two men. Actually, it was of Hare and Brenton. The mistake was almost inevitable, so interlinked has the work of the two men been. So much so, that it is surprising – especially given that they have not only worked on shows together, but have directly collaborated on four plays – just how different the work of the one is from the other. If it is the epic model, with its opening-out of the scale of political debate, which has come increasingly to interest Brenton, the same cannot be said of Hare. Where Brenton has seen his 'acceptance' by the National Theatre, for instance, as a challenge in terms of potential cast growth and territorial aggrandisement, Hare's plays, with one notable exception, have remained consistently scaled-down in format, the action confined in rooms populated by small groups of people with tangled emotional relationships the likes of which are only to be found in Brenton's least characteristic play, *Sore Throats*.

Crudely, Brenton's characters are conceived from the outside, as embodiments of the various and conflicting strands of social reality. They are ideologically determined rather than psychologically explained, leading many critics, looking in vain for the conventionally peopled stage of the 'well-made-play', to talk absurdly of stereotypes. Now, curiously, it is just this tradition of the well-made-play that is most frequently invoked in what scant critical attention Hare has received, his name being linked with that of Osborne and even Rattigan. Such a response is an attempt to assimilate the plays back into the mainstream by stressing their wit and polish, at the expense of attention to what it is that the characters are so articulate about. It ignores the deliberate sabotage that Hare deploys on the expectancies of a straight-line plot development – the *status quo*, disruption of the *status quo* by a solvable moral dilemma, explication and resolution of situation – of the standard model. Ansorge makes the point well:

> In more conservative theatrical circles, which includes the vast majority of playgoers and critics, there has been much admiration expressed for the wit and bite of Hare's dialogue ... tempered with regret over his nagging refusal to lower the tone of his moral voice which is constantly to be heard wise-cracking away in the plays. (*P & P*, Apr 1978)

In truth Hare is every bit as aware of and as interested in ideological conflict as Brenton, but, where the latter is concerned primarily with characterisation as a product of social reality, Hare works from the inside. He is intensely interested in the particular individuality of the individual, and most of his central characters are misfits, living out their disillusionment through the dismal unrolling of post-1939 British history. His characters do not embody the confusion of social reality but struggle against it, and it is in this clash that Hare seeks to define the arena of political debate. This raises particular problems because most of his plays are located almost symbolically in the camps of the enemy; in an exclusive girls' school (*Slag*, 1969); in the Hampstead home of a politically bankrupt Labour MP (*The Great Exhibition*, 1972); in the City-commuter land of Surrey (*Knuckle*, 1974); in Jesus College, Cambridge (*Teeth 'n' Smiles*, 1975); and in an English country-house (*Licking Hitler*, 1978). The debate, although occasionally interrupted by outside voices, is almost entirely contained within the precincts of what is clearly seen as the ruling-class.

This is nowhere more apparent than in *Slag*, the play which first introduced Hare to an other than Portable audience. Although it is set in an exclusive girls' school, it rapidly emerges that Hare is less interested in the specific details of locale – we never see any of the pupils, all of whom have anyway reportedly left by the end of the play – than in its potential for enclosing the debate within a tiny area of a social model that is recognisably English.

I'm fascinated by self-enclosed societies – a very middle-class obsession. There has to be a degree of parody about plays with that theme. My plays are intended as puzzles – the solution of which is up to the audience. . . . *Slag* was about all educational establishments which I've known, including Cambridge, where there is a very self-regarding obsession with personal relationships.   (*P & P*, Feb 1972)

The play opens with the three women teachers, Joanne, Elise and Ann, promising, in a parody of the beginning of *Love's Labour's Lost*, to renounce men and sexual intercourse. Joanne wishes to tie this specifically to 'the establishment of a truly socialist society', though Ann rejects the extension, pointing out that, anyway, the only men they see are the parents.

From the outset the humour of the play derives from the gap between theory and practice: Elise knitting a baby's bootie is told by Joanna, 'All you need now is a fuck'; and Ann's desire to start from scratch, 'spend the time creatively', 'build a new Brackenhurst', is undercut by Joanna's reference to Robinson Crusoe – the point being that Crusoe too was without a sexual partner, and when he 'landed on a desert island, his first instinct was to create a perfect embryo of the society he had escaped from'. The various changes they propose – Joanna has 'renamed her study the Women's Liberation Workshop. She says she's teaching dialectics this week instead of gym' – will bear no relation to any outside reality, nor will they even be of value in a school which is progressively denuded of pupils as scene follows scene. Joanna, the most militantly feminist character, who has driven away the 'Royal Child' by teaching her to masturbate, is presented as no more in touch with the possibility of change than the others. Her *Robinson Crusoe* analogy is drawn from Bunuel's movie seen during her employment as a cinema projectionist, and we discover that all her ideas are taken from films, possessing no greater validity than the fantasies of Ann or Elise; 'the Women's Lib thing was much more of a character device than a polemic. But that whole discussion about genetics (the superiority of the female to the male chromosomes) was painstakingly researched. It was meant to be elastic – to see how far people can stretch themselves and an argument' (*P & P*, Feb 1972).

The isolation of the characters is important. They are shut off from a larger social world, teachers with nothing and, ultimately, no one to teach. Joanna, who in the first scene of the play had declared, 'This is the battle-ground of the future. . . . It's between intercourse or isolation', talks as they watch the First VII (all that are left by this point) of wanting to teach the girls a separatist programme, 'to work in a community that was feminine by necessity and make it feminine by choice', and then attempts to break out over the wire, only to be pulled down by Ann – 'everyone tries a breakout at one time or another'. The wire has a double function: it preserves the old order from the invasion of the new, and it prevents what insights are achieved within its exclusive grounds from being disseminated elsewhere. It is a confusing metaphor for the state of an England in which a Brackenhurst can still operate, as in Shaw's *Heartbreak House*, as a reasonable symbolic location. As Joanna says, 'At Brackenhurst nothing ever happens. The tedium is quite a challenge, quite an experience. The distinctive English sight of nothing happening and nothing going to happen.' The faded gentility of an exclusive school ruled over by would-be progressives – the paradox is impossible and deliberate; in Brackenhurst and in England nothing ever changes. The debate is of course unfairly presented – Hare's main concern is to satirise a liberated consciousness whose mattress is still the soft lands of the Home Counties – and *Slag* is in no obvious sense *about* feminism or anything else. It is the sterility of the debate that is stressed. These are bankrupt teachers caught up in their own ridiculous dreams; like Crusoe's, their model society can only exist away from that absolute essential of political life, human contact.

Hare elaborates further on this theme in *The Great Exhibition*. In a *'comfortable'* London flat, dominated by a *'rather weary looking cannabis plant'*, Hammett acts out his last hours as a Labour MP. He has not left the house for six weeks, and has not visited his Northern constituency for so long that eventually the Home Secretary arrives to suggest that he resign. 'It's a long way and when you get there it's a dump.' Hammett protests, 'And the people resent me because I'm not working class.' His desire for isolation – he hides the telephone under a biscuit-box and talks of working on a 'letter-box for the front door that will burst into flames twice a day and incinerate the contents' – is a recognition of the extent to which he is cut off from what, as a socialist, should be his roots. In part, then, the instigation for the play is close to that of a number of plays of the period – most obviously Brenton's *Fruit*, which Hare directed. 'I think it was to do with Labour and politics generally in the sixties. The only political experience I had was believing passionately in the Labour Government of 1964, and watching that government sell everything down the river. So the play was about a disillusioned Labour MP' (*TQ*, v, no. 20, 1975).

Certainly Hammett is a product of a consciousness which predates that exemplified by the debate between the three women in *Slag*: 'I decided to be a politician about three days before the rest of the world became revolutionaries', he announces rhetorically. What he is most articulate about is not his loss of commitment but his complete lack of it from the outset. He is neither an old socialist, with his origins in traditional trade-union and working-class activity, nor a member of the New Left. He had become a socialist 'like other people go into the law', as a profession, 'half out of eloquence, half out of guilt', and had subsequently realised his complete failure to relate to the historical period through which he is crawling towards death. 'I sat down at the age of twenty-one and I thought I'm going to need some enthusiasms to get me to the grave. And I chose three. Food, sex and socialism.' The wilted cannabis plant, never used by him, is the nearest he has approached to the 'alternative society', and his political education was received on the Aldermaston March. 'We moved on to rip up a regional seat of government. That's a place where old Tories go to die. After the bomb drops – remember the bomb?'

It was on the March, we learn, that he first met his wife;

in the following weeks I talked to her about socialism, and as I talked I became so convinced, it became so clear, that I decided to be a politician. My own eloquence, you see. The platform, the business of speaking, it all delighted me. I courted Maud with public speeches. My actual proposal drew heavily on *Das Kapital*.

What chiefly preoccupies Hare is the analogy between public life and acting. Much of the power of the play comes from the dramatisation of this analogy, and also many of its problems. That I can quote Hammett's words with such ease freely of any context points to what is a central weakness of the play. Much of *The Great Exhibition* is in effect a long monologue of wit and despair. It scarcely matters who Hammett is addressing; he is an actor for whom all speech is a disguise. His wife is now a casting-director. When she first enters, she announces that she is tired because she has been auditioning for *King Lear* all day. Hammett recalls to Jerry, Maud's Australian hippy

66

lover, how he first saw her at drama-school in the role of
Cordelia.

> The man who was playing Lear opposite Maud, and I
> mean dead opposite Maud, arrived at rehearsals with
> some charts under his arm. He then laid them out on the
> stage and retraced the very steps Sir Barry Jackson had
> used with the Birmingham Repertory Company in 1924.
> The moves turned out to have a kind of triangular zest. I
> loved it. It seemed to me at the time that the theatre put
> to good use could be the most sophisticated possible
> means of ignoring what people were actually like.

Hammett's articulation of the falsity of acting as a useful
way of dealing with the impossible confusions of reality is
reinforced by his very articulateness. Maud tells him, in
their first interchange in the play, that for eight years he has
been her only contact with reality. 'I've always said there
are two kinds of people. Human beings and actors.' But
Hammett, as we have seen, is only an actor. He had entered
Parliament in the landslide of '66, and he talks about it as a
'debating society, some ghastly boys' school'.

The play's two acts are labelled 'Public Life' and 'Private
Life', and much of the excitement derives from the way in
which the two are connected. The narrative of the play
parallels Hammett's demise as a politician with his hiring of
a private detective to spy on Maud, who has been planning
to leave him. 'Hammett feels himself to be an exhibitionist
both in his public life and in his private life. He feels
conscious that he's performing in parliament, and conscious that he's performing in front of his wife' (*TQ*, v, no.
20). His one attempt to break out from the restraints of the
room that he has created for himself is when he goes to
Clapham Common, in a parody of Lear's 'unaccommo-

dated man' speech used as the prefatory epigram to the play, and exposes himself before an indifferent audience.

His attempt to render himself naked before his public – a nakedness which is echoed in the Polaroid shots of Maud and Jerry taken for him by the private detective – is a dismal failure. He meets Catriona, an old upper-class friend of his wife's, whose introduction into the narrative allows him a few nostalgic blasts at the parliamentary opposition, but then discovers that she has been following him around to recruit him on behalf of her father, who is Chairman of the Confederation of British Industries. The play ends with Hammett and Maud, now firmly cut off from any role in the public world, seeing a future if only they can 'lose our personalities', and then repeating each other's name. Any move towards a dramatic resolution has already been scuppered by Hammett's realisation that Catriona has all the time been manipulating the plot of the play to her own ends, and that there is nothing new to be learned from it.

Maud used to appear in plays by Ibsen in which the characters would come on stage and tell each other what they perfectly well knew already. 'It is ten years today, Mrs Rummell, since the terrible snowdrifts during which Little Eywolf fell off the kitchen table while Gregors and I were copulating thereby damaging the nerves in his leg, which accounts for the limp with which he now walks.' And in would come Eywolf, limping like mad. That's how I feel with you, Catriona. It was called exposition. But it turned out you already knew.

The Great Exhibition is, then, for all its verbal dexterity a flawed play. It is a *tour de force* which remains contained within the confines of its isolation. Hare recognised its necessary limitations, locating the problems in its inability to overcome its format.

> I think people have expectations of plays with one set and a limited number of characters, and I think those limitations are impossible to resist. And although *The Great Exhibition* starts in a room, and then deliberately explodes and opens out to try and confound the audience, I don't think it really succeeded. ... There is something about the ritual of a play in which there is this guy at the centre of the stage with all the best lines, who's being witty at everybody's expense, and whose uniquely subtle psychology we're going to explore during the course of the evening, which is limiting, which is dead. Because it stops the audience thinking – or rather, they imagine they're there to find out what this man on the stage thinks. They're not: they're there to find out what *they* think.   (*TQ*, v, no. 20)

It is difficult to engage with *The Great Exhibition* other than on the level of exposition. Hammett simply will not take the strain of acting both as Hare's spokesman and as a character in a narrative. What is notably lacking is dialogue in the sense of genuine conflict. To this point, *The Great Exhibition* was Hare's largest sustained piece of work – it took him about a year to write – and it is the last of his plays to place the emphasis on a single character, a process that had begun with his work with Portable – primarily shows about individual literary figures, on Kafka, Genet and Strindberg ('once we were even going to do Lawrence Durrell' – *TQ*, v, no. 20) and later *What Happened to Blake* (1970).

What Hare attempts in his subsequent work is a series of perspectives of the political state of the nation which does not accord to either the psychological model – the reduction of politics 'to wearying personal fetish, or even chronic personality disorder' – or the tradition of agit-prop which dominates so much alternative theatre in the seventies: 'if a play is to be a weapon in the class struggle, then that weapon is not going to be the things you are saying; it is the interaction of what you are saying and what the audience is thinking' ('A Lecture', in *Licking Hitler*). Hare has talked frequently of himself as a writer of history-plays. It is a useful description, pointing as it does to his concern with the presentation of things as they are in the context of how they might have been, rather than to any idealist notions of how they should be. 'I write tribal pieces, trying to show how people behaved on this island, off this continental shelf, in this century. How this Empire vanished, how these ideals changed' (ibid.). 'How things should be', Hare suggests, is as much the business of the audience as the writer. What concerns him is not street politics but personal despair, 'and it is to that despair that as a historical writer I choose to address myself time and time again' (ibid.).

The first of these new approaches is *Knuckle*, completed after, and clearly influenced by, his collaboration on *Brassneck*. The location is the City-commuter world of Guildford, but a Guildford that is seen through the eyes of a character, Curly Delafield, who is modelled on the Continental Op. tough-guy heroes. The effect is to articulate the corruption that Hare finds beneath the civilised veneer. The housekeeper of Curly's father, Patrick, tells him that he is a 'cultured man', to which our hero replies, 'Who ran Auschwitz? A pack of bloody intellectuals.' In the first scene Curly arrives at the Shadow of the Moon Club in search of the truth about his sister Sarah's disappearance. Although she never appears, the image of Sarah is at the centre of the play. She is that figure of despair, a product, as is Curly, of an unbrave new world of commercial ruthlessness, the world of 'John Bloom and Jack Cotton'. Jenny, whom Curly meets at the Club, tells him that Sarah 'used to say life was a plush abattoir', that 'she'd recognize a moment of happiness because – she remembered having one in nineteen-sixty-five, and if another came along, she could remember'.

The plot of *Knuckle* is modelled on the forties American detective movies, but Curly is not the conventional modern knight-errant of the Chandler tradition. His reaction to what Sarah is reported as describing as Surrey's 'contagious diseases – moral gumrot, internal decay' had been to run away and become an international armament salesman. Sarah's sole gesture, as Jenny tells Curly, was when 'she ran away to Surbiton. That's the scale of her life.' Ansorge makes the point well:

> In Hare's later work the guardians of our most protected institutions like Patrick, who reads Henry James by night and ruins men by day, speak powerfully in defence of ruthlessness. Clearly idealists like Sarah go under. Hence Curly's belief in his 'guns', both real and metaphorical, his dependence on a life-style based on cynicism and disgust but providing the only weapons which might one day defeat his father – using evil to fight back at evil. (*P & P*, Apr 1978)

Hare uses the detective-quest motif gradually to strip away the comfortable exterior; Curly's search takes him into a shabby world of blackmail, crooked property-dealing and murder, all of which are quite directly linked to the everyday life of the City financier. Patrick attempts to tell Curly that the world has changed, but his prior knowledge is implicit in the aggressive role he has chosen to play. 'The city of London once enjoyed a reputation for unimpeachable integrity. . . . But in the last twenty years we've been dragged through the mud like everyone else. The wideboys and the profiteers have sullied our reputation. We work now like stall-holders against a barrage of abuse.'

Curly eventually learns of the final meeting, between Patrick and Sarah on Eastbourne beach, after which Patrick had left her to commit suicide. He had attempted to tell her about the harsh reality of City life – 'Those who wish to reform the world should first know a bit about it' – and challenged her to suggest how it might ever be changed. Then, in a brilliant exchange of clichés, Curly and Patrick put forward all the usual arguments against the possibility of change, the whole dialogue only serving further to stress the strength of Sarah's and, as we have seen in a rather different way, Curly's conviction that change must still be thought to be possible.

> CURLY: Tell me of any society that has not operated in this way?
> PATRICK: Five years after a revolution . . .
> CURLY: The shit rises . . .
> PATRICK: The same pattern . . .
> CURLY: The weak go to the wall . . .
> PATRICK: Someone's bound to get hurt . . .
> CURLY: You can't make omelettes . . .
> PATRICK: The pursuit of money is a force for progress . . .
> CURLY: It's always been the same . . .
> PATRICK: The making of money . . .
> CURLY: The breaking of men . . .
> PATRICK: The two together. Always. The sound of progress.
> CURLY: The making of money. The breaking of men.

72

Having unearthed the truth, Curly realises the futility of publishing it:

> Somewhere every so often in this world there will appear this tiny little weed called morality. It will push up quietly through the tarmac and there my father will be waiting with a cement grinder and a shovel to concrete it over. It is inadequate. It cannot help us now. There are no excuses left. Two sides. Two sides only.

Humanism is finally rejected, and with it the warm overcoat of morality, and in a final soliloquy Curly prepares to leave Guildford with the only solution that he has – although it is, of course, not the only one posited by the play as a whole.

> Why should I feel ashamed of myself? Why should I feel inferior? Why should I believe her? And, anyway, Sarah was alive. It was autumn again. In the mean square mile of the City of London they were making money. (*Smiling*.) Back to my guns.

The same dialectic of idealism and despair is present in *Teeth 'n' Smiles*, represented by the song-writer, Arthur, and the self-destructive singer, Maggie.

MAGGIE: If there was going to be a revolution it would have happened by now. I don't think 1970'll be the big year.

ARTHUR: Leonardo da Vinci drew submarines. Five hundred years ago. They looked pretty silly. Today we are drawing a new man. He may look pretty silly.

MAGGIE: You still want it to mean something, don't you.

73

Teeth 'n' Smiles is the first of the history-plays not to be set in the present. Although first performed in 1975, the play concerns the attempts of a rock-group to get through their two sets at a May Ball in Jesus College, Cambridge, in 1969. The earlier hopes of the alternative society are caught in that moment of containment, one year after the Paris Spring of 1968. 'Would you say the ideas expressed in popular music . . . have had the desired effect of changing . . . society in any way?' asks Anson, the bumbling medical student who is organising the event, and Maggie's response is to take him off and screw him. From the outset it is evident that not much is to be hoped for from a band that is uncertain whether it is in Cambridge or in Canterbury, and the first scene of the play is dominated by a demarcation dispute about whose job it is to fix the one plug that stands between them and their public. Their particular brand of unthinking destructive anarchy is powerless against the less obvious but infinitely elastic establishment represented by the College. They set out to smash the place up, but succeed only in smashing themselves.

ARTHUR: They invent a few rules that don't mean anything so that you can ruin your health trying to change them. Then overnight they re-draft them because they didn't really matter in the first place. One day it's a revolution to say fuck on the bus. Next day it's the only way to get a ticket. That's how the system works.

As the long night proceeds the band experience the impossibility of affecting anything. Blocked off by a sea of drugs and alcohol from the unreality which they attempt to assault, all their worst efforts are met with indifference or containment. The first set is a disaster, 'like floggin' a corpse'. Wilson: 'Do you know, some woofter comes up to

74

me after the set, says I expectin' somethin' altogether more
Dionysiac, I says Thursdays we're Dionysiac, Friday's
we're just fuckin' awful.' Arthur's songs are as powerless as
the band's aggression in the face of the University establishment's ability to soak up anything. After they have been
busted, Maggie goes berserk during the second set – '(*She
holds up the whisky bottle.*) This is a depressant, I take it
to get depressed' – and sets fire to the tent, while all around
the rest of the band set off on an orgy of looting and sex.
But, as Arthur tells her, nothing has been achieved. 'They
all love it you know. Dashing about in the smoke. They're
hoping to make it an annual event.'

The economic context is provided by Serafian, the aging
entrepreneur acting as their manager. He arrives unexpec-
tedly with his latest protégé and the intention of sacking the
increasingly unreliable Maggie. It is his commercial cynicism that adds the edge to Arthur's, and to some extent
Maggie's, defiant despair. Where Arthur can offer an
analysis of how things might develop, alongside his hopes
for the emergence of the 'new man' – 'I can see us all.
Rolling down the highway into middle age. Complacency.
Prurience. Sadism. Despair' – Serafian has never conceived
of anything beyond the uneasiness of the *status quo* in the
pursuit of money, which is all that the activities of the band
represent to him.

He tells Maggie a long anecdote about being in the Café
de Paris when it was bombed in 1941. As the smoke cleared
he felt his ring being lifted from his finger and realised that
the bodies were being looted, 'and my first thought is: I'm
with you, pal'. Once he was clear of the building he hailed a
taxi, but the driver, seeing the blood on his dinner jacket,
'the exploded wealth', refuses to take him. Serafian was
happier in the old days of popular music when the lines
were more obviously drawn – 'It was organised crime' – but

is quite ready to agree with Maggie that to him the band is 'just merchandise . . . soapflakes we could be'. Maggie's rejoinder, 'What a critical insight . . . and what did you do in the next *thirty years*?', has a double-edge. What really has changed during this time? The ball-room in the Café de Paris had been a perfect reproduction of that of the Titanic, and Cambridge in 1969 hears as the final song in the play Maggie's 'Last orders on the Titanic'; but if the nation, symbolised in these institutions, has been steadily sinking, the top deck is still populated as it always has been. Arthur's qualified idealism and Maggie's gesture of accepting the prison sentence for the possession of drugs look rather minimal compared to the ability of the old establishment and the new commerce to come to terms – as in *Knuckle* – rather than yield to change.

Hare's insistently empirical observation of despair as the only honest response to a bankrupt culture is best articulated in the two companion plays, *Plenty* and *Licking Hitler* (1978), where for the first time he looks at the larger historical perspective, tracing the decline from the war years. It is an important development, and reinforces his claim to be fundamentally a history-writer.

> If you write about now, just today and nothing else, then you seem to be confronting only stasis; but if you begin to describe the movement of history, if you write plays that cover passages of time, then you begin to find a sense of movement, of social change, if you like; and the facile hopelessness that comes from confronting the day and only the day, the room and only the room, begins to disappear and in its place the writer can offer a record of movement and change.   ('A Lecture', in *Licking Hitler*)

This sense of the 'movement of history' is most obvious

in *Plenty*, which covers, in a series of jumps, the period 1943–62. The play opens in a room in Knightsbridge in 1962. Susan Traherne is about to leave both house and husband. The first 'has been stripped bare', and the second lies naked and asleep. In packing-cases are collected all the material goods that the couple have accumulated in the post-war years. The contrast is striking, the apparent 'plenty' of the 'never had it so good' years mocked by the real naked impoverishment of both individual and location. That the location is specifically England is stressed from the opening words of the play, delivered by Susan's friend, Alice: 'I don't know why anybody lives in this country. . . . The wet. The cold. The flu. The food. The loveless English.' This is England before the alternative euphoria of the late sixties and, more importantly, immediately before the Labour administration of which Hare had briefly entertained such hopes, an England still living in the aftermath of war. It is, furthermore, an England seen firmly from the perspective of the establishment rather than the shop-floor, and the lives of all the characters are inextricably linked with the failure of English diplomacy either to succeed or to give way to change. Just as the lives of the characters are firmly rooted in the past, so are the explanations of continuity and decay.

The second scene takes Susan back to 1943, as an agent in occupied France, the only time in her history when she was able to believe that what she was doing had any point, that there was a cause worth fighting for. Her experiences in the war provide the only thing for her to hang on to, at first optimistically but finally in despair and a peculiarly refined English version of madness. 'The most unlikely people. People I met for only an hour or two. Astonishing kindness. Bravery. The fact you could meet someone an hour or two and see the very best of them and then move on.' Her work as an agent had of course been one of deception, and what Susan comes to experience subsequently is that in the business of government and commerce there is only deception, that the necessary lie does not conceal a greater truth. By 1952, working on copy for an advertising agency, she is well able to make the connection:

> In France . . . I told such glittering lies. But where's the fun in lying for a living. . . . To produce what my masters call good copy, it is simply a question of pitching my intelligence low enough. . . . This is all the future holds for any of us. We will spend the next twenty years of our lives pretending to be thick.

If Susan's central discovery is the inadequacy of idealism, her husband, Brock, starts with fewer illusions. He is fascinated by her circle of literary and intellectual friends, but places all his hopes on inherited privilege and the accumulation of wealth. 'I think everyone's going to be rich very soon', he tells Alice in 1947, 'Once we've got over the effects of the war. It's going to be coming out of everyone's ears.' Post-war society, as conceived by all the characters, has nothing to do with the construction of the Welfare State and the early dreams engendered by the Labour administration of 1945. Even Brock's vision of wealth is set securely within the portals of the Diplomatic Service, in which he has made his career. Their world is that of the old England that will continue to administer the stranglehold over all attempts to change. One of Brock's colleagues in the Service, Darwin – described by Brock as a 'modern Darwin who is in every aspect less advanced than the last', an evolutionist too unsophisticated to be aware of the possibility of revolution – talks of building the new Europe.

For him, it will be a programme along traditional pater-
nalistic lines, about as wrong as it was possible to be about
the new Europe. His imagery takes us steadily away from a
present of road-building, through the peasant fields of the
Empire, to the inevitable and carefully placed tray of
civilised drinks. 'Massive work of reconstruction. Jobs.
Ideals. Marvellous. Marvellous time to be alive in Europe.
No end of it. Roads to be built. People to be educated. Land
to be tilled. Plenty to get on with. (*Pause*.) Have another
gin.'

For Darwin in 1947, such an idealistic vision of what is
essentially the continuation of Empire is still a possibility.
Its public manifestation is the Festival of Britain, in 1951,
but Hare significantly uses the celebrations as a back-drop
for the beginning of Susan's personal disintegration.
Beneath the celebratory fireworks of the Festival she
negotiates the fathering of her child in exchange for a deal
involving 500 cheese-graters. But it is the Suez crisis of
1956 that is the personal and political breaking-point. As a
military manoeuvre it was misconceived and shambolic,
and Hare uses it to demonstrate the complete misreading of
history, and in particular of Britain's role, in the post-war
world, as exemplified by such as Darwin and the earnest
representative from the once-ruled territories, Mr Wong.
At the height of the crisis Susan and Brock hold a dinner
party for some of their fellow diplomats. A stage direction
describes Susan as '*dangerously cheerful*'; the parallels
between the Suez invasion and her own adventures in
France are irresistible, and push her over into an excited
madness. Wong puts forward a thesis about the American
and English partnership – the Americans are the Romans,
'power, armies and strength', and the English the Greeks,
'ideas, civilisation, intellect' – which is immediately undercut by the entrance of Darwin. The images of classical

nostalgia collapse against Darwin's realisation that the whole campaign is a fraud, not the glorious cause that Susan would like it to be.

Darwin's crisis is that of the old ruling class. He had been against the campaign from the outset, but has subsequently discovered that the government has lied. Greeks and Romans give way in the new world to Hollywood stereotypes. 'I would have defended it had it been honestly done. But this time we are cowboys and when the English are the cowboys, then in truth I fear for the future of the globe.' Darwin's notion of the traditional English code of fair dealing disintegrates around him faced with a final revelation of what had always been the political reality of deception, and the disintegration is mirrored dramatically by the break-up of the dinner party into shouting and abuse. As Darwin leaves to resign, Susan makes the connection between the parachute descents into occupied France, where 'we were comparatively welcome', and those into Egypt. Her final words before the interval now appear heavily ironic in their attempt to reconcile her and Brock's ideas of 'plenty'.

> Isn't this thrilling? Don't you think? Everything up for grabs. At last. We will see some changes. Thank the Lord. Now, there was dinner. I made some dinner. . . . A little ham. And chicken. And some pickles and tomato. And lettuce. And there are a couple of pheasants in the fridge. And I can get twelve bottles of claret from the cellar. Why not? There is plenty. Shall we eat again?

The crazily expanding meal, the feast of expediency in the ruins of idealism, is the first manifestation of Susan's insanity. Throughout the second half of the play, her attempts to come to terms with a world of lies and deception provide a perfect image of the larger context of decay. Her efforts to advance her husband's career in the Service founder because of her refusal to lie, to understand that public life is simply a game with rules that may not be articulated. 'Do you never find it in yourself to despise a profession in which nobody may speak their mind?' she asks Brock's superior, Sir Andrew Charleson.

> That is the nature of the service, Mrs Brock. It is called diplomacy. And in its practice the English lead the world. . . . As our power declines, the fight among us for access to that power becomes a little more urgent, a little uglier perhaps. As our influence wanes, as our empire collapses, there is little to believe in. Behaviour is all.

Diplomacy is revealed not as compassion and tact, but as duplicity and deception.

Susan has nothing with which to counter this. Her threat to shoot herself is rightly seen as silly and in bad taste. The elastic establishment will continue to preside over the final years of plenty. Her final words in the play, as she is transported back into wartime France after a final impossible attempt at an emotional relationship with Lazar, the man who has carried so much of the symbolic weight of her idealism, underline the irony. A brief moment of rapport has been established with a French farmer, and she addresses him and the audience, 'My friend. There will be days and days like this.'

Although this brief analysis of *Plenty* almost inevitably reads as though it seeks to place it in the Shavian tradition of 'theatre of ideas', this is not the whole truth. Certainly a sustained debate dominates the play, but Hare's creation of characters who demand a complicated sense of involvement from the audience – in a way that none of the other playwrights I shall be considering does – means that the debate is never an enclosed one. Ansorge talks of the ending in terms of an illusion that the audience has already had shattered, but this is to miss the point. The irony derives not from the fact that the audience has already had revealed to them that things did not work out as hoped for – which is to reduce the play to the level of simple exposition – but that it has been given a chance to evaluate the essential falsity of Susan's idealism. It looks as though, on a narrative level, there is only a choice between the cynical manipulation of the establishment and romantic idealism. The more subversive suggestion can be drawn from the sub-text of the play, that interaction between play and audience that Hare talks of, that there was a possibility of something else happening, that the presentation of English history is not only that of a pessimistic procession towards decline, but also there to be learned from.

This feeling is reinforced by *Licking Hitler*, which is exclusively concerned with a version of the war far removed from dreams of glory. It is set in an English country house, requisitioned for use as a radio propaganda unit to broadcast, from supposedly German sources, a dialogue of lies and defamation to demoralise the enemy. A picture of Goebbels replaces the ancestral portraits, and a new meritocracy with its roots in the diplomatic world, the traditional land-owner, Lord Minton, whose deafness and dumbness symbolise his ineffectualness and his inability to communicate with the new. Minton is ushered indirectly on his way by the man effectively running the broadcasts, Archie Maclean: 'Tell him we appreciate the sacrifice. Having to spend the rest of the war in that squalid wee end in Eaton Square.' The bitterness is important, and places Archie apart from both the old and the new ruling class. He is, we learn, 'from Glasgow, from the Red Clyde', a

82

journalist whose class and nationality cut off all contact with the continuity of the English *status quo*. His brilliance at his job stems from his absolute lack of belief in any lip-service to the moral tenets of the class that he sees as the real enemy. In the country house, as in the Diplomatic Service in *Plenty*, the lie reigns supreme, but for Archie it is unencumbered by any sentimental attempts to pretend that there is any larger morality. He argues successfully that, instead of propagandising against the German invasion of Russia on the demoralising grounds of its evident stupidity, they should be aiding it because it *is* stupid.

Into this setting is introduced Anna, whose uncle is Second Sea Lord. Her total lack of contact with ordinary life has caused her to remain ignorant of the existence of electricity-bills, and her efforts to make a pot of tea lead her to pour cold water over the entire week's rations. She represents very easily for Archie both the privilege and the helplessness of the old order he is really fighting. He tells her,

> I set myself the task. Get through the war. Just get through it, that's all. . . . This house is the war. And I'd rather be anywhere, I'd rather be in France, I'd rather be in the desert, I'd rather be in a Wellington over Berlin, anywhere but here with you and your people in this bloody awful English house.

Archie breaks into her room and substitutes himself in bed for her childhood teddybear, and their relationship stays at the level of aggression. No communication occurs, and he has Anna removed from the project when the possibility of real emotion proves a threat to his careful world of lies.

The play, which was produced on BBC television, ends, using the technique of many seventies quasi-documentary movies, in the present day, with a voice-over to describe what has subsequently happened to the major characters. Archie moved into making evocative films of his working-class roots, but is now working in Hollywood – sentimentality giving way to the lie – and Anna went to work in an advertising agency, 'increasingly distressed by the compromises forced on her by her profession. In 1956 she resigned and announced her intention to live an honest life.' The activities of the unit are shown to have been those which formed the basis of post-war society. The residents in the country house have spread through all positions of influence. 'Many of the most brilliant men from the Propaganda and Intelligence Services went on to careers in public life, in Parliament, Fleet Street, the universities and the BBC.' The inference is that these were logical continuations of their profession of lies and propaganda, that they are perfect examples of a society founded on dishonesty.

The last words are those of Anna, reading from her final letter to Archie. They resemble those of Maggie to Serafian in *Teeth 'n' Smiles*.

Whereas we knew exactly what we were fighting against, none of us had the whisper of an idea as to what we were fighting for. Over the years I have been watching the steady impoverishment of the people's ideals, their loss of faith, the lying, the daily inveterate lying, the thirty-year-old deep corrosive national habit of lying and I have remembered you.

The country house is Hare's most successful historical location, linking the old with the new, in an account of English history that is both disturbing and challenging. Hare's English plays offer not a programme for change, but rather a gauntlet thrown down, demanding an analysis that

84

must be made before any thought of change is possible. Their dramatic effectiveness must be judged by the extent to which they succeed in making an audience question the premises of the institutions to which, all radical and alternative politics notwithstanding, it still clings desperately.

Hare's determination to chronicle the contradictions of English society, rather than attempting a neat theatre of political idealism, has taken its toll, and it was with relief that, in 1975, he turned away from post-war Britain to look at the Chinese Revolution.

> I was sick to death with writing about England – about writing about this decadent corner of the globe. The excitement of *Fanshen* was to write about a society and to cover a period of time in which one felt that people's lives were being materially and spiritually improved, in a culture that was completely different to anything we knew about.   (*TQ*, v, no. 20)

Fanshen was commissioned by Joint Stock as their second production, and was based on William Hinton's account of change in China from the early years of the Revolution through the first half of the century, as experienced in a single village, Long Bow. The play was unusual for Hare, in that he spent five weeks attending rehearsals with the actors and directors (Bill Gaskill and Max Stafford-Clark), working from Hinton's book, before the play was started. Hare claims that he made no special concessions to the company's wishes, and the text he produced was, remarkably, little altered before the first performance at the Crucible, Sheffield, in April. It then transferred to the Institute of Contemporary Arts, London, and was then revised slightly for a season at the Hampstead Theatre Club, followed by a short tour and a televised production.

Fanshen is quite unlike his other work. His concern with dominant individuals is nowhere evident. The play has a cast of more than thirty, but was played with only nine actors (seven in the revised version). This was not just a conventional doubling-up of roles in the usual interests of economy. *Fanshen* is not about individuals as such. Little attention is paid to the development of character or to psychological distinction. Hare is more concerned with the interrelationship of the people in the village as they grapple with the common experience of change. In the community, as in the production, the total is far greater than the sum of the parts. Characters come and go from scene to scene, sometimes, though not always, introducing themselves to the audience, and a near anonymity is achieved by the uniformity of dress. Gaskill: 'The centre of our work on *Fanshen* does not lie in character at all and I think it has been an important thing for the actors to have discovered how to work and to be excited by working without "character" being the mainspring' (*P & P*, June 1975). Most of the scenes show the villagers arriving at decisions, in particular undergoing group appraisal and self-criticism, and many of these techniques were adapted as a part of the rehearsal process. For the actor, as for the villager, it was not enough to understand change; it was important to experience it directly. In Chinese *fanshen* is change; literally it means to 'turn the body', or to 'turn over'.

Fanshen opens in a characteristically low-key manner. As the audience settles, the actors walk on one by one, introducing their initial role, filling in with supplementary information, and placing themselves in the hierarchy as presently constituted. It is their social and economic role that is stressed. We learn nothing else about them. Introductions over, they set about their tasks in the village economy. The stage is bare throughout save for a raised platform from which the landlord watches them. The build-up is slow, fixing an image of the structure of the old order, the peasants working, the land-owner overseeing from above. The landlord leaves, and only now do the house-lights dim, conventionally signalling the start of a performance. The play will not be concerned with the old order, though we will hear frequent complaints about it. The lights down, we go straight into 'fanshen'.

T'IEN-MING: There will be a meeting. There will be a meeting today. In the square after the noon meal. There will be a meeting.
The men look up from their work.
FA-LIANG: A meeting.
TUI-CHIN: Twenty years ago we had a meeting.
CHENG-K'UAN: About the church, about who owned the vegetable patch.
TUI-CHIN *shrugs and smiles.*
TUI-CHIN: Another meeting.

The stark simplicity of language is in marked contrast to the wit and articulation of Hare's other plays. No particular attempt is made to produce an English version of Chinese speech-patterns, and the villagers swear at each other in familiar Anglo-Saxon terms, but the effect is to slow the pace, to force the audience to think out events along with the villagers. We know no more than they do, are learning alongside them, a process aided by having the audience virtually surround the cast. The sardonic humour of the surprise that a meeting has been called when there was one only twenty years before again forces the audience to accept a change of pace. The play will progress through a long time-span, and the experience of this in a theatre is in itself an argument against the idea of instant solutions. 'Fanshen' is a laborious act.

As they move to the meeting, the next scene develops. Kuo-Te-Ye, a collaborator with the Japanese, is brought in under guard. He is placed on the platform, trussed, and then flung in front of the assembled villagers. They demand violent revenge, but T'ien-Ming tells them that they must provide the evidence, that they must undertake the revenge, for themselves.

We are asking for your help. No one has ever asked your help before. Look at him. There's nothing to fear. You can touch him. Everyone here has a grievance, everyone here has the right to accuse, we have all the same thoughts in our heads. Those of us who fought in the resistance are now asking for your help. You must be the ones to beat down traitors, you must accuse. Who will be the first to accuse?

The calmness of the exposition does nothing to allay their fears; they are still living in the old world. T'ien-Ming unties the prisoner and demonstrates that there is nothing to fear. At last a man stands.

YU-LAI *looks round, then walks up.* T'IEN-MING *places him dead opposite* KUO-TE-YE.
T'IEN-MING: Was this man a collaborator? (YU-LAI *nods*.)
Did you suffer at his hands? (YU-LAI *nods*.)
Did he steal your harvest? (YU-LAI *nods*.)
Did he butcher your friends? (YU-LAI *nods*.)
Accuse him.
A pause. Then YU-LAI *strikes* KUO-TE-YE *across the face.*

> *Then he smashes a fist under his jaw.* KUO-TE-YE *falls back. Then picks him up, hits him again.*

T'IEN-MING: Accuse him.

> YU-LAI *stands him unsteadily on his feet, then takes a pace back.*

YU-LAI: She So-Tzu was tortured for eighteen days, starved and shot. He was responsible. He betrayed him to the Japanese. I saw the body. I know it happened.

T'IEN-MING: Name him.

YU-LAI: Kuo-Te-Ye.

> YU-LAI *goes back and takes his place in the crowd. Silence.*

Cautiously, other villagers stand to accuse and to name. The first step has been taken. The repeated use of 'then' in the stage directions is a cue to the way the scene was played. Each move, each gesture, each short piece of speech, is separated off. What is revealed by the stripping away of extraneous matter is the bare logical outline of the move towards articulation. The style is almost ritualistic. Yu-Lai's violence is a shock, carefully unprepared for. It precedes his account of the torture and murder, which will in turn precede the main point of the exercise, not revenge but a changed society. It is a gut-reaction insufficient to produce 'fanshen', and it will later rebound on him when he is accused of corrupt leadership in the post-'fanshen' community. Its deployment prevents the villagers from being convenient mouthpieces for a simplistic didactic argument. Real pain has produced an action which may be unhelpful but is understandable. These are not just political pawns.

Hare makes a similar use of comedy in the play. It is never directed against the villagers, and it allows the audience to see that the urge towards change is complicated and not always pure. Later a meeting is called to redistribute resources by classifying the peasants as poor, middle or rich. The blacksmith presents a problem. He doesn't work the land, and so is not a peasant of any kind, but equally he is not a land-owner. The attempts of the chairman to find him a status are frustrated by the villagers' insistence on giving him the worst possible designation, if only they could decide which it is. They are not bothered about the classification, only about his work.

OLD LADY WANG: You . . .

HUAN-CH'AO: Very happy to hear what you think.

OLD LADY WANG: We think . . .

HUAN-CH'AO: Yes?

OLD LADY WANG: We think you're a disgraceful black-smith.

HUAN-CH'AO: I see, yes, that's very interesting.

OLD LADY WANG: And we wouldn't trust you to bang a nail up an elephant's arse-hole.

HUAN-CH'AO: I see. Yes. That's very clear. (*Laughter.*)

The chairman tries to bring them back to the main question. It doesn't matter in determining his status whether or not he is a good blacksmith. But the old lady is determined. When a tentative agreement is reached, she still will not give way.

HOU: Good and bad don't come into it.

YUAN-LUNG: Call him a poor peasant . . .

OLD LADY WANG: Who must improve his work.

HOU: You're a poor peasant who must improve his work.

The blacksmith's calm acceptance of the attack on his work is, of course, not at all what is intended by self-criticism, and the laughter comes from this and from the old

90

lady's graphic depiction of his lack of skill. Ultimately the decision is deferred, but the villagers have made their point. Change for them is a qualitative as well as a quantitative thing. The humour displays the gap between their leaders' oft-spoken desire to accede to their wishes, and their attempts to direct those wishes towards an already programmed course. The villagers are not symbolic figures. They are recognisable people engaged in politics as it directly affects them. Sometimes they are subsequently seen to be limited in their analysis, but equally the format of the play, screening the great event, the Revolution, through the eyes of the one village, raises questions about the reliability of the Party leadership. This tension is of crucial importance in *Fanshen*, and was responsible for most of the discrepancies between the book and the play, discrepancies which Hinton argued against and which to some extent were resolved in the revised version.

The leadership insist continually that it is only from the people, and not from the Party cadres, that real change can occur, but Hare brings into the Chinese play his own experience of post-war Britain, and in particular a grave suspicion about the words of all leaders. The leaders are not presented unsympathetically, however; they are articulate on their own problems, and on its inherent ironies. After the first meeting we learn that T'ien-Ming, who had come to organise the Long Bow Peasant Association, is a member of the Communist Party. Before he can recruit in the village, he is a witness to the first signs of corruption amongst the new leadership. Yu-Lai thinks there should be some perks to go with the responsibility, otherwise he is better off being a plain peasant. T'ien-Ming agrees but tells him that he must wait until the people make the suggestion.

YU-LAI: I think we should get something. Not for

91

ourselves, more for expenses, for the Association. If we took over the inn, managed it, that would help pay for the school, pay for the oil we need for lamps for Association meetings. We're going to have to make some money somehow.

CHENG-K'UAN: Take over the inn?

YU-LAI: Why not?

A pause.

CHENG-K'UAN: Put it to the people?

YU-LAI: I thought we were waiting for them to put it to us.

They smile.

CHENG-K'UAN: Take over the inn.

The scene stops abruptly at that point. There is no need for elaboration. Yu-Lai's consciously ironic echo of T'ien-Ming's declaration is allowed to carry the weight of the contradiction. Later, we shall watch Yu-Lai being brought back into line by the villagers, but from the outset Hare has worked hard to present him not as a man dead-set on corruption, but simply as a man upon whom leadership is thrust. The corruption that ensues is not inevitable, but always possible.

Where Hinton had seen a steady development towards communism, Hare is less certain. Again, Hare's starting-point is outside the events through which Hinton had lived, but this doubt is of central importance to the play. It is particularly apparent at the end. At the Second Lucheng Conference, Ch'en argues against the impossibility of complete egalitarianism at that stage. 'Equality cannot be established by decree. . . . The strong, the ruthless would soon climb to the top; the weak and the sick would sink to the bottom. Only in the future when all land and productive wealth is held in common and we produce in great abundance will equality be possible.' 'Fanshen' has gone too far, too quickly, he argues: some of the more enthusiastic redistributions will have to be reversed. In the original version, Hare saw Ch'en's words in an unsympathetic light, those of a leader temporising yet again. After talking with Hinton he attempted to remedy this, but the nagging doubts remain even in the revised version.

The play ends pretty much as it began, not because nothing has changed, but because real change is the result of a long, and often tedious, struggle. The Party cadres arrive back in the village to explain that mistakes have been made. They are uncertain, blaming themselves, blaming the Party, blaming Ch'en. He attempts to explain why they must go back.

Land reform won't ever be a solution to people's problems. Land reform is just a step towards socialism. And socialism itself is transitional. It's unstable. It may be developed into communism, but also at any time, in any of a thousand ways, even by default, it may fall back. Because it's fraught with the contradictions of change and still loaded down with the culture of the past. . . . Is the pistol fired and the race underway, every one starting at once? Or is our land one day to be held collectively, by all of us, all land owned in common. You see the question has barely been asked. We haven't begun.

The cadres meet the villagers, attempting to justify the past mistakes. The peasants are working in the fields. The words of the cadres are heard in a rising crescendo, heaped one on top of another until, just before they drown each other out, their final pleas are heard:

I'd like to know what you think.
What do you think.

93

Tell me.
Let me know what you think.
What do you think about this?
Then they drown in sound and light.

The emphasis is placed back on the peasants. The leaders have returned to learn. But it is impossible to ignore the question that Hare leaves hanging. Is real change ever possible? The resonances of that question take the play out of its specific historical context, and relate it to the same set of problems that Hare has been worrying away at throughout his career. 'I had deliberately written a text that was as resonant of Europe as was possible, so that people might make their own analogies, about political leadership and so on' (*TQ*, v, no. 20). In *Fanshen*, history is not presented as a determined series of events. We do not know how the struggle will end, for the play ends with all manner of possibilities left open. But set against the frustrated hopes of Hare's English plays, the direct grappling with the urge to change is something quite refreshing in the contemporary theatre, and the result was one of the most peculiarly gripping evenings that I spent in a theatre in the entire decade. Although Hare has more recently devoted as much time to directing as to writing, and he is anyway by no means a prolific writer, there is every reason to suppose that he will continue his historical questioning.

4
Coming to Terms with the Seventies: Fusions

Working inside the establishment is always a contradictory process. The basic compromises necessary to
present politically committed work inside an alien
system will mute, if not silence, the radicalism of the
dramatists. On the other hand the system will have to
change to accommodate them.

(Clive Barker, 1978)[1]

The Churchill Play (1974) and *Fanshen* (1975) will serve to
signpost the end of the first period of post-'68 political
theatre. They represent a change of direction not only for
the two writers, but also in the essentially 'fringe' tradition
in which they had developed. From 1974 on, the term
'fringe' is used less and less, as the concept of an alternative
theatre, working alongside and, largely, in opposition to
the mainstream gains credence. Transfers from the alternative to the mainstream are not uncommon, but in practice it
is always possible to point to the distinction. The development of an alternative circuit depended on three chief

factors – apart, that is, from an audience interest: the growth of less casually organised touring-circuits, the creation of permanent or semi-permanent company-bases, and the increased accessibility of the larger subsidised theatres to alternative productions. It is important to note that the commercial theatres play almost no part in this development.

In great part this development is related to changes in the funding of the arts, and certainly throughout the 1970s there was a steady, if not spectacular, increase in the money available via the Arts Council and the regional arts bodies for theatre associated with the alternative companies. Not that this should be overstressed.

> In 1973/74 the fringe received £250,000: sixty companies had to share an amount equal to only half the grant to the National Theatre (i.e. £500,000). In 1977/8 between them the National Theatre and the RSC had £4.2 million – all of the rest of drama £6 million. Of that £6 million, £4.75 million went to theatre buildings; touring (thirty-three companies) received only £872,000. New projects (58) received £229,251.[2]

There are two obvious stings in this tail: first, the emphasis placed on the building and maintenance of new theatres, many of them, such as the Nottingham Playhouse and the Sheffield Crucible, planned as monuments of civic pride in the financially rosier years of the sixties; and, secondly, that placed on the work of the National and the RSC at the expense of the rest. Charles Marowitz, Director of Open Space: 'the establishment powers . . . do not really want healthy small-scale alternative threatre in England. They would be happy with the National, the RSC, Covent Garden and perhaps half a dozen "okay" producing organisations with respectable credentials.'[3] In fairness, the two provincial reps cited above did stage the first productions of *The Churchill Play* and *Fanshen* respectively, but a careful scrutiny of their later mainhouse repertoire will reveal an increasing dependence on safe revivals and already-proven commercial hits as the harsher financial realities of the latter half of the decade began to bite. And, although it is true that the National and the RSC were more receptive to the work of new writers, it has hardly dominated their output.

In this context, Brenton's comments on David Hare's production of his *Weapons of Happiness* as the first new play at the National take on a peculiar resonance.

> I know I'm in an exposed position but someone's got to go in first and start doing something. The question is, will new writing actually work on a big stage at the National. . . . I mean, can you take 15 actors and put them on at the Lyttleton with a new script and make an audience want to come? If we can't we're in trouble: if the National is to be in any sense national, then it's got to be about England today and that means new writing.

This defiant expression of willingness to take on the establishment within its own citadels must be balanced against the economic argument that accompanies it.

> You can go on forever as a playwright earning your living in cultural cul-de-sacs playing to 30 people a night: I now want to be tested on a big scale and that means using the kind of money and resources that only the National or the RSC can provide. You can of course pick up subsidies in smaller theatres, but you can't go on for ever having your work cornered like that.[4]

97

The event was heralded in *The Sunday Times* the following day with an article by John Peters on the new dramatists, headed 'Meet the Wild Bunch'. The Peckinpah reference suggested that from now on the flood-gates were open.

In his feature Peters sought to introduce 'a new generation of British playwrights' – and in particular, Brenton, Hare, Howard Barker and Snoo Wilson – that had in reality been firmly established in the alternative theatre circuit for several years. It posits a clear distinction between two kinds of theatrical arena, the establishment and the non-establishment, strongly intimates that the barriers between the two were about to crumble and that, furthermore, the occurrence might well be a bloody one. It is in a similar spirit that Brenton had talked (in *The Times* article) of himself, Hare, the cast and the production team 'as an armoured charabanc . . . parked within the National walls'. And, just as Peters now had felt the need to alert the Sunday bourgeoisie to the new danger, so Sheridan Morley in the article in *The Times* cited above, had set out to introduce 'The man behind the Lyttelton's new play'.

There is agreement, then, on all sides that new territory was about to be taken, and subsequent events give some plausibility to this view. Brenton's new work was increasingly to use either the National or the RSC, and writers such as Hare and Bond were to be seen not only as playwrights there but also as directors. Indeed, Bond's own production of his *The Woman* (1978) saw the potential of the Olivier Theatre at the National properly realised for the first time. But we are not concerned here with a simple movement up the Theatrical League table. The shift in emphasis by writers such as Brenton away from the alternative to the major subsidised London theatres has important political implications, not the least being that it allowed critics such as Peters and Morley an apparent confirmation of their centrist position; for implicit in both their articles is a belief that it is in London, and above all in the National–RSC axis, that the real theatrical 'state of the nation' is to be tested, a fact palpably untrue for the new drama to this point.

It is worth considering *Weapons of Happiness* more directly at this point, for, if it is true that the very fact of the production has an almost emblematic significance for the mainstream critics, equally Brenton set out to present a play which would celebrate the conflict between the National and, if you like, the reputation which preceded him. In it Brenton sought quite consciously to confront one set of expectancies (those of the international culture that the National embodied) with another (the anarchic energy of his earlier plays). Where *Magnificence* had opened with a long first scene in the Royal Court house-style, precisely in order to disrupt the naturalistic expectations of its audience, so, in *Weapons*, the audience is deliberately misled.

The play opens with a man, alone on stage, addressing, if anybody, and the uncertainty is important, the audience. His theme is his own isolation in London, and by extension the isolation of England in the wider political and historical context of Europe. The isolation is reinforced both by the unexplained nature of the opening, and by the un-Englishness of his rhetoric.

> I don't sleep. I walk about London. So many people, sleeping. Around you. For miles. After so many years, it is better to be tired. Not to think or remember. Ten million, asleep, around you, is warm. The ignorant English, like a warm overcoat. About me. It is better. While in the nightmare of the dark all the dogs of Europe bark.

Before the audience is properly able to take stock of his words, a factory-door is opened and the man is challenged. In the stumbling conversation that ensues it emerges that the newcomer is the man's boss, that he runs a potato-crisp factory, that Frank has been working there for a week, and that Ralph mistakenly believes him to have come from Hungary. Frank corrects him: 'Czechoslovakia. The Czechoslovakian Socialist Republic.' Ralph's discourse is at odds with that of Frank. They are two men inhabiting the same stage but with, it is already evident, no point of connection. Ralph's embarrassed parting-shot to his strangely uncommunicative employee ('Tuck yourself up. Good book, hot drink and a packet of crisps. Ha!') prefigures a separation of experience that will be crucial to the play.

As Ralph walks away he is attacked and the briefcase containing plans to close the factory is stolen. He appeals to Frank for help:

FRANK: I plead.

RALPH: For godsake, what's the matter with you?

FRANK: I plead guilty of being a war criminal. And of committing a whole number of grave crimes for the benefit of the US imperialists. To the detriment of the working people of Czechoslovakia and the whole peace camp. All the dogs of Europe.

And at that point the first scene ends, abruptly. It has been brief – three pages of printed dialogue – and confusing. For the audience the overall experience is one of displacement; put crudely, it does not know what kind of play it is watching. It is an experience that is carefully worked for.

Brenton then serves up his National audience with a largish portion of the sort of lumpen pudding they had been expecting. The second scene is set in the factory-yard, in the lunch-break, with the workers playing a shambolic game of cricket. The dialogue is superficially in an established tradition that dates from Bond's *Saved* – the predominant mode is aggression as the only plausible form of communication in the world of controlled play at work – but contains a great deal of the wryly ironic sub-text of Brenton's early plays. The older Billy, for instance, looking back dreamily to his personal sixties.

LIZ: How old you then, Billy darling?

JANICE: Pretty ancient actually. Do you know he remembers Bob Dylan?

LIZ: COO. Bring out your dead.

BILLY: He could 'a changed the world, Dylan. Still could if we'd let him. (BILLY *hits the guitar. A horrible chord.*)

JANICE: Sad.

LIZ: Make you weep.

JANICE: Yeah.

LIZ: Saw my Mum in the bath the other night. You know, nude.

JANICE: Sad.

LIZ: Like curried chicken.

JANICE: Really sad.

For the young workers age does not represent any access to history or to knowledge, simply physical decay; Billy's frantic holding onto an immediate past that has not even taught him basic guitar-techniques offers little hope for any visionary alternative. Theirs is a bleak world, a logical progression from that of the childhood and adolescence presented in Brenton's earlier plays; they have learnt nothing at school, and they will learn nothing at work. Brenton sketches in their alienation with economy, concentrating in particular on their sense of personal futility, rejecting traditional politics as they prepare for the factory-occupation which will follow.

This is the first account of contemporary English society to be seen at the National, and its supreme importance lies in its aggressive rejection of the essentially liberal-humanist philosophy of mainstream theatre. If it shocked, and it was meant to, it did so in ways which connect it with all Brenton's earlier work. It was, in other words, what the audience had expected to have placed before them. But through all this wanders Frank, the absolute embodiment of the physical decay associated by the young workers with age, an as-yet unexplained figure in isolation. And it is with Frank that Brenton was going to open up the play into a wider international context.

In the third scene he is called into the office to help with enquiries into the attack on his boss, there to be confronted by Ralph, a union representative, and a world-weary but not heavy police-inspector ('Just a public servant with his thumb in the dyke', as he explains). Frank's recoil from the soothing questions strikes an uneasy note. No one accuses him, no one threatens him. Suddenly the scene changes without explanation, and we are present at a real interrogation in 'a bare, dirty room with a naked light bulb', Frank standing as if handcuffed. As before, the effect is of dislocation, a process aided by having the other three actors already present take on the role of harsh interrogators. Brenton seeks in this way not to make a connection between past and present, but to emphasise a difference.

Frank's presence as a ghost from a past in which 'revolution' was more than a glib phrase from an alternative rhetoric acts as a chilling commentary on the fag-end of the politics still being depressingly played out in and around the crisp-factory. For the kids, zonked on booze and pills, politics is an anarchic lark, to be swooped down upon on fast motorbikes, and to be supported by slogans culled second-hand from the sixties. The play's title derives from the words of the terrorist, Jed, belatedly argued against by Brenton, in *Magnificence*. Their absurdity is made doubly so by the involvement in the contemporary action of a man who was briefly at the centre of real political struggle:

> Oh we had the world to remake. The universe in our hands, history was water in a cup, we had only to drink. Who could have, then, imagined this dereliction. This filthy empty room, the broken doors, the exasperation. Too much lost, too much blood. Now, I do not even want revenge on all that I once believed in. I wish only to lie in the sludge of the debris, of what was once a fine building. Miles deep, stirring only for a little warmth.

The role of Frank is based on that of Josef Frank, a dedicated communist worker who was imprisoned, tortured and later hanged in the Prague Treason Trials of 1952. His intrusion, fictitiously, into the present brings with it a futher ghost, that of Stalin, frequently literally present on the stage. It raises questions that go far beyond the local issues of contemporary South London, and open the National Theatre to an international context very different from that anticipated by its management.

Although Frank subsequently forms a brief liaison with one of the workers, Janice – who, unlike her colleagues, has at least smatterings of historical knowledge, and who ironically takes him to look at the universe on their first date, at the London Planetarium – he can offer little more than a puncturing of their dreams. Unwillingly he compromises his desire to be left alone and joins them in the

103

factory-occupation; but he is unable to support their simplistic plans for continuing production. Frank has been a true political believer, and central to his belief had been an understanding of the day-to-day practicalities of change.

> FRANK: And how do you run the factory? And how do you buy the potatoes? And the cellophane, for the packets? And pay the printers, for the funny faces in pretty colours, upon the packets? And the oil in the vats?
>
> JANICE: What you saying?
>
> LIZ: 'Let go', he's saying.
>
> BILLY: Course he's saying 'let go'. They all say 'let go' in the end. Even Dylan, his last three LPs. . . . He said 'let go'.
>
> FRANK: You do not have the chance for revolt often. And, often, it is ridiculous. Fleeting. Difficult to think through. But it is rare. And not to be thrown away. It is the most precious thing on earth.

Frank's presence in the play focuses attention on a new strand in Brenton's work, one which moves his version of *avant-garde* theatre towards the territory more usually associated with agit-prop. The play posits no solutions, but it argues strongly for the need to ask questions. The occupation is abandoned and the kids make for the countryside – the open-ended conclusion to so many of Brenton's later plays – leaving Frank alone again. In a last flash-back, this time to Prague in 1968, a Russian tank appears on stage. In a final act of defiance, Frank runs at it and flings his coat over the gun-barrel. Stalin, who is standing by the tank, addresses him directly for the first time – 'Incurable romantic' – but Frank is already dead. In the final scene the kids find a deserted farm-house in

Wales, and the last words of the play are Janice's, in response to Billy's query about Frank, 'What was he?': 'He was a Communist.'

The play's conclusion harks back to Brenton's own words of 1974: 'If you're going to change the world, well there's only one set of tools, and they're bloody and stained but realistic. I mean communist tools. Not pleasant. If only the gentle, dreamy, alternative society *had* worked.'[5] Frank has fought in a political world quite unknown to the kids in the factory, and Brenton has chosen the National venue to argue for a need to return to a properly Marxist base of political struggle; but the choice of venue is the problem. To what audience is the play addressing itself, and with what aim? To shock (the *avant-garde*), or to educate (agit-prop)? Frank's role as opposition to the mindless politics of the alternative society is clear enough, as is the play's articulate presentation of the bloodiness of the tools; what is less so is any sense of future direction.

There is arguably an inevitability about this confusion, one that arises from Brenton's decision to 'take the theatre way'. *Weapons* is struggling towards an articulation of a political way forward in an arena that many would consider could not be more inappropriate. Sandy Craig, one of the founders of 7:84, argues the need for a crucial distinction between political *drama* and political *theatre*.

> Political plays seek to appeal to, and influence, the middle class, in particular that section of the middle class which is influential in moulding 'public opinion'. The implication of this is that society can be reformed and liberalised, where necessary, by the shock troops of the middle class. . . . Political theatre, on the other hand, as embodied in the various political theatre companies, aims – with varying degrees of success – to appeal to, and

105

to be an expression of, the working class. Its underlying belief is that the working class is the progressive class within society.[6]

For Craig, the appearance of *Weapons* at the National would doubtless perfectly illustrate the first part of this argument. But it scarcely describes the play that Brenton produced. There is no urge towards reformation and liberalisation. It could be argued – and indeed was by critics of both left and right persuasion – that the play is essentially negative, offering no solutions; but there is then the danger of arguing in mutually contradictory ways. *Weapons* is a much more open-ended play than either of these positions will allow for. More attention needs to be paid to this open-endedness, and this would involve direct considera-tion of the structure of the play, rather than the production of a simple gloss of the 'meaning' which is the major obsession of most critics.

What the National gave Brenton above all was the space, the facilities and the size of cast to work properly for the first time on the creation of an 'epic' structure that he had been moving towards in the plays immediately preceding. In *Weapons*, there is no single voice on which the audience can rely. There is a huge, and endlessly shifting, space on which contradiction flourishes. The separate viewpoints are shown to have arisen from the very different *social* experiences of the various protagonists. This multiplicity of viewpoint is central and is reinforced at narrative level by the constant disruption of the 'story', and by the historical jumps. Each scene, in classic Brechtian manner, is in effect a separate discourse with the audience; and the audience is being asked to consider a series of virtual contradictions, which in turn form a larger discourse. No single 'reading' of the play is possible.

Now none of this may answer the particular objections of the proponents of 'political theatre' over 'political plays', but it may take on more force when we realise that many of the problems that Brenton faced on his debut at the National had their counterparts in the development of agit-prop theatre throughout the decade. In other words it is not simply a matter of types of venue, and types of audience. There is an external and constantly changing social reality which is in large part held in common. The question of audience is an extremely problematic one. The auditorium was not filled with quite the same mix for *Weapons* as for, say, a Restoration-comedy revival. Belts and Braces entered the eighties with a long London West End run, with *Accidental Death of an Anarchist*, and 7:84 is a not infrequent visitor to the Royal Court. A performance by Pirate Jenny of Edgar's *Our People*, about a strike of Asian immigrants (seen by me in a West Indian Working Men's Club in Sheffield) had an audience that consisted almost entirely of white salaried workers and students – as did a performance at about the same time by CAST of a play about a factory-closure, this time in an upstairs room in a pub.

However, throughout the decade, away from the National–RSC axis and, largely, from the subsidised circuit, agit-prop groups did continue to develop – sometimes as new companies, and frequently as splinter groups from existing ones. So, for instance, the Scottish 7:84 Company formed by John McGrath led to the creation of an English 7:84, and from that Belts and Braces, which in turn produced the feminist group Monstrous Regiment. All, having undergone many changes, are still active. Many of the newer agit-prop groups were committed to a particular perspective: most importantly, feminism, gay rights and racism. But, as I argued in the first chapter, the Conserva-

107

tive victory of 1970, and the subsequent build-up of industrial conflict, culminating in the miners' strike and defeat of the Heath administration, is the prime cause of this proliferation of a theatre agreed on versions of the traditional class-based view of political struggle.

It is the work of John McGrath in particular that best illustrates opposition to the infiltration of the subsidised theatre as attempted by writers such as Brenton. He has always argued strongly the need for a separate political theatre, which, whilst it is loosely within an agit-prop framework, sought a new form of relationship with an audience that was to be defined politically rather than theatrically.

I believe theatre can best achieve its independent artistic objectives by becoming a part of [the] hugely complex movement towards a developed, sophisticated but liberating form of socialism which is happening all over Europe, East and West, and in many other parts of the world. Without it, the end of the twentieth century is going to be a grim time to be alive. This does not mean that I insist that all plays should be recruiting meetings for a party that does not exist. It is simply that to be good as *theatre*, plays must now ruthlessly question their ideological bases, the set of assumptions about life on which they are built, and should have a questioning, critical relationship with their audience, based on trust, cultural identification and political solidarity. These attitudes behind the play are always what plays are really 'about'.[7]

McGrath's new company took its name from a statistic: 7 per cent of the country owning 84 per cent of its wealth. In 1973, it toured Scotland with *The Cheviot, the Stag, and the*

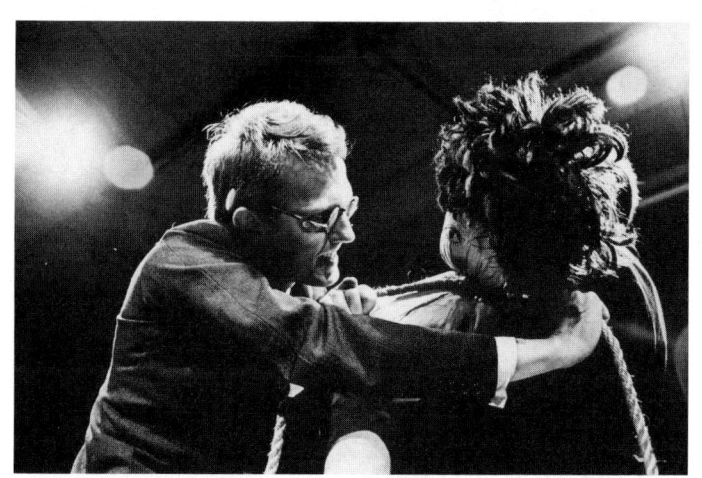

1. *Christie in Love* by Howard Brenton, Royal Court Theatre Upstairs, 1970; William Hoyland (Christie).

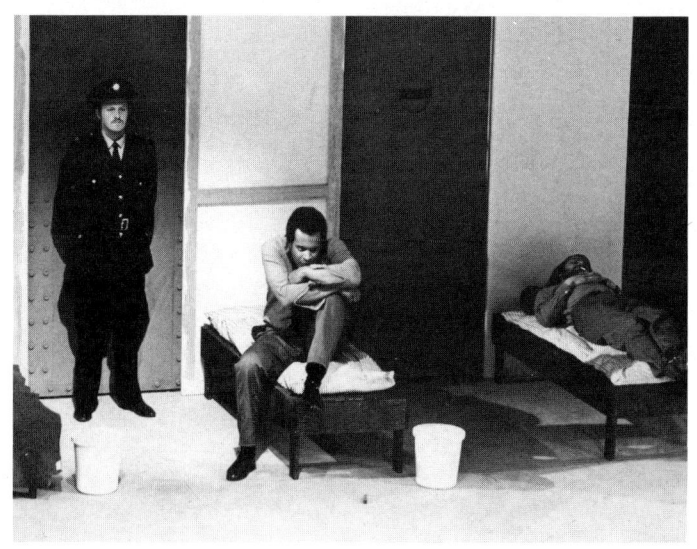

2. *Measure for Measure* by Howard Brenton and William Shakespeare, Northcott Theatre, Exeter, 1972; Neville Aurelius (*centre*) as Claudio.

3. *The Churchill Play* by Howard Brenton, Nottingham Playhouse, 1972.

4. *The Romans in Britain* by Howard Brenton, National Theatre (Olivier), 1980; Stephen Moore (Thomas Chichester).

5. *The Genius* by Howard Brenton, Royal Court Theatre, 1983; Trevor Eve
    (Leo Lehrer) and Joanne Whalley (Gilly Brown).

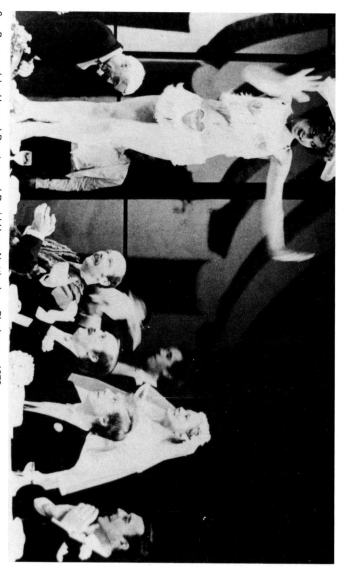

6. *Brassneck* by Howard Brenton and David Hare, Nottingham Playhouse, 1973.

7. *Teeth 'n' Smiles* by David Hare, Royal Court Theatre, 1975; Hugh Fraser (Peyote) and Helen Mirren (Maggie).

8. *Fanshen* by David Hare, Crucible Theatre, Sheffield, 1975, Joint Stock.

9. *Licking Hitler* by David Hare, BBC TV, 1977; Michael Mellinger (Karl) and Hugh Fraser (Langley).

10. *Saigon: Year of the Cat* by David Hare, Thames TV, 1983.

11. *Comedians* by Trevor Griffiths, Old Vic, 1975; Jimmy Jewel (Eddie Waters), Dave Hill (Ged Murray) and Jonathan Pryce (Gethin Price).

12. *Comedians*, Old Vic, 1975; Jonathan Pryce (Gethin Price).

13. *Through the Night* by Trevor Griffiths, BBC TV, 1975; Alison Steadman (Christine Potts) and Dave Hill (Joe Potts).

14. *Oi! for England* by Trevor Griffiths, Central TV, April 1982; (*left to right*) Adam Kotz (Finn), Richard Platt (Landry), Ian Mercer (Swells), Neil Pearson (Napper).

15. *Destiny* by David Edgar, BBC TV, December 1977; Colin Jeavons (Turner) (*right*) and Joe Blatchley (Maxwell).

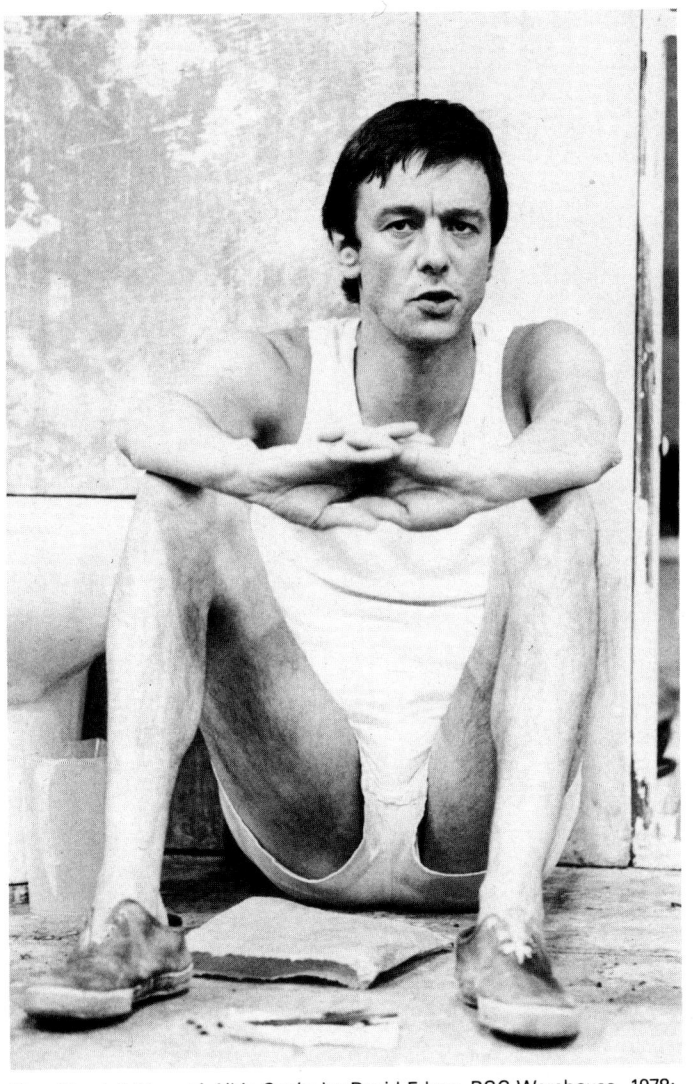

16. *The Jail Diary of Albie Sachs* by David Edgar, RSC Warehouse, 1978; Peter McEnery (Albie Sachs).

17. *Mary Barnes* by David Edgar, Royal Court Theatre, 1978; Patti Love (Mary) and Timothy Spall (Laurence).

Black, Black Oil. It sought out non-theatrical venues in an attempt to reach the people whose history, struggles and culture are the subject-matter of the play. *The Cheviot* was the first of a succession of plays that attempted to relate contemporary political struggle to the wider history of the movement, and as a general model it was very influential. For, just as the shock-tactics of the fringe were becoming predictable, so the combination of propaganda and natural-ism offered by so many of the agit-prop groups was beginning to provoke little more than yawns. If the former promised increasingly futile bouts of anarchistic energy – increasingly futile in the harsher face of contemporary politics, and the collapse of the 'alternative' dream – then the latter usually delivered nothing much beyond a certain dull realisation that yet again the correctly socialist line had been moulded onto the particular factory-closure, strike, or whatever. From the outset, 7:84 sought to go beyond the merely propagandist, and to this end the company utilised techniques culled from genuinely popular culture as well as from the earlier years of the fringe. Their intent, above all, was to involve the audience in the questions.

Richard Seyd summarised the problem of contemporary agit-prop well in 1975: 'if people don't think that capitalism is an absurd and damaging way of organising society, then very little that one does is going to change their minds'.[8] But the problem is a larger one than this. The bulk of early-seventies agit-prop theatre was essentially undynamic, preaching patterns of repetition rather than change. Since then, far too much feminist theatre has followed the same course – precisely because it is caught in the trap of wishing at the most basic level to persuade the 'unconverted' whilst at the same time offering the possibil-ity of a rather more accurate reflection of the very important complexities of feminist politics in a period of

109

rapid ideological transition. For the last year or so, the most acclaimed show to come from the alternative circuit has been Clare Luckham's *Trafford Tanzi*, transferred to the Mermaid from the Half Moon. Immensely successful at the box-office, it offers a view of sexual relationships in terms of a series of wrestling-bouts as Tanzi develops through childhood to a brutalised marriage. By way of suggesting the limitations of such a banally low level of analysis, I can do no better than quote Clare Colvin's enthusiastic review:

> I am sure that some radical feminists will sneer at this play as being too 'soft', and for giving the audience an opportunity harmlessly to let off steam rather than offering any solutions. I don't agree. By its broad and showbiz-flavoured appeal, the play reaches a far wider audience, and its points go home amidst the laughter.[9]

Colvin completely misses the point here. It is not the failure to provide solutions that makes it 'soft': it is its absurd simplicity. It suggests an accessibility to change by an individual – stand up to the wrestling husband and beat him at his own game – that is unrelated to any larger analysis of change or to any awareness of the complex dynamics of such activity. Ironically, as it continued to play to packed audiences, a play that concerned itself with the more complicated struggle of real feminist politics in a hostile world, Marcella Evaristi's *Commedia*, was allowed to drift through London with little more than a respectful nod from the critics.

Now I don't wish to dwell on *Trafford Tanzi*, but it illustrates well the sort of problems that have confronted crude attempts at agit-prop during the last decade. David Edgar: 'specifically, the techniques of agit-prop are incapable of dealing with questions of consciousness, precisely

110

because they portray only the assumed objective essence of a situation, rather than the dynamic between how people subjectively perceive that situation and the underlying reality'.[10]

This stress on audience as a fluid and questioning presence, as virtually a sub-text of the play, is a gradual development. It certainly owes something to a more sophisticated understanding of Brecht's adaptation of epic theatre – not the Brecht as perceived in the polar carica-tures of Stalinist hard-man or liberal humanist, but the Brecht who, as Althusser argues, 'wanted to make the spectator into an actor who would complete the unfinished play'.[11] Groups and writers learnt as they developed that to use the audience as either a vehicle for assault – to be abandoned anyway once the audience has been educated in the techniques of assault – or for preaching at is to avoid the central preoccupation of all political theatre, the urge to change. Where the *avant-garde* had been concerned essen-tially with the subjective approach, and agit-prop with the objective, the dynamic that Edgar refers to would be produced by a fusion between the two.

At the outset few of the new playwrights would have admitted to any debt to Brecht's work. Brenton's reaction, as late as 1974, is not untypical. 'I think his plays are museum pieces now and are messing up a lot of young theatre workers. Brecht's plays don't work, and are about the thirties and not about the seventies, and are now cocooned and unperformable.'[12] It is evident that, in his move towards the reformulation of an 'epic' theatre, Brenton's ideas have undergone change. In addition to his adaptation of a seminal modern epic text, Buchner's *Danton's Death*, he has also produced a version of Brecht's *Galileo*. But the debt is not as direct as this might suggest. The very move of contemporary political drama towards an

111

epic stance necessitates a coming to terms with the work of the most immediately important epic writer; just as writers such as Brenton and Bond had found it necessary to reassess the achievement of Shakespeare, one of Brecht's most obvious predecessors.

One of the most influential productions in the move towards the rethinking of the epic style was that by 7:84 of Arden's reworking of his own *Sergeant Musgrave's Dance*, *Sergeant Musgrave Dances On* (1972), which Brenton has described as 'a shattering experience, one of the great shows'.[13] Arden had been experimenting with versions of epic since the original *Musgrave*, and he had frequently though misleadingly been described as the English disciple of Brecht. This reworking followed several years of rethinking on Arden's part, in part in response to the critical reception of his later work, but chiefly in response to the changing political struggle. He was clear about the significance of the break: 'Twelve years ago I looked on at people's struggles, and wrote about them as an onlooker. Without consciously intending it, I have become a partici- pant'.[14] His collaboration with 7:84 had been preceded by a rather less happy involvement with CAST, but it is no less true for Arden than for the other writers in this book that the post-'68 years created an altered political stance – in his case from uncertainly pacifist humanist to revolutionary socialist with a strong interest in the Irish struggle.

Sergeant Musgrave's Dance, though written in the shadow of Cyprus, had been historically unlocatable, a difficult political allegory that had been crudely assimilated into the mainstream humanist tradition. The reworking offered no escape into a world of moral generalities: it dealt uncompromisingly with the immediate situation and its possible outcome. A key play of the fifties revival, by then safely enshrined as a classic on the 'A' Level syllabus, had been reanimated and used to confront the audience directly with the miners' strike and the shooting of 13 people by the British Army in Londonderry, of 1972. In the same year he produced *The Island of the Mighty* and *The Ballygombeen Bequest*, followed by a series of plays of crucial importance, almost totally ignored by the critics, before he produced his full-scale epic, *The Non-Stop Connolly Show* of 1975 (all with Margaretta D'Arcy).

It is likely that the epic style of *Sergeant Musgrave Dances On* was directly influential on the collaborative *England's Ireland*. What is more easily demonstrable is that from this point on political theatre generally was moving ever closer to versions of the epic. Bond had already produced *Narrow Road to the Deep North* in 1969, a parable play owing much to Brecht's 'Lehrstuck'; and he followed this with a series of plays using an epic format: *Lear* (1971), *Bingo* (1973), *The Fool* (1975), *The Bundle* and *The Woman* (1978). Even David Edgar, a writer whose early work was entirely in an agit-prop vein, was, by about 1974, beginning to question his work with General Will; and to move away from plays in which almost desperate attempts were made to lighten the ideological pudding, with surrealism and naturalism being played one against the other. And Edgar was not alone in realising that, for all their temporary relevance and popularity, shows such as *The National Interest* (1971), *State of Emergency* and *Rent; Or, Caught in the Act* (1972) were not breaking new ground, were not attempting to involve the audience in any form of dialogue. He has gone so far as to argue that his work 'broke the form', and has described jokily the ultimate agit-prop play.

I had a fantasy at that time that I wanted to do a play which had no people in it at all, in which everybody was

113

either an aeroplane or a graph of labour migration from the north west in the 1960s – an entirely economistic kind of play, because I was getting kind of pissed off with reviews which complained about my writing two-dimensional characters, when actually I'd tried very hard to write two-dimensional characters.[15]

This kind of critique of the limitations of agit-prop lies behind the 'play within the play' in *The Churchill Play*; in the rehearsal for the Yalta Conference sequence, for instance:

MIKE: What's the bath symbolic of then, eh Joby?

JOBY: (*he thinks. Then he kicks the bath*): Europe, Europe, sat upon by 'bums a Super Powers.

MIKE: And the bathwater? What's the bathwater symbolical of?

JOBY: (*he thinks. Then*): People a Europe! Displaced by . . .

MIKE: . . . Great bums a . . .

JOBY: Ay.

But this comic deflation of agit-prop is not the only level on which the prisoners' entertainment is to be understood. They are rehearsing a surrealistic version of agit-prop theatre in preparation for an audience, the Parliamentary Commission, that could not be less sympathetic, less prepared to question. That they do so watched by a further audience, that in the theatre, only serves to compound the irony. Joby's play can and does achieve nothing, either as 'piss-taking' (the *avant-garde*), or as an urge towards change (agit-prop).

Of course, this 'play within the play' does contain in a joky form that 'movement through history' that was

114

beginning seriously to preoccupy agit-prop theatre, and which provides the very basis for 7:84's work, for instance. And it is here that most of its real energy is located, offering as it does an aggressive reinterpretation of 'official' history. As the immediacy of the confrontation politics of the early seventies receded, leaving only a local and easily compromised victory, the need to redefine past socialist history, as the editors of the *May Day Manifesto* had urged back in 1968, becomes more apparent. The point is well made in the preface to the published text of Red Ladder's *Taking Our Time* of 1978, a play about the impact of new technology in the cotton industry of mid-nineteenth-century England:

> The decision to make a history play based on past events in the West Riding was taken with the intention of reconnecting our audiences with that past. But the period we chose needed to have specific resonances with the contemporary experience of our audiences if it was to be of more than passing interest to them. So we chose the 1840s with the aim of drawing from that time some useful parallels for today and some challenging ideas for tomorrow.

The re-examination of history is not unique to agit-prop. The alternative circuit produced a mass of plays that looked beyond the immediate struggle, seeking in the past both a starting-point for debate and a way of reanalysing history. Where Brenton and Hare had scoured post-war Britain, Griffiths had from the outset been concerned with the origins of the British and European socialist movement. As early as 1973, Steve Gooch's *Female Transport* presented an episodic account, from a feminist perspective, of the transportations to Australia; and Caryl Churchill's *Light*

115

Shining in Buckinghamshire (1976), one of several plays
re-examining the English Civil War with a radical eye, can
be compared with her *Vinegar Tom* of the same year, a play
which is in effect a feminist critique of Arthur Miller's *The
Crucible*. All these plays were performed at venues such as
the Half Moon, the Traverse and the Royal Court Theatre
Upstairs, venues which bridged the mainstream and the
agit-prop circuit.

This capture of an historical purchase is in itself a major
factor in the move towards an epic structure. By expanding
the time-scale, and stressing historical and political causation, rather than the conventionally psychological, playwrights were in effect forced to come to terms with epic.
And in so doing they were of course not only rediscovering
their political roots but their theatrical ones also. The shock
of the new was inexorably wearing off, and the more recent
drama has reflected the need for a more sensitive awareness of the complexities of the struggle.

In the second half of the decade, then, a greater degree of
sophistication is to be found in both the *avant-garde* and
agit-prop traditions, not the least reason being that it begins
to be possible to talk about an established tradition. A
generation of older and wiser theatre writers and workers
were discovering in the only way possible, through their
own experiences, that there were no short cuts, theatrically or politically. But it was a generation that had found
an audience, or rather a variety of audiences, and its success
gave it access to venues and to financial support that
allowed for the public opening up of a more complicated
discourse; a discourse that was anyway being enforced by
the changing political climate.

Although, throughout the seventies, there had been a
well-organised attempt at Constituency level to move the
Labour Party towards a properly socialist programme – an

attempt largely stage-managed by previously non-aligned members of the left, refugees from the alternative politics of the late sixties – this reaped few rewards at national level. The Callaghan administration that followed that of Heath was very much in the mould of Wilson's, and the gap between right and left in the Party grew publicly wider. The defeat of the Labour government and the beginnings of the Conservative monetarist experiment was accompanied by the formation of the Social Democratic Party, led by right-wing figureheads forced out from the Labour Party. All this took place in the shadow of a growing recession that did not produce the working-class militancy confidently predicted by many activists. Unemployment rose as British manufacturing industry collapsed. To many on the left the mood in the country seemed bitter and resigned, rather than prerevolutionary. The late seventies was no time for millennial politics, and political theatre began increasingly to move away from the here-and-now, to rethink itself in a larger theoretical and historical arena. Change was not for the moment to be sought for in the immediate future. The new drama was coming of age, and a harsh age it was.

5
Trevor Griffiths:
Strategic Dialectics

I'll probably never complete a play in the formal sense. It has to be open at the end: people have to make choices, because if you're not making choices, you're not actually living.

(*Times Educational Supplement*, 25 June 1976)

Although Trevor Griffiths has worked on two plays with Brenton and Hare, *Lay-By* and *Deeds* (1978), as well as having a touring production of *The Party* directed by Hare, he is a political playwright of a very different kind from either of them. His plays possess from the outset a commitment to the harsh cut-and-thrust of political struggle that is scarcely to be found in the early work of either of the others. And again, although *Occupations* has been toured by the 7:84 Company, Griffiths cannot be fitted into a straight agit-prop slot.

Like Brenton and Hare, Trevor Griffiths first started to work seriously as a playwright in the immediate post-'68 period. Before this he had written three plays, only one of which he would later defend, *The Daft 'Un*, 'which was about – surprise surprise – my brother and me, or people like my brother and me' (*TQ*, vi, no. 22, 1976). He had come to playwriting late, one of the first products of the 1944 Education Act, progressing through university, National Service, teaching and journalism scarcely touched by the theatre. As late as 1976 he claimed only to have seen about fifty plays. In 1967, by then working as an education officer with BBC Radio Leeds, he was encouraged by Tony Garnett to write another play for Kestrel, a production company formed by Garnett and Ken Loach after the success of the film *Kes*, based on Barry Hines's novel *A Kestrel for a Knave*. Sticking to Garnett's dictum to write about what he knew, he wrote *Love Maniac*, about a teacher in a new comprehensive school.

The indirect connection with Hines's novel is interesting, because, unlike those of Brenton and Hare, Griffiths's roots as a writer are to be found not in the theatre at all, but in that tradition of the English novel – later transmuted into films – that dates from Lawrence's early work and continues through the late fifties and sixties with such writers as Stan Barstow and Alan Sillitoe. Indeed it was Barstow who encouraged Griffiths to write his next play, *The Wages of Thin*, an uncharacteristic 'experiment' about three lads in a lavatory, with half-conscious borrowings of menace from Pinter.

The tradition that Griffiths drew from was concerned with the detailed reconstruction of Northern working-class communities, of the England – away from what is too often still taken to be the mainstream of English culture – left behind by so many of the characters in the work of David Storey and David Mercer. Mercer, whom Griffiths regards as his immediate predecessor as a writer, provides the model for the drunkenly despairing northern émigré playwright in *The Party*. In 1981 BBC television screened Griffiths's serialisation of *Sons and Lovers*, a project he worked on for two years. He is easily able to make the connection between Lawrence's world and his own:

> There is no point where *Sons and Lovers* seems anything but the truth, honestly perceived, interesting also because that life is still available, that deeply apolitical life, that idea that life is about close communal relationships, about honour, respectability and getting on. (*Socialist Worker*, 23 Jan 1981)

In *Sam, Sam* which, though not performed until 1972, is the earliest of his produced plays, Griffiths comments drolly on the connection. In the first act Sam offers a short tableau of life in his home as a child – a dialect confrontation between his father and himself after his mother's eye has been blacked – before turning on the audience with

> How's that then? That a bit better? That a bit closer to your authentic working class drudgery, is it? 'Course it is. Come on, own up, that's the real thing, innit? Eh? Who was it said Lawrence was more authentic than life itself? That were Lawrence that – 'Sons and Lovers' actually.

The provocation is deliberate; the presumed middle-class audience are served up with what they have come to accept as northern social realism. The point is made even more acute when we realise that Griffiths was writing the play around the time of Peter Gill's introduction of Lawrence's plays to the theatrical canon in the Royal Court season of 1968.

But, if Griffiths was well capable of standing expectation on its head, his commitment to a tradition which is

120

studiedly unexperimental and totally dominated by naturalism has never wavered. He was never a part of a London
avant-garde, and has relied on variants of the naturalistic
format as the most accessible and economic way of opening
up the discussion that is at the centre of all his plays. Even
Apricots (1971), the nearest Griffiths approached to
writing a fringe-play, can be seen, once the impact of the
sexual explicitness has receded, as a naturalistic account of
one evening in the life of a marriage – rather like the last act
of *Sam, Sam* or the opening of *The Party* – where the
alienation of the two partners serves as a 'metaphor of life
in capitalistic, bourgeois society'.

Sam, Sam has been described by Griffiths as the biography of about 5 million people, those who, as a result of the
1944 Education Act, have pulled themselves up into the
professional middle classes. Versions of this theme –
usually complete with the brief and impossible visit back to
the North – in the novels and films of the tradition I have
discussed are too numerous to need particular citation. The
play examines the lives of two brothers – both played by the
same actor – one of whom has made it up the ladder, while
the other has not. The first half is a short show put on by the
unemployed brother who stayed at home, a typical Friday
night of fighting to be next in the bathroom, which is put
into perspective by his bitter analysis of how the situation is
perpetuated. The style is a mixture of naturalism and
stand-up comic business which prevents the audience from
ever simply looking in on the action. The second half is
reminiscent of the later Osborne, a non-dialogue between
the brother, prosperous and despairing, and his up-market
wife. Significantly, one critic has suggested that the play
could be subtitled 'Friday Night and Sunday Morning'.

What the play offers is, in effect, two suggestions of how
a single life might develop given different environmental

121

conditions. The prosperous Sam is about to be adopted as a Labour Party candidate but lacks any political energy or any insight except into himself, while his brother still possesses not only the political analysis but an uneasy sense of still belonging to something. Unemployed Sam ends his section of the play conducting Beethoven's Choral Symphony, whilst his upwardly mobile counterpart fills his empty house with the impossibly nostalgic sounds of the Brighouse and Raistrick Brass Band played on his expensive machine, '*black gunmetal base, large gold and red magnetic circles*'. That the conflict is an important one politically for Griffiths is seen by his recurrent use of it – with the biographically based brothers in *The Daft 'Un*; with Bill, the militant Labour MP, and his apathetic but eventually politicised brother, Eddie, in the *Bill Brand* TV series; and, most obviously, with Joe Shawcross and his brother visiting from the North in *The Party*. It is a conflict between the old and the new worlds of political struggle which is seen in historical as well as personal terms, and it provides the starting-point for all his work, in which he visits the two poles with a pendulum-like regularity.

The Party, first produced at the National in 1973, owes its genesis to the events of 1968, and uses them as a basis for debate. The action occurs during the first night of the Paris barricades during the May of that year. A group of people, representing various shades of the left spectrum, meet at the house of Joe Shawcross, a TV director from the North, now domiciled in London. The expensively functional living-room gives the impression '*of purpose narrowly triumphing over comfort; of rich ease scored by persistent puritan principle*'. They are meeting to discuss the possible formation, in the light of current events, of a united left party committed to political revolution. In the event they do not even get as far as agreeing an agenda. Always in the room, and switched on from time to time, is the television, bringing the BBC version of events across the water, already being encapsulated as 'history'. Before the 'party' begins, Joe and his wife, Angie, have an unsuccessful encounter in the bedroom, and the image of impotence remains associated with Joe throughout the play in all his attempts to arrive at some form of political commitment. 'We do this like we do everything else. It's a game', he tells his ex-wife, Kara, later, 'It's an intellectual pursuit. Or something worse. It's part of being . . . bourgeois. Peel the onion: find the nuance beneath the hint, the insight in the discrimination, the complexity below the conceit.'

His inability to choose between the various options that are to be offered him during the course of the eventing is put into relief by the presence of his brother Eddie, who has come down to borrow £300 to start a small business. Eddie expresses no interest whatever in the meeting, and disappears for a night on the town whilst Paris erupts on the television. Although *The Party* is fundamentally concerned with a political debate, it is evident that its origins lie for Griffiths in the predicament of himself and his generation, caught short in what might just prove to be a significant historical moment with no analysis to offer.

It started with a number of images . . . and what happened to me, in 1968, in France. And the American universities, the Blacks in Detroit, Watts. It started with the experience of the Friday night meetings at Tony Garnett's where sixty or seventy people would crowd into a room . . . to do more, to get it right, to be correct, to read the situation as a first step towards changing it utterly. . . . And with it all, the faint sense of, not silliness, exactly, but lack of candour that people proffered. For example, in relating their life-roles to their abstracted revolutionary role. The lack of connection between what they did day-by-day and what they did night-by-night. (*TQ*, VI, no. 22)

This sense of duality – the wish to be involved, to believe that what was happening was a new political departure, set against a strong feel for the absurdity of living-room revolution – is important, and is reflected in the play, for, unlike the new writers of the London fringe, Griffiths's political and cultural education did not start around 1968. His continual intellectual reference-points amongst English writers are Raymond Williams and Edward Thompson, and his first direct political experiences were gained in the North in the late fifties and early sixties, with CND and the 'Committee of 100', and then with the emergence of the old 'New Left' – the years of the *New Reasoner* and the beginnings of the *New Left Review*. 'And by about 1960–1 I was chairman of the Manchester Left Club, and about a year later I was acting editor of Labour's *Northern Voice* and Labour's *Voice*. . . . It began to increase experientially my preoccupation with politics and my understanding of it to some extent' (*TQ*, VI, no. 22). The excitement over the *événements* in Paris in *The Party* is always tempered by a larger analysis drawn from the earlier years of political activity, and by the time it was written 1968 was, anyway, part of history. The concern is not, as with his younger contemporaries, with the celebration of the spectacle, but with a discussion of its significance in an historical framework.

The debate that ensues captures both the urgency and the absurdity that Griffiths recalls from the meetings at Garnett's house. The uneasy atmosphere is frequently punctured by Sloman's increasingly drunk and bitter meanderings around the group. The first half of the play is dominated by an argument between Ford, a sociology lecturer from the London School of Economics, and Tagg, an old-style Trotskyist, who is, it transpires, dying of cancer. Ford, late-*New Left Review* and post-Marcussian with Situationist tendencies, rejects the traditional Marxist analysis of revolution based on class-conflict, seeking to redefine the terms, just as he argues Lenin has done before him. He argues that in a world of advanced capitalism the urban proletariat is no longer to be looked to as the vanguard of change, that it has become completely assimilated into the consumer society, and that the real battles will now be fought elsewhere, in the Third World.

> Our function, in the old centres, is to assist, however we may, the final victory of those anti-capitalistic, revolutionary movements. Whether we are Blacks in Detroit or white proletarians in Manchester, that is our sole remaining revolutionary purpose and duty. And . . . we must not seek to impose upon these movements the theoretical and organisational patterns elaborated for and applied to the strategy of metropolitan areas; such as city-based leaderships, centralised party control, and all the dead wood of European practice.

Tagg's response is to admit that some rethinking may be necessary given his observation of the 'revolutionary potential . . . growing among sections of the population whose relation to the working class is either non-existent, or extremely tenuous, or positively antagonistic'. However, he then sets out to refute Ford's argument point by point, reaffirming the need to build a disciplined and non-spontaneous party-organisation, based on the working class, but freed of any vestiges of Stalinism. The argument of spontaneity against discipline is echoed in the various members of the group's reactions to Tagg's attempts to alter the free-for-all discussion to a formal meeting with a chairman. Ford sees it as simply a power gambit, whilst Grease, the agit-prop theatre-man, wakes up sufficiently to communicate for virtually the first time. 'You want us to number from the left or something? . . . What do we need a chair for? Jesus Christ. There's *ten* of us man. Suddenly we need a bureaucracy.'

Tagg's commitment to his programme is reinforced in the second half when we hear him on the 'phone to Paris, agreeing with the decision made by his group to withdraw from, and not contest, the barricades.

So those brave and foolish youths in Paris now will hold their heads out for the baton and shout their crazy slogans for the night. But it won't stop them from graduating and taking up their positions in the centres of ruling class power and privilege later on.

What is remarkable about this argument in theatrical terms is the amount of uncompromising space allowed it. Each man talks, virtually without interruption, for about fifteen minutes. It is a use of the stage as an arena for the discussion of political ideas without parallel amongst Griffiths's contemporaries, and it is characteristic of all his plays. His characters have an amazing facility for remembering and quoting long extracts of prose – even down to the doctor spouting from Hippocrates in an attempt to explain the inevitable lack of humanity in the modern hospital-system to a woman who has just undergone mastectomy in *Through the Night* (1975). It does not always fit easily into the naturalistic framework of the plays, although in *The Party* Griffiths succeeds in achieving a mixture of emotional engagement with the situation and analytical interest in the arguments that prevents the play from becoming simply a series of linked monologues.

Again, Gramsci's address to the factory-workers in *Occupations* (1970) works through the sheer wit and power of the rhetoric, where elsewhere the play falters as Griffiths resorts to rather limp methods of conveying information – 'perhaps you would be good enough to fill in some of the background now', 'it's in Russian, so I'll have to translate', and so on. What is certain is Griffiths's determination to push debate to the centre of his plays, and this is a major part of their dramatic success. For what is unusual is that the arguments are open-ended, not convenient set-pieces laid out by the writer to prove a point. The audience is provided with no neat solutions. After Tagg's telephone-call to Paris – the man of theory suddenly in touch with events – the second half of *The Party* is largely given over to a sober conversation between Joe and Sloman, a conversation which gives biographical flesh to their particular dilemmas, and moves the debate even further away from abstractions.

They talk about their past lives, and Sloman gradually moves towards his response to the arguments of the first half, a response which includes his radical critique of a Wordsworth ballad. He rejects all theory in favour of an almost biological determinism coupled with undiluted faith in the potential of man.

There'll be a revolution, and another, and another, because the capacity for 'adjustment' and 'adaptation' within capitalism is not, contrary to popular belief, infinite. . . . And they'll find the 'germ' from inside the class, not from 'outwith'. Because the germ's there, the virus is there, and however many generations of workers

127

are pumped full of antibiotics or the pink placebos of late capitalism, it will persist, the virus under the skin, waiting.

Although the argument virtually concludes the play, it is not intended as a conclusion, as a correct line, but as a further part of the debate. Its strength lies in its patent sincerity in comparison to Ford's well-rehearsed lecture; its weakness is the way in which Sloman continually talks of 'they'. He, and by association Joe, the writer and the director, have only the role of fatalistic voyeurism left.

In Griffiths's debates then, there are no clear winners. This is in part a reaction to what he had come to see as the shortcomings of his political journalism, born of the feeling that necessarily only one aspect of the question could be presented – and doubtless also his work as a teacher had taught him much about the didactic potential of drama. Griffiths's objections to journalism are very different to Hare's more general critique, that it trivialises and simplifies the complications of reality. Griffiths narrows the area of debate. He did not in any easy sense decide to become a playwright. Rather he resorted to drama as a way of discussing those issues that seemed important.

I just had a load of sap that wasn't being used, that just presented itself as a dialogue. I mean I've always thought about opposites, about the possibility of opposites for ideas. And after a couple of years of writing this political journalism I suppose I just wanted to say something that was other than that. (*Gambit*, VIII, no. 29, 1976)

This commitment to dialogue is a constant in all his work, and is at the centre of *Occupations*, a play which can be seen as a companion-piece to *The Party*. It is set in Turin in

1920, at the time of the factory-occupations. Griffiths has chosen a moment when history could go either way. Karbak, a communist agent, arrives to encourage the socialist leaders to widen the scale of their offensive. *Occupations* poses the same central problem that Griffiths had considered on a smaller scale in the English context of a factory-strike at the time of the Industrial Relations Act in his radio play *The Big House* (1969): whether to embark on an all-out pre-emptive strike, with the possibility of failure in the short term and disintegration in the long, or to settle within the system for temporary improvement of wages and conditions, and the possibility of consolidation for the future struggle. Parallels with France in 1968 are always apparent, with the Old Fox waiting in the wings, like De Gaulle, to arrange a referendum to subvert the struggle, and, more ominously, with the slides and music anticipating the Fascist backlash which is about to occur.

Karbak attempts to persuade Gramsci to risk all in the cause of his scientific version of Marxism, accusing him of loving the people too much. 'You cannot *love* an army, comrade. An army is a machine. This one makes revolutions. If it breaks down, you get another one. Love has nothing to do with it.' Politically, one strand of Karbak's argument leads to Stalinism. That it leaves out all human considerations is emphasised by his treatment of his mistress, a Russian aristocrat dying of cancer whom he abandons when his work in Italy is complete, and of Polya, her servant from the old order, whose body is simply used by the representative of the new as required.

The connection between the public and the private is similarly explored in Griffiths's account of the 1903 Social Democratic Conference in the BBC play *Absolute Beginners* (1974), which traces Lenin's break with Trotsky, and his moves to form a strong centralised Party-organisation.

Human considerations cannot be allowed to interfere. His closest associates are removed from influence if they offer opposition, whilst usefulness to the Party will excuse any personal shortcomings. Lenin rounds on Trotsky at the end of the play – his words are much the same as those of Karbak: 'You seem to think a party is an organisation for the deliberation of complex moral choices, a sort of political sewing circle.' Even Lenin's wife's night-time query, 'Do you want me?', takes on ironic undertones with her later offer of secretarial assistance, 'Do you need me?'

This harsh view of the revolutionary programme forms a continual part of the dialectic in all his plays. The nearest Griffiths gets to a deliberate negation of the position is in *Thermidor* (1971), a preliminary investigation for a Stalin show trial set in 1937. Here the logic is pushed to its historical limit. The interrogator, Yukhov, having told Anya that 'intellectual digressions will not be welcomed', is only temporarily put off by her revelation that they had been friends and comrades in 1924. His pursuit of logic in the wrong cause will not allow him to move from his carefully laid-down bureaucratic procedures. In *Occupations*, Gramsci opposes Karbak, and refuses his consent. 'I thought, how can a man love a collectivity, when he has not profoundly loved single human creatures. . . . Treat masses as expendable, as fodder, *during* the revolution, you will always treat them thus.' Thus thwarted, Karbak, in a secondary strategy, turns to the Fiat management to organise a deal that will strengthen the Russian state. He is a man whose 'occupation' is revolution; if temporarily it cannot be advanced, then it must be consolidated.

However, Karbak is never just the fall-guy for Gramsci's arguments. He is the central character in the play, much of the force of his argument is historically undeniable, and, as in *The Party*, the single voice is only one part of the dialogue. The key distinction is that Griffiths sees the debate as being exclusively of the Left. Although he is always careful to allow the capitalist establishment a reasonable voice – the plans of the Fiat representative for a model workers' welfare scheme is a case in point – he never feels the need to argue the case for change, only the ways in which it might be best achieved.

> My plays are never about the battle between socialism and capitalism. I take that as being decisively won by socialism. What I'm really seeking is the way forward. How do we transform this husk of capitalist meaning into the reality of socialist enterprise. (*TQ*, VI, no. 22)

The dilemma for Griffiths, and the instigation for his work, is summed up well by Albert Hunt:

> Griffiths is concerned with marxist thought as a basis for action. He uses the theatre to examine the apparent contradictions in the way marxist ideas have been handled; and in so doing, he examines the way those contradictions are reflected in himself as an individual. But there is no central tradition of marxist thought in Britain. Griffiths is aware of a hole in our culture where Karl Marx ought to be. His plays are a conscious attempt to fill the hole. (*New Society*, 16 Jan 1975)

That this is a problem for him can easily be seen in *The Big House*. The strike he follows has obvious analogies with the situation in *Occupations*, but there comes a point, in the context of English political empiricism, when he can develop the argument no further. Frustrated in his attempts to escalate the struggle, the militant organiser, Jack, arranges a walk-out at the leaving-party of Commander

Percy, a personnel officer of the old brigade who runs his job as if he were running a ship. The demonstration achieves the desired embarrassment within the walls of the factory, but a newer, more subtle management is slowly assuming control, and the play ends with Jack and a mate watching a carefully doctored news-item on the retirement on a pub television. Questioned on the changes he has seen, the Commander says all the right things: 'For a start, management has become a more exact science' – and the pair are left to vent their anger on the broadcast. Their attempt to look forward in hope rings self-consciously hollow:

> YATES: One day somebody's gonna say it the way it really is, Jack. And all the sets in England'll explode with the impact.
> JACK: That'll be the day, Tom.
> YATES: Aye. That *will* be the day.

It is not that the conclusion is pessimistic exactly – the struggle to reinstate their fellow worker has succeeded after all – but its tongue-in-cheek realism is a concession to the impossibility of pushing it any further. In *Such Impossibilities*, written for the BBC in 1971 but never produced, Griffiths looks back to 1911, and shows Tom Mann, Secretary of the Transport Workers' Federation, supervising the Liverpool seamans' strike. Despite all setbacks – including Mann's imprisonment for 'incitement to mutiny' – the strike is a complete success. All demands are acceded to, and the movement is shown as gathering strength as a result. The day-to-day activities of the strike committee are shown in detail and the connection made with the larger analysis. The play would have ended with Mann's words on the roll:

Political and industrial action must at all times be inspired by revolutionary principles. That is, the aim must ever be to change from capitalism to socialism as speedily as possible. Anything less than this means continued domination by the capitalist class.

Not only is Griffiths making the connection with present struggle quite explicit, but by its attempted placing in a series called 'The Edwardians', which concentrated on such figures as Baden Powell and Conan Doyle, he is offering a view of the English past which tears the audience away from the usual cosy, establishment nostalgia. In his introduction to the published play Griffiths was clear on his intentions: 'to restore, however tinily, an important but suppressed part of our collective history; to enlarge our "usable past" and connect it with a lived present; and to celebrate a victory'.

Much of Griffiths's work has been precisely an attempt to restore a part of our collective socialist history – Edward Thompson's *The Making of the English Working Class* was an early influence. When he submitted *The Party* to the National it was as a result of a commission to write a play about Kronstadt, and he has been working on a play about the English Revolution for several years. Frequently this has involved him in moving the action into the larger arena of the European Marxist movement, including his screenplay for *Reds* (1982), based on John Reed's account of the Russian Revolution in *Ten Days that Shook the World*, but always with the avowed intent of making the connection with the here and now. Thus there are deliberate echoes from one play to another – for instance, both *Thermidor* and *The Party* use the same quotation from Trotsky's address to the 13th Party Conference on the role of the Party. The intention is to create a dialectical structure not

only within each play, but through the whole developing
body of work.

Griffiths's preoccupation with the origins of the Labour
movement is, then, one which causes him to see-saw back
and forth through history. In *All Good Men* (1974, BBC
'Play for Today'), the connection between past and present
is made in a specifically English context. Edward Waite, an
early Labour Party and union leader, is living out his
retirement in his Surrey home – *'twelve usable rooms, good
lawns front and back'*. As the play opens he is talking,
'quietly, as though to a question', about the General Strike
of 1926. His accent, a mixture of Manchester and standard
English, indicates his uneasy move away from his Northern
urban and industrial roots. The images of compromise
accumulate throughout the play. He is seated surrounded
by all the apparatus of film-making, an old man in a wicker
chair, literally exposed to the camera. These first few
moments are crucial, for they promise the audience from
the outset that the presentation of one man's political
career will occur within a structured account of the process
that eventually brings the programme onto the screen.
Waite is immediately joined by the TV-producer Massingham – Winchester and Oxford – and they discuss the points
to be raised in the following day's interview.

The contrast between Waite's retired opulence and the
early hardships he describes is a further cue leading to an
expectancy of a simplistic account of the sell-out of the old
Labour order. It is a feeling that is reinforced when we
learn that Waite has been offered, and intends to accept, a
life peerage. But Griffiths sets up this expectation only that
he may the better come to terms with the reality of the
history. For Waite is not just a convenient fictionalisation
of Labour Party compromise. It is gradually revealed that
Massingham's motives in making the programme are not as

impartial as he claims – indeed that they could not be – and that he is planning a demolition-job on Waite, that very account, though from a right-wing perspective, that the audience has been led to expect. He is apparently aided in his task by Waite's son, William, whose researches into early Labour history have unearthed what he claims to have been a betrayal by his father of the working class at the time of the General Strike, a betrayal which he argues is symptomatic of the overall failure of the Labour Party to effect real change.

However, Griffiths does not allow the attack to go unchallenged. Waite defends the Party's necessarily com-promised efforts, and contrasts the achievements with what he sees as an academically messianic vision on the part of his son.

> You sit there behind your little desk in your little ivory tower and you read your Marx and your Trotsky and you get your slide rule out and do a couple of simple calculations and you have your blueprint. Revolution. Total change. Overnight. Bang. Especially bang. You have to have your bit of theatre as well, don't you? . . . Reality isn't like that. Reality is . . . taking people with you.

The tension between the two positions is one which Griffiths was to explore in more detail in the Thames TV series *Bill Brand* (1976), in which a newly elected MP with a political position close to that of William – the MP's name is even the short form of that of Waite's son – is faced with the application of his ideas in the day-to-day compromised reality of Westminster. Certainly the suggestion in both *Bill Brand* and *All Good Men* is that parliamentary struggle alone will not effect real change, but no simple conclusion is

135

intended. Waite and his colleagues *were*, in their way, 'all good men', and they have a position that can be defended; it is the situation that has changed. Waite's defence is only partially successful, just as William's revolutionary stance is only partially appropriate. What the play stresses is that Waite and his son still have a dialogue, albeit an angry one, that their debate is still a live issue.

In contrast, it is Massingham who is left with nothing to contribute, nothing to say. He is in the business of communication, and not of communicating. When questioned by Waite's daughter, Maria, as to what *he* thinks of the old man, his reply is evasive: 'That's not my brief. I present; others judge.' He attempts to argue for a role of dispassionate observer, as he later reiterates to William: 'I'm simply the film camera, the tape recorder, the lighting man.' William's response attacks the very basis of supposed objectivity on which the ideology of Massingham, and behind him the entire structure of public-communication networks, is built. 'If you want to write the history, you have to say who was right, Mr Massingham. You have to *choose* your spokesman.' Massingham can only respond to the argument he has witnessed in terms of a personality struggle – 'So you hate your father' – and William's riposte goes unanswered: 'You listen but you don't hear.'

Versions of this critique of the role of television are to be found frequently in Griffiths's work, and I have already cited a number of instances of the intrusion of the television into the sub-text of several of the plays. They are there primarily because of his belief in the potential of the medium. Griffiths is unusual in the context of this book, in that all the other writers I discuss have attitudes ranging from indifference to outright hostility towards it, even though one of them, John McGrath, started out as a television-writer. Griffiths has no strong brief for the theatre at all, and has increasingly concentrated his activity on writing for television, arguing correctly that for most people drama is exclusively associated with this medium.

Part of the attraction for him is the access it provides to an audience that a theatre, both in terms of size and social range, cannot; *Through the Night* was watched by an estimated 11 million people. But more important for Griffiths is its subversive potential for what he describes as 'strategic penetrations': 'I simply cannot understand socialist playwrights who do not devote most of their time to television. . . . It's just thunderingly exciting to be able to talk to large numbers of people in the working class, and I can't understand why everybody doesn't want to do it' (*Gambit*, VIII, no. 29). That he is aware of the problems is obvious: they are well articulated by Sloman's response to Joe's demand for a play from him, in *The Party*. 'Wednesday Plays? It's the Liberal heartland, Joe. Every half-grown pupa in grub street is in there fighting with you. It's the consensus. It's the condition of our time.' Sloman's expression of the deradicalising effect of television is close to that of David Edgar's response to what has probably been Griffiths's most successful penetration to date, *Bill Brand*.

> The inherent problem with television as an agent of radical ideas is that its massive audience is not confronted en masse. It is confronted in the atomised, a-collective arena of the family living room, the place where people are at their least critical, their most conservative and reactionary. (*TQ*, VIII, no. 32, 1979)

Sloman's objections to attempts at a socialist TV drama are telling, although they are addressed specifically to the politically impotent Joe: 'You occupy the same relationship to the means of production as every other . . . producer in that golden hutch at Would Not Lane you call the Centre. Socialist? A socialist producer? What's that? It's irrelevant.'

But Griffiths opposes the implications of Edgar's argument, that the audience is an atomised passivity sucking up uncritically all that is offered. The difference between their positions is that, whereas Edgar is looking for an immediacy of action, Griffiths talks more about a gradual process of insinuation.

> To argue . . . that television is part of a *monolithic* consciousness industry where work of truly radical or revolutionary value will never be produced is at once to surrender to undialectical thought and to fail to see the empirical evidence there is to refute such an argument. . . . To work in television as a playwright will be to seek to exploit the system's basic 'leakiness', so to speak . . . to (though it must in time be *with*) the many millions of cohabitants of one's society who share a part of a language, part of a culture, part of a history, with oneself.   (Author's Preface to *Through the Night*)

The argument has clear echoes of the attitudes expressed by Brenton and Hare in moving from the fringe to the establishment theatre. It is for Griffiths, quite specifically, the creation of a revolutionary drama in a non-revolutionary culture, and inevitably the paradox colours even his most optimistic pronouncements – even to the extent of virtual contradiction within the actual plays.

One of the obvious attractions of television for Griffiths is the potential that it affords for a more pressing version of the dialectic. Unlike theatre, television can be easily utilised to present a multiplicity of viewpoints, so that a viewer is not looking in on the total event but is able to become involved to some extent with the experience and analysis of a number of differing characters. On stage, the writer, and indeed the actor and director, has at his disposal any number of ways of focusing attention on the individual – the power of rhetoric, the use of soliloquy, techniques of blocking, lighting effects, and so on – but no way of enforcing it in the way that film or television can. This is not just to talk about talking heads. Rather, it is its ability to present events from different perspectives that is important.

After Christine's mastectomy, in *Through the Night*, her next contact with the hospital establishment is the doctor's round the following day. The round is not filmed looking in on the event but from Christine's bed, the camera and microphone taking the place of the patient. In this way the complete lack of comprehension on Christine's part, and of communication on that of the medical staff, is not just witnessed, but experienced. The viewer can see or hear no more than she can, and there is no possibility, as there would be on stage, of discovering any other perspective through which to attempt to make sense of the scene. In the text Griffiths indicates by the use of brackets what it is that the staff are saying and that Christine and we cannot hear.

REGISTRAR: (No problem with the) wound, sister?
WARREN: (None) at all, doctor.
SEAL: (Is she de)pressed, would you (say)?
WARREN: (Just a bit) down, doctor. (It's only) natural, I (sup)pose.

This capacity for shifting perspective serves not only to present a keenly realised dialogue between different individuals in the television-plays, but also to demonstrate graphically the dialectical relationship between the objective event and its subjective apprehension. Thus when, in *Such Impossibilities*, Tom Mann first arrives at the Inspection Hall in the Liverpool docks, the cameras would have moved between his observation of the seamen being stripped for a humiliating medical inspection and his reaction to the event. It is a film-technique so familiar as to go unremarked by what is now an exceedingly sophisticated viewing-audience, but its effect is to suggest a relationship between abuse and analysis which will lead to action. In addition it provides great scope for sustained examination of the public/private tension that informs so much of Griffiths's work.

So, in *Through the Night*, the availability of detailed responses from staff and patients alike allows Griffiths to demonstrate that Christine's distress does not arise from the ill will, incompetence, or whatever, of any individual or individuals – all are seen genuinely to be doing their best – but from the very nature of the institution. The patient's role is summed up well by the friendly Dr Pearce:

> Mainly, I think, it's because we have lost all idea of you as a whole, human being, with a past, a personality, dependents, needs, hopes, wishes. Our power is strongest when you are dependent upon it. We invite you to behave as the sum of your symptoms. And on the whole you are pleased to oblige.

This comes in the middle of a long expository speech which is completely at odds with the rest of the play. It is a curious intrusion, looking back to the very different demands made by the theatre in Griffiths's early work. It is not that what Pearce has to say is irrelevant or uninteresting – simply that it does not need this intensity of articulation. The matrix of interrelated perspectives that makes up the rest of the play allows the audience virtually to share the complexity of the experience for themselves, and it should be from this and not from a heavy piece of foisted stage didactism that the analysis should arise. The play was screened in the same year as Griffiths's last stage-play – with the exception of his collaboration in 1978 with Brenton, Hare and Ken Campbell, on *Deeds*, a farewell to Richard Eyre at the Nottingham Playhouse – and Griffiths now sees himself almost solely as a television dramatist. It will be exciting, especially given the evidence of increased pressure on the potential politicisation of television drama, to see how he sustains the challenge (compare Hare in *Ah! Mischief*).

Curiously, Griffiths's latest stage-play, *Comedians* (1975), owes much of its genesis to television, and yet is the most uncompromisingly theatrical play of his career. First produced by Richard Eyre at Nottingham, it was revived in London, and taken, in an American version, to Broadway, before eventually being televised, though with less than complete success. One of the instigations for the play was the popular TV series *The Comedians*, a weekly bout of stand-up comics drawing heavily on the Northern club-circuit, produced by the Manchester-based Granada company. The jokes, as always, relied almost entirely on sexual and racial fears, but seemed to Griffiths to express a new degree of hate: 'they brought a heightened realism, and a heightened cynicism and a heightened bitterness into the common colloquy in ways that hadn't been there before – or at least that had been suppressed' (*TQ*, VI, no. 22). From this and his desire to write about a teacher came the central structure of *Comedians*.

The first act is set in a secondary-school classroom in Manchester, a room created with the most meticulous attention to naturalistic detail in the Nottingham production. The play opens with a caretaker cleaning obscene graffiti off the blackboard prior to the start of an evening class. The same caretaker will end the play removing the unpleasant reminders of the evening's attempt at educa-tion. The class is the last in a course taught by Eddie Waters, a once popular but prematurely retired Northern comic in the tradition of Frank Randle, to a group of aspirant comedians. The night's session will be followed by their public debuts at a local working-men's club, where they will be vetted for future employment by a London-based agent, Challenor.

As the members of the class assemble it is evident that Griffiths has brought them together as an apparent embod-iment of the various stereotypes upon which the humour of the TV series depended – there is one Jew, two Irishmen, a milkman, and so on – and much of the edge of the dialogue comes from the comedians' ability to deploy and frustrate the expectations of the comic stereotyping. The most self-confident, the Ulsterman George McBrain, swaggers in, already virtually into his stage-act. The attempt by the insurance-agent Phil Murray, to put him down – 'You get more like Paisley every day' – is picked up by him and returned with the unmistakable accent of the Protestant leader: 'Mock not the reverend doctor, Mr Murray. There's not many left of us can walk on water.' His riposte is a good example of the essentially humanist approach to comedy that Waters attempts to instil in them: 'most comics *feed* prejudice and fear and blinkered visions, but the best ones . . . illuminate them, make them clearer to see, easier to deal with'. What he stresses is the connection between the public act and the personally felt experience from which it should derive.

Ironically, the best illustration of Waters's point is provided with the late arrival of Phil's brother, Ged, soaking wet and still in his milkman's outfit, just as Waters

announces the first exercise. Ged wanders through the
room, offering a series of friendly explanations, completely
unaware that he has disrupted proceedings, a natural comic
describing what has happened to him.

GED: Sorry I'm late. It's bloody pissing down out there. I
fell asleep on the settee watching *Crossroads*. So I had
to nip down t'depot and borrow a float to get here.
And t'bloody battery were flat. Got stuck on the old
road. Walked the last sodding mile. Evening, Mr
Waters. Evening all. (*A big friendly grin*.)
ALL (*in chorus*): Good evening, Mr Woodentop.

As the class proceeds the differing attitudes of the comedians gives substance to Waters's teaching. Sammy
Samuels, the Manchester Jew, has an ambition which
would not allow him to appear in the sort of club he runs;
McBrain cannot admit of the possibility of commercial
failure; and Connors, the man from Eire, sees his act as the
only way he can ever escape from the building-sites. The
soft Ged is the closest to Waters's humanist position, whilst
the abrasive Gethin Price is the one on whom Waters pins
all his hopes.

The confrontation between these last two finds early
expression. Waters responds to Price's deliberately provocative impromptu limerick, the opening rhyme of which,
'pratt' and 'hat', promises the inevitable conclusion, with a
blow-by-blow analysis, concluding that 'it's a joke that
hates women *and* sex'. Price's reaction indicates the
beginning of a rift that is to assume central importance.
McBrain tells a joke about a deer-poacher, and Price offers
a dead-pan parody of Waters's conclusions.

Now, Mr McBrain, you must see that the joke is totally

143

supportive of all forms of blood sports. Besides which it undoubtedly hints at the dark secret of animal buggery. . . . A *comedian*, George, would have carried all this out into the open where we could all see it . . . so that we'd all come to realise what should've been obvious from the start, or from the Middle Ages, whichever you prefer: namely, deep down we all want fucking up the arse by antlered beasties. It's a joke that hates *deer*, George.

It is only Price who understands what Waters is intent on in his set of unannounced diatribes against the Irish, Jews, negroes, cripples, defectives, the mad, women and workers. Connors asks after the first, 'Would that be Southern Irish or Northern Irish', and it is left to Price to cut through the resultant strained silence with the explanation, 'Lesson Three: "Stereotypes" '.

Although Waters has been a successful comic, at no point in the play does he tell a joke. It is his role as a teacher that is stressed. His aims in the classroom are essentially the same as those of the conventional imparter of liberal wisdom more usually to be seen performing there. Even the tongue-twister he gives them to practise – 'The traitor distrusts the truth' – unites moral intent with comic skill. In the 'class' room he stresses the unifying function of comedy and not its potential for commercial gain. 'When a joke bases itself on a distortion – a "stereotype" perhaps – and gives the lie to the truth so as to win a laugh and stay in favour, we've moved away from a comic art and into the world of "entertainment and slick success".' The problem for the comedians is that they are to be judged by the values of market capitalism and not of liberal idealism, by a Challenor committed to a view of the comic art that stresses the lowest common denominator, that confirms the 'stereotype' rather than questioning it.

Challenor and Waters are old adversaries. Where Challenor has moved down south and into management, Waters has stayed put. Challenor's final words to them before they leave for the club offer a possible access to fame and fortune diametrically opposed to that of Waters's teaching. He tells them that they are not there to make the audience think, but to give them what they want:

> We're servants, that's all. They demand, we supply. Any good comedian can lead an audience by the nose. But only in the direction they're going. And that direction is, quite simply . . . escape. We're not missionaries, we're suppliers of laughter. . . . Perhaps we can't all be Max Bygraves. But we can try.

The presence of the commercial entrepreneur causes consternation and this is reflected in the performances that follow in the second act. The curtain opens on the stage of a working-men's club. The theatre audience is addressed by the Concert Secretary as though it is a real club audience. He apologises for the break in the bingo and promises that the interruption will not last more than half an hour. It is a bold stroke by Griffiths, setting up a tension between the two audiences that culminates in Gethin Price's act. That the tension is there is evident from the suppressed laughter that greets the Club Secretary's words in the theatre, and this despite Griffiths's firm note that he should be played 'real, not caricature'. This is not a world or a culture that the majority of the theatre audience have access to. Its inappropriateness produces a laughter that illustrates graphically the class-division that Waters wishes to eradicate, and that Price will shortly articulate.

145

The second act consists entirely of the comedians' performances. Connors opens with a long monologue, more 'honest' than comic, about the strangeness of being an Irishman in England, and he is followed by Samuels, who, after starting a similar act drawn from his own Jewish culture, suddenly lurches into a series of sexist and racist jokes – including his version of McBrain's deer-poaching gag – offering the agent what he has appeared to demand, and turning away from Waters's teaching. He is to be rewarded with the promise of a contract: 'it was a different act, the wife, blacks, Irish, women, you spread it around', Challenor tells him in the third act. Phil and Ged Murray's double act collapses when Ged, playing a dummy on his brother's knee, refuses to similarly compromise their routine when Phil introduces a joke about a Pakistani on a rape charge. He comes out of role and demands that his brother tell the joke, which white-faced and completely unfunnily Phil does. The theatre audience is caught up in the contradictions of the event, recognising the terms of the dilemma and responding directly to the embarrassment. Griffiths follows this with a beautifully polished performance by McBrain, turning it on as he has always seemed likely to do, and treading a fine line between Challenor's and Waters's positions in order to do so. The audience relaxes back into the safety of his professionalism, and then stunningly the entire atmosphere is changed.

Gethin Price appears. His hair is cropped short and his face is a white expressionless mask. He is dressed like a surrealistic Manchester United 'bovver boy', with echoes of *Clockwork Orange*, and he carries a tiny violin and bow. He says nothing, prepares to play, notices a thread hanging from the bow and attempts to pull it off. It resists all his efforts and he sets fire to it. As the bow begins to burn, the violin starts to play a complicated piece unaided. Seemingly in desperation, Price crushes the violin beneath his boot. Then for the first time, but still ignoring the audience, he speaks. 'Wish I had a train. I feel like smashing a train up. On me own. I feel really strong. Wish I had a train. I could do with some exercise.' As he goes through a Kung Fu routine, two larger than life-size dummies of a couple in full evening dress are wheeled on – clothed as though they have just come from a theatrical performance perhaps.

As he becomes aware of their presence he leaves off the exercises, moves over, and attempts to communicate with these inanimate creatures from another world. Through them he addresses the reality of the audience in the theatre, no longer allowed the luxury of the social mobility of club *and* theatre. 'Cigarette? . . . No? . . . Taxi! . . . Are you the interpreter, then? Been to the match, have we? Were you at t'top end wi' lads? Good, wannit? D'you see Macari? Eh? Eh? . . . P'raps I'm not here. Don't you like me? You hardly know me.' Faced with the complete impossibility of communicating across the class-barrier, the confrontation becomes more direct. He takes a cigarette from the man's pocket, offers to discuss his wife's sexual potential, wonders whether to thump him, invites the woman to join him in his British Rail delivery-truck, and finally pins a flower onto her breast. As he steps back, blood oozes onto the white dress. Price is left in a single spotlight, addressing the audience directly for the first time.

I made them laugh, though. Who needs them? Hunh. . . . U-n-i-ted. Un*i*-ted. You won't keep us down there for long, don't worry. We're coming up *there where* we can gerrat yer. . . . I shoulda smashed him. They allus mek you feel sorry for 'em, out in the open. . . . (*Pause. He looks after them. Calling.*) National Unity! Up yours, sunshine.

He picks up another violin and plays 'The Red Flag', before concluding reflectively, as stunned as the audience, 'Still, I made the buggers laugh.'

I have dwelt on Price's act because it is the pivotal point in the play, a sustained theatrical enactment of opposition to all that Waters has argued for. Its impact is if anything even more electrifying seeing it a second and third time, producing on at least one night an intervention from a member of the audience, a measure of the directness of the assault. Price's skinhead articulates a disturbing continuation of the class divide – one nation confronted by the delinquent version of the other – that will not be contained by all the humanist persuasions of the classroom, and it is this alone that prompted Griffiths to add a third act. The original clash had been between Waters and Challenor, 'the man who was uncorrupted and the man who was deeply corrupted', but 'something comes up that transcends the level of consciousness and understanding of these two guys' (*TQ*, VI, no. 22).

The third act returns the characters to the school, where Challenor offers a predictable analysis of the acts as marketable properties. McBrain and Samuels are promised contracts, and one by one the comedians make their uneasy exits until only Price and Waters are left. Gethin can see that the rest of the class have opted either for Waters's programme or for compromise, but this is no longer the point for him. Connor's and Ged's integrity is irrelevant because it will not lead to change: 'they stayed put because they've nowhere else to go'. Waters had thought his performance brilliant but repulsive: 'It was ugly. It was drowning in hate. You can't change today into tomorrow on that basis. You forget a thing called . . . the truth.' Price's notion of the truth is not that of Waters's 'beautiful'

148

ideal, however, but a product of the hard experience of social reality that he claims the teacher has forgotten.

> Truth was a fist you hit with. Now it's like cow-flop, a day old, hard until it's underfoot and then it's . . . green, soft. Shitten. Nothing's changed, Mr Waters, is what I'm saying. When I stand upright – like tonight at that club – I bang my head on the ceiling. Just like you fifty years ago. We're still caged, exploited, prodded and pulled at, milked, fattened, slaughtered, cut up, fed out. We still don't belong to ourselves. Nothing's changed. You've just forgotten, that's all.

Waters's response, to tell how a visit to a concentration-camp after the war compromised his ability to make jokes, is inadequate. By now the weight of the dialectic has moved away from the teacher to the activist, even though the attempted empathy of many critics towards Waters's political position prevented them from comprehending the shift. What is at stake is no longer a debate about rival theories of comedy, but the conflict between reformism and revolution that had preoccupied Griffiths in more abstract form from his earliest work. What singles *Comedians* out is the way in which political debate is entered at a tangent, so that the audience is involved in the implication of the struggle through a structure of plot and characterisation which is apparently at one remove from the world of the earlier plays, many of which had the effect of plunging into the dialectic head-on.

Waters ends the play listening sympathetically to a Pakistani student's version of an old Jewish joke. He offers him a lift home and a place on his next course. The teacher has learnt nothing, and can only envisage a perpetuation of the liberal paternalism that is at the heart of his ideology. Gethin has already left, his personal and public life in ruins about him, having learnt from his first engagement:

> I found this in another book. I brought it to show you. Some say the world will end in fire. Some say in ice. From what I've tasted of desire I hold with those who favour fire, but if I had to perish twice, I think I know enough of hate to say that for destruction ice is also great and would suffice. (*He folds the paper, puts it back in his pocket, moves to desk, picks up his bag, rather casually.*) It was all ice out there tonight. I loved it. I felt . . . expressed. (*Pause, lifting suddenly.*) The Jews still stayed in line, even when they knew Eddie! What's *that* about? I stand in no line. I refuse my consent.

Gethin has crossed the dividing-line; what will happen to him and to the struggle he has embraced, he knows no more than Griffiths. But his commitment to the struggle is absolute, and the continued articulation of the need to nag at the terms of that struggle will ensure that Griffiths's work, whether or not he ever returns to the theatre, will occupy a central place in the development of political drama.

6
David Edgar:
War on All Fronts

I do like agitprop, and I'm fond of my agitprop plays. I'm fond of that period. There may again be a period when agitprop will have more relevance than I believe it does now. But I don't think I'll ever go back to it, because the sort of subjects that I want to deal with now won't take it.

(TQ, IX, no. 33, 1979)

David Edgar's words, quoted above, were spoken when he had three plays running simultaneously in London theatres. This success was not untimely, for, although he did not start writing until 1970, he was to prove the most prolific, and the most frequently produced, playwright of his generation. By the end of the decade some forty of his plays had been staged.

However, the three London productions represent something more than a simple recognition of his emergence as a major writer. They also signal a change of direction in the work of a man whose roots are solidly in the agit-prop tradition. Most of his early plays were 'occasional' pieces, often specifically commissioned by individual groups, written quickly in response to a rapidly changing political situation. All written from a committedly left socialist position, they nevertheless show evidence of Edgar's willingness to enlarge the thematic scope of political drama in a quite unprecedented way. Throughout his career it is evident that the source for his work is very often issue-related, and there have been plays on a bewildering array of topics – on baby-snatching, on field sports, on political imprisonment, and so on. This is obviously related to his original writing-career as an aspirant investigative journalist, but it also helps to shed light on Edgar's dramatic aims.

Many of his plays have as a starting-point what is effectively a newspaper story, the bare outlines of an event that demands more than the superficial explanation or analysis conventionally offered. This is most apparent in his straight agit-prop plays – about industrial agitation, government legislation, and so forth – but in all his work what chiefly preoccupies Edgar is the desire to explore, on as many fronts as possible, the struggles of a socialist philosophy at large in a confusing world of late capitalism. If his socialism provides the overall didactic structure of his plays, it is the confusions of the material world that creates most of their dramatic interest. For, even in his earliest work, Edgar was never a crude ideologue.

He is younger than the other playwrights in this book – in 1968 he was an undergraduate, studying drama at Manchester. Like them, however, his early work was very much a part of a post-1968 consciousness, though his starting-point was rather different. Edgar has described his political activities at university as undirected; he felt himself swept along with the fashionably radical current:

I don't feel that until I left university my socialism developed beyond combining being quite a good public speaker and quite a good polemical writer with a sense of social injustice, emerging from horror at the hydrogen bomb, plus a sense of disillusion with the Labour government and of outrage at the Vietnam war. (*TQ*, IX, no. 33)

This expression of a broad-based leftish disaffection is familiar, but Edgar never saw himself as involved in the more optimistic elements of the alternative culture. By the time he left university, to become a journalist, the atmosphere had changed. As a journalist, he was involved with some of the early investigation of the Poulson corruption scandal, one of the instigations for Brenton and Hare's *Brassneck*, and it is from this period that his first activity as a playwright dates.

He came to play-writing by a natural progression. Unlike Griffiths, he had been from his early years an avid theatre-goer, and certainly his work exhibits, even more than Brenton's, evidence of a man who is familiar with earlier English drama. Once at Manchester he tried his hand first at acting and then at directing, without deriving any real satisfaction from either. In Bradford his work as a journalist brought him into contact with the University drama, originally as a theatre-critic, and later as a writer.

By 1970, when Edgar began to write for groups associated with Bradford University, the political climate on the left had changed, though he believes that most practitioners of left theatre were slow to realise it. But his first two plays, both of that year, *Two Kinds of Angel* and *A Truer Shade of Pale*, which owe much to the encouragement of Chris Parr (then a fellow at Bradford), are loosely comparable to the early work of Brenton and John Grillo, also commissioned by Parr at this time. Although the nearest that Edgar ever formally got to the kind of theatre associated with Portable was as a part of the team-effort on *England's Ireland*, elements of the Portable style coexist in his work with a commitment to agit-prop theatre. *Acid* (1971) was still in the broadly Portable school, a play about terrorism, full of fire and rhetoric, with an ending, 'the daughter basically giving the line of the piece to these three Charles Manson-type monsters, I now find embarrassing' (*TQ*, IX, no. 33). In *The End* (1972) – a play commissioned, like Brenton's *Wesley* and *Scott of the Antarctic*, to play in a specific public environment – Edgar utilised the University computer-console to present a piece that incorporated scenes in a Polaris submarine. But his work was beginning to change in response to his observation of the political changes around him.

Edgar saw, in the aftermath of the Conservative victory of 1970, a need to return to the traditional arena of class conflict, and to abandon the notion of an *avant-garde* counter-culture opposition. He came to believe, as he expressed it in 1978, 'that reports of the death of working-class militancy had been much exaggerated' (*TQ*, VIII, no. 32, 1979). He was not alone in this feeling. The Election result was a shock to the Left. Wilson's government may have lacked any serious socialist credibility, but there was an overriding sense of inevitability about it struggling through into the next decade. The real politics, most activists argued, would take place outside of Parliament. Heath's struggle with the miners, and the introduction of the three-day week, suddenly brought the trade-union movement back into the forefront of the struggle. Richard Seyd of Red Ladder later argued that they were taken by surprise: 'we had to relate to working people through their own organisations and not stay on the outside of the Labour movement' (*New Edinburgh Review*, 1975). He was by no means alone. Richard Muldoon: 'rich situations like Heath versus the miners went untouched by us' (*P & P*, Jan 1977).

Despite this early commitment to agit-prop, there was something almost accidental, if inevitable, about Edgar's first attempts at the form.

> It happened that a group of people wanted to set up a new theatre company arising out of Bradford, and this became the General Will: but the first performances of *The National Interest* were under the auspices of Bradford University. And really the whole series of work for the General Will came out of that coincidence. It might have been that a group interested in another kind of work might have done another kind of play of mine, and that would have been the line of development. (*TQ*, IX, no. 33)

The National Interest (1971) was written in response to the first year of the new Conservative administration, and it was followed by a succession of plays all of which were concerned directly with contemporary issues – so much so that the output of Edgar and General Will in this period is more like a continuing serial than a sequence of distinguishable plays. As one piece was taken out of the repertoire, another replaced it. It is the nearest that modern agit-prop has got to a 'living newspaper' tradition, with the scripts of plays being emended and added to as political events changed.

None of them was written, however, in a straightforwardly documentary style. Other agit-prop groups had realised the need for a lightening of the didactic load with accessible comic routines, and Edgar did more to develop this aspect than anyone. Where McGrath has argued that his use of popular culture forms – the traditional music of *The Cheviot*, for instance – is a deliberate attempt to communicate with his desired audience in terms of its own 'popular' culture, Edgar is more catholic in his range. His presentation of *Rent, Or, Caught in the Act* (1972) as a series of music-hall turns was done, he explained, simply because it was funny; and not with any idea that he might be utilising a relevant cultural form in political terms. A direct result of this is that, in the plays with General Will, Edgar completely bypasses the kind of social realism that was to become such an important feature of his later work. He argued later that at the time he felt that television, a medium to which he has always been hostile, had captured the naturalistic play, showing people's behaviour as conditioned 'primarily or exclusively by individual factors' while he sought a form 'which demonstrates the social and political character of human behaviour' (*TQ*, VIII, no. 32).

In his agit-prop plays, Edgar's characters are not, then, presented as psychologically convincing individuals. His frequent use of doubling parts – which in any case is forced upon companies economically by the vast size of his casts – helps to reinforce the sense in which the actors are simply presenting a character to the audience. George, at the beginning of *Wreckers*, introduces the action to the audience, before announcing his first role: 'And I, for the time being, am George. Occupation, Detective Sergeant in the Metropolitan Constabulary. The Force. London's Finest. The Boys in Blue. Or, as they call us round here, the Filth.' At the beginning of the second act the same actor announces that he is now playing a newspaper reporter. The rather heavy suggestion is made to the audience that both roles are essentially concerned with policing society, but Edgar does not allow the actor space to develop the characters as individuals. The emphasis is on externals; continually Edgar strives to deny his characters relationships that are other than material and political. Of course, in any play dealing with human activity, some indications of personal lives will appear, but Edgar was anxious to eliminate them as far as possible. He has enlarged on this with reference to Turner in *Destiny*:

> I'm not going to give you the opportunity to say Turner is a fascist because his wife is a gorgon, or his child is a mongol, or his son was run over, or whatever. I'm not going to do it. You are not going to know. He could be single. He could be gay. I'm going to treat everything else about him in a very complicated way, but you're not going to know anything personal or intimate, because, if you do, you'll run up that blind alley for psychological explanations. (*TQ*, IX, no. 33)

Because Edgar set out to create two-dimensional characters, he was heavily reliant on the comic potential of language to involve an audience more accustomed to looking for psychological rather than material motivation. Most of the characters in the early plays have a carefully constructed ability to deal with their own caricature-like quality. They frequently turn jokes in on themselves. The posh girl selling the *Workers' Vanguard* in a pub in *Wreckers*, for instance, presents her worry about her sales-technique in a way that can only come from the actress's awareness of the contradictions inherent in this activity. 'I really ought to sell another five before closing time. You see, I've come last but one in our selling group three weeks running, and if I don't up my sales I'll be liable to compulsory self-criticism.' In such a statement the line between the world of the sales-rep. and the revolutionary becomes very faint, and the audience is able to explore, and to enjoy – or perhaps even to recognise in embarrassed familiarity – the contradiction.

Edgar further prevents his characters from 'establishing' themselves for an audience by the sheer pace of the plays. The scenes progress in a series of rapid transformations of theatrical styles. Narrative jumps are frequent, and explained by characters stepping out of role to explain the new circumstances – in itself, a device to prevent identification. For his agit-prop plays Edgar grabbed around in all directions, and many of his borrowings were to become standard features of the later work of many other groups – the explanation of productivity deals in the form of 'The Generation Game' in *The Dunkirk Spirit*, for example. In his career so far, Edgar has utilised virtually every literary and theatrical *genre* going, from the spy-story to the love-story. *The National Interest* portrayed the Conservative government as Chicago hoods, whilst *The Rupert Show* (1972), which examined sexual politics, was presented in the form of a church-service. For *Rent, Or, Caught in the Act*, Edgar set out to explain the workings of the Housing Finance Act to tenants' associations by raiding the conventions of Victorian melodrama.

We got a link-up with the Child Poverty Action Group . . . and the play was a series of scenes from Victorian melodrama putting the Harddoneby family through a series of situations – in a squat, in a rented house, in various sorts of council housing. It was a very mechanical piece, but it did actually explain a complicated Act of Parliament in reasonably simple terms. It played to thirty tenants' groups, and it got its audience. It went down very well, and was very useful.   (*TQ*, ix, no. 33)

This last sentence goes a long way towards explaining the tension that is to be found in all of Edgar's early work. Because he was intent on writing for an audience whose interest was, in a general sense, political rather than theatrical, he relied enormously on the parody of pre-existing dramatic (and especially television and film) forms with which even a non-theatrical audience would be familiar.

> We began to realise that our shows had to do two things –
> to be entertaining in commenting on things the audience
> would know about, and to provide a context in which to
> view events – a political, theoretical context. And
> because of these factors, the plays worked best with what
> the jargon calls 'advanced workers' . . . they worked
> badly with fairly apolitical workers. (Edgar, quoted in
> Itzin, *Stages in the Revolution*)

The reliance on parody was, as Edgar came to realise, extremely problematic. In 1972 he used an updated version of *Romeo and Juliet*, in *Death Story*, about the Irish struggle; and then in *Tedderella*, a reworking of the pantomime, *Cinderella*, he presented his account of Ted Heath and the Common Market negotiations. But he reached the high-point of the form, and also its end, in *Dick Deterred* (1972).

In this play Edgar moved beyond casual parody to direct takeover. Shakespeare's *Richard III* was twisted, mangled and rewritten to provide an account of King Richard Nixon and his dealings before, during and after Watergate. It is a very clever, and a very funny play, but its cleverness is ultimately its problem. The tone is set by the first entrance of Richard:

Now is the winter of our discontent
Made glorious summer by this Texan bum
And all the crowds that didn't duck the draft
Vacating are the bosoms of Saigon.
Our brows now bound with wreaths of compromise,
Our bruised armies are demobilised,
Our napalm bombs are changed to Paris meetings,
Our My Lai massacres to diplomatic measures.
But I, that am not shaped for aught but tricks,
Nor made to court an amorous CBS,
I, that am rudely stamped, and want capacity
To strut before a wanton East Coast liberal . . .

and so on. From now on, it is evident, all the surprises will
be theatrical surprises. The attention of the audience will
be held firmly on Edgar's ability to transpose Nixon's
activities onto the pre-existing structure of Shakespeare's
play. Little in the way of political sophistication is to be
expected, and little is forthcoming. There are, it is true,
some glorious pieces of paralleling from the original;
Richard's wish,

Let me have men about me that are thin
Crew-cutted yes-men, Christian Scientists

for instance, or the echo of Hamlet's anguish:

To bug or not to bug, that was the question.
Whether 'twas nobler in the mind to suffer
The slings and arrows of the *New York Times*
Or, 'neath the veil of national security,
By surveillance end them? To bug – to tap –
No more! It's not my fault, I'm not to blame,
It's Kissinger what did it.

160

And Nixon's Press Secretary, Ron Zeigler, converted to
Catesby, and asked by the White House Chief of Staff, Bob
Buckingham, to serve his King in the only way he knows, by
lying:

> BUCKINGHAM: Good Catesby, when I took thee from my
>   firm
>   Of advertising agents, for to serve the King.
>   I knew thee as a marv'llous PRO
>   For playing down the defects of a product
>   And playing up its virtues. Now's your chance
>   To prove my faith to you.
> CATESBY: But, noble lord,
>   I must myself have knowledge of the truth
>   If I'm expected to deny it.

In such ways Edgar does go a little beyond a superficial
explanation of how the Nixon administration came to be,
and what it represented, but his invocation of the worlds of
commerce, publicity and Ivy League dual morality is not
sufficient to open up the play as a genuine political tool.
The play is a game, the result of which is already known to
the audience; all the pleasure is in watching the execution,
and not in moving towards an analysis. The play cannot
develop politically beyond the confines of its restrictive
parental structure (Edgar: 'essentially form preceded content there' – *TQ*, IX, no. 33). That he was aware of the
problem is shown by the ending when, after the King has
been mourned in song by the Democratic and Republican
groupies, Anne and Elizabeth –

> Take a last bow
> But Richard you see
> It's definitely
> All over now

– the audience is left with a final image. Richard rises out of the coffin and addresses them directly – 'Wanna bet?' – as the Cops turn and train their guns on the auditorium. Dramatically it is a stunning conclusion, but politically it suggests an almost desperate straining after a possible message. Ironically the play never got its planned production in the States, because of Nixon's sudden resignation.

Although *Dick Deterred* is the furthest that Edgar ever pushed the line of parody, the problems raised by it politically are to be found on a smaller scale in all the work that he produced for General Will. His final piece for them was *The Dunkirk Spirit*, which played until the 1974 election which returned the moderate Labour administration under Callaghan. In this play Edgar moved away from the immediately contemporary for the first time, whilst still remaining in an agit-prop mould. Edgar has described it as being 'really a history of British capitalism since the war'. It was more elaborate than anything that he had previously attempted, and looks forward to the large-scale historical sweep of *Destiny*. It proved to be the final straw in a deteriorating relationship with General Will, for Edgar was discovering, as Brenton had done with the Brighton Combination, that they were heading in different directions.

> What happened was that after *Dunkirk* I got obsessed with slickness. I was fed up with seeing agitprop plays that were messy, and also I was increasingly thinking that the politics you could get across were very crude, whereas the world about us was getting more complicated. (*TQ*, IX, no. 33)

This desire to present a more complex view of political struggle was one which would take Edgar inexorably away from agit-prop as most usually conceived in this period. His two final efforts at the kind were *The Case of the Workers' Plane*, about Concorde, written shortly before *Dunkirk Spirit* in 1973, and *Events Following the Closure of a Motorcycle Factory* (1976). In both cases, although Edgar believed that they had been well received by the immediate audiences for whom they were intended, he was concerned that they had little to interest a more general audience, something that was beginning to preoccupy him more and more. He was aware that they were attempts to write a new kind of play, but attempts that were subverted by the agit-prop expectancies of the form.

With both *Events* and *The Case of the Workers' Plane* there were plays weaving through which the form couldn't take. There was a play about people who loved making expensive, sophisticated aeroplanes, but realised that it was a social disaster to do so. And there was a much better play in *Events*, about the conflicts between different sets of workers – the actual way, aside from the slogans, in which sets of workers allow themselves to be divided, and indeed want to be divided one from another. And both those plays weren't the plays that eventually hit the stage. (*TQ*, ix, no. 33)

The tension in the early plays between the urge towards agit-prop as a politically 'correct' medium, and the increasing desire to deal more honestly with a complex political argument does not have only structural implications. A closer examination of Edgar's use of dialogue will amplify the point. He shares with many writers of his generation an enjoyment of the way in which comic stereotypes can be manipulated. In most agit-prop theatre there is a tendency to reserve such stereotyping for the political 'villains' – the

163

land-owning squire, the exploiting boss, the government minister, and so on. And Edgar can more than hold his own in this. In *Blood Sports* (1975), a conversation between two grouse-beaters is halted when the younger one, Ralph, is accidentally shot by the land-owner.

In the surrealistic conversation that follows between the Bane and Oliver, Edgar creates for the former an absurd version of the clipped language of authority, translated in square brackets:

> RALPH *dies. A* HUGE DOG *rollocks on to the stage and finds the grouse. A* BUSH *slides on.* OLIVER *bemused.* THE BANE *stands up in the* BUSH. *He has a gun and a glass of sherry, wears a kilt, carpet slippers and talks in an upper-class English accent.*
>
> BANE (*as the* DOG *bounds over to him*): Hell one, Grover, hell one. [Well done, Rover, well done].
>
> (*He takes the grouse from the* DOG. OLIVER *looking at the* BUSH. *To explain*) His eyes. Toe-while nut. Loo a heater? [Disguise. Mobile Butt. You a beater?]
>
> OLIVER: Ar.
>
> BANE: Sell fun, Plover. Might. Sets woe. [Well done, Rover. Right. Let's go.]
>
> (*Notices* BODY) Sky Shod. [My God.]
>
> Why splean, tots cat? Cry odd. [I mean, what's that? My God.]
>
> OLIVER: I'm sorry, sir, for spoiling yourn shoot, sir.
>
> BANE: Wry bod. [My God.]

The audience is left in no doubt as to where its allegiance should lie, the parody of the voice of authority being reinforced by the continued subservience after the shooting of the older beater. But it does not advance the understanding of the audience in any way – any more than the presentation of conservative politicians as Chicago hoods would: you are still left free to agree or not. However, more interesting than this is the way in which Edgar so often plays with the language of characters with whom the audience might be expected to sympathise, and with ideas with which they might be expected to agree. *Blood Sports* (originally called *Summer Sports*) consists of a series of one-acters dealing with issues of class and politics in a light-hearted romp through English outdoor pursuits. In another one, *Ball Boys* (which was subsequently published separately), two ball-boys murder a famous Swedish tennis-star. In his introduction Edgar hastens to assure us that more serious matters are at stake:

> *Ball Boys* is an attempt, through the story of two unlovely orphans in a tennis club locker-room, to expose the essential contradictions inherent in late monopoly capitalism, to analyse the role of neo-colonialism in confirming the repressively-tolerant ideological inter-face between superstructure and base (while remaining not unmindful of the need to be fully cognizant of the essential dualism of the decaying bourgeois apparatus), to express implacable hostility to the running dogs of craven reformism in the labour bureaucracies, and to stress the vital need for alternative modes of leadership to pose the essential question of state power.

Edgar's careful conclusion to his gloriously theoretical introduction – 'It is arguable that in this project the play is not totally successful' – is almost Swiftian in its manipulation of the reader's response. This willingness to experiment with verbal confusion is, however, never merely a game. In part it derives from the sense of being pulled in two directions at once that I talked about earlier – a desire to make the committed statement fighting a fear of

165

simplistic reductionism – but in his later work it begins to operate as a more positive tool. A comparison of two theoretically similar confrontations will serve to illustrate this. The first is from Brenton's *Revenge*. The newly released villain, Hepple, confronts his ex-gang-members, Rot and Bung, in a billiard-hall:

> HEPPLE (*deadly*): You cough out of turn, one cough, and my friend here, my very good friend here. (*Nods to* BUNG.) Hello, Bung, how are you? . . . Takes you apart and puts you together again. Don't let that happen. I guess his notions of anatomy are very crude. And another thing, don't call me Adam. Call me Chief. No call me Mr Big. No, call me Chief and Mr Big.
>
> ROT (*aside*): I was having a game of billiards. Quite good form. When in walked death. My game never got back to scratch.
>
> HEPPLE: First call my place. Then when night falls on London Town, and the Mums and Dads are tucked up and cats put out, and the bobby's on his beat and the moon's a mysterious pallor over the chimney top, I'll strike my blow, MacLeish . . . Don't hang about. We got offences to commit.

The language here is enclosed. Its archaic rhetoric drawn from a comic-book world of simple heroes and villains suggests both the out-of-date nature of Hepple's vision and its practical limitations. It is effective as comedy but it has no reference outside of the conventions it appropriates. And nor, to be fair, was it intended to. Brenton is precisely stressing the redundancy of a cops-'n'-robbers world-view. If we compare this with the play that Edgar produced immediately after *Destiny*, *Wreckers* (1977), we can see a rather similar play of language being put to a very different end. It is worth noting that *Wreckers* was written for, and in collaboration with, 7:84, by then well-versed in the conventions of agit-prop. The scene this time is a pool-room in a pub; Labour Party activists gather to plot:

> GEORGE: Paul Johnstone. 32 years of age. Stated occupation: polytechnic lecturer. Hobbies: the Cinema, chess and militant entryism. (*Helpfully.*) A bedsitter infiltrator. Johnny-come-lately-Trotskyist. Self-appointed samurai. (*Enter* HUDI.) And this one, you know.
>
> HUDI: Paul Johnstone.
>
> PAUL: Gerry Neil. (*He shakes* HUDI's *hand.*) I'm an armchair revolutionary.
>
> HUDI: Oh, nice. I'm a mindless militant.
>
> PAUL (*waving a cue*): You play?
>
> HUDI (*taking it*): You bet.
>
> GEORGE: The conspiracy is forged, in smoke-filled rooms behind closed doors.
>
> HUDI *turns towards the exit.*
>
> PAUL: Leave the door, mate, gets like an oven in here.
>
> HUDI *comes back.*
>
> GEORGE: In well-ventilated rooms behind half-open doors.

Here, and in the rest of the scene, which is set in 1975 and is concerned with the plans of left activists to dump their moderate Labour MP, the audience is presented with political information by characters who articulate clearly a caricatured version of what Edgar is asking it to consider quite seriously. The language in this instance is culled from the right-wing British press. But the game is not an enclosed one, as it is in *Revenge*. A multi-layered structure of meaning is created within which the audience must perforce wander. The sincerity of the characters is not called into question by their ability to project their own caricature-counterparts. Rather, a sense of complexity is created, stressing the difficulty of relating the apparent logical and intellectual clarity of a given action to the complications that occur when such a programme is, as it must be, transmuted into human action. Furthermore, the humour here suggests the need for the individual activists to be self-consciously aware of the dangers of using a quasi-revolutionary rhetoric in what is evidently not a revolutionary situation.

More than any of the other writers discussed, Edgar has always responded directly as a playwright to the political changes he has discerned around him. So, it is no surprise that his final disillusionment with the agit-prop form should coincide with the defeat of the Heath administration, and the end of a period of considerable working-class militancy. Callaghan's was an essentially middle-of-the-road administration, in effect a continuation of Wilsonian pragmatism; and, although the next five years witnessed what may yet prove to be the final battle in the long struggle between the right and left wings of the Labour Party, there was little evidence of a leftward movement at the level of public policies. In this sense, *Wreckers*, which is almost exclusively concerned with this internal struggle in the larger political context of events from 1972 to 1975, continues the argument which Griffiths had developed in *All Good Men*, and was about to expand on in *Bill Brand*.

Much of the militant-left activity of the earlier part of the decade was rechannelled into the internal Party struggle, and this at a time when rising unemployment and successive waves of inflation made action on the industrial front ever harder to sustain. Agit-prop is most effective – other than on specifically localised pressure-group issues – during a period of direct class-struggle. This was not the situation during the second half of the seventies, and Edgar's work reflects this.

This helps to explain something else about the language of *Wreckers*, a play that was written after *Destiny*, but which is still attempting to come to terms with his work prior to it. Because it is not only a 'history' play – tracing events from the Industrial Relations Act of 1972 through to the first two years of the Callaghan administration – but is also trying to come to terms with the significance of these events in theatrical terms, Edgar finds it very difficult to achieve a consistency of approach. There is throughout a slightly uneasy feeling about the kind of manipulation of language that I talked about earlier. In parts it sounds like virtually a parody of the agit-prop form that he had previously relied on, and was now in the process of rejecting. It is frequently uncertain of its audience, seeking to bludgeon a point home and at the same time retain a tongue firmly in the cheek as a defence against any charge of simplification. By the time of *Teendreams* (1979), Edgar had moved so far away from the form that he is able to include a comic parody of an agit-prop rehearsal within the narrative.

From now on, Edgar's plays were not going to be simplistic, either in terms of their argument or of their form. With *Destiny*, Edgar turned away from the small halls of the agit-prop circuit, and set out to write a big play for a big space. It was an urge that created grave problems for him, and the play had a chequered history of broken promises and rejections before it finally opened (really rather unsuitably) at the Other Place, Stratford. Even this production occurred only because he was assured that it would transfer to the new Warehouse theatre in London. In the event it went to the Aldwych, and finally onto the smallest space of all, the television.

Destiny had been a long time in the making. The continued hold-ups on a production enabled it to be changed and revised frequently. At one time it had a projected running-time of five and a half hours, but, if it was the most ambitious play Edgar had ever worked on, the delays meant that it was also the most carefully constructed. After its opening, in September 1976, he would never again produce plays at his previous rate. Its success gave him a reputation which could demand and get more time to work, but this is not the whole answer. Edgar observed around him an evermore-complicated political struggle, and this in turn demanded more complicated political responses. An unchanging political commitment would be backed by even more intensive research, leading to a more questioning analysis on stage.

In *Destiny*, Edgar utilised many of the features of agit-prop, but in ways which move the form towards what he and others have described as 'faction' – the combination of fact and fiction. It is not an attempt to reproduce history as such, but involves the creation of a fictional set of characters to demonstrate the workings of the meticulously researched material. His general model is a variant of the epic, with frequent changes of location, and a series of jumps through history before eventually concentrating on a brief period in contemporary England. The effect is to show the way in which a current political reality is a product both of previous history and of the particular interventions and interrelations of individuals acting within that history. The objective history is enmeshed with subjective responses. So, although Edgar is scarcely more interested in individual psychology here than in his earlier plays, more scope is allowed for the development of character. The use of epic-devices, in particular the continual breaks in the action, does, however, prevent such development from taking the edge off Edgar's insistence on a material and social explanation of behaviour.

The direct instigation of *Destiny* was the growth of increasingly well organised right-wing, 'populist' groupings in England. Although the extreme Right had made occasional public inroads from the fifties on – at the time of the 1958 Notting Hill riots, for instance – the thread connecting it to the activities of Mosley's Blackshirts of the thirties was in practice a thin one. However, as the fuller implications of successive governments' policies of open access to immigration for citizens of the old Empire, and the newer Commonwealth, began to be observable, so the Right began to mobilise. Essentially peripheral organisations such as the League of Empire Loyalists, the White Defence League, and the National Labour Party started to find common ground, culminating in the formation of the National Front in 1967 – just three years after Peter Griffiths's racist-inspired victory in the Midlands, location of Edgar's play, and one year after the Labour Party had followed the 1962 lead of the Conservatives to introduce agreement on limitations on immigration.

The following year, Enoch Powell made his famous 'rivers of blood' speech on the anniversary of Hitler's birth, the coincidence of which is used by Edgar to telling effect in *Destiny*. Part of the university agitation of 1968 resulted initially from Powell's presence as a speaker on English campuses, from several of which he was 'seen off' or excluded. By 1971, the Conservatives had introduced an Immigration Act which, to most people on the left, confirmed the consensus of the two major parties on a qualified institutionalisation of racial prejudice. Subsequent legislation throughout the seventies, by both parties, has done nothing to remove this feeling.

The fact of Powell's speech is in one sense the starting-point of Edgar's play, for it represented for the first time the voice of respectable British politics openly declaring itself in agreement with the opinions of the extreme Right. At the end of the first act, Edward Drumont of the Canadian Action League interrupts the Nation Forward's celebration of Hitler's birthday. He brandishes a newspaper report of the speech at the participants dressed in National Socialist gear as confirmation of his earlier dismissal of their nostalgic antics.

> OK, now take off that stuff . . . Shirt, armband. All that fancy dress . . . Right. Comrades. For years you have been battering against a bolted door. And now it's open. You can join, and build, and move. To do so, you must spurn the trappings. Spurn the fripperies. But not the faith. Not, absolutely not, the faith.

As one of the members repeats the phrase 'rivers of blood', the scene freezes and Khera, a foundry-worker, enters. We have seen him previously only in the opening scene, a native servant being ordered around by his British Army 'superiors' on India's Independence Day, 1947. He announces to the audience in the monologue-form used by Edgar to introduce all his colonially located characters back into England, his decision to come 'home':

> Gurjeet Singh Khera
> Once a slave
> Returns to haunt the Empire's grave

A voice is heard off, shouting for Khera, and Platt, works-manager and local Conservative election-agent, comes on stage. Khera ends the first act, as he had started it twenty years earlier, being screamed at by a white boss.

This kind of transition is typical of *Destiny*. It emphasises Edgar's central preoccupation in the play with causation. So it is logical, for instance, that a play which will ultimately concentrate on the race-issue in the context of a seventies' parliamentary election should start where the issue starts, with the British Empire. But, equally, the format of the play also suggests an opposite way of considering events – that the end of what was represented by Empire is racial hostility in an economically declining England. It is the intervention of individuals within these causal chains which prevents the structure from being merely deterministic; history will show us not only how things are, but how they might have been different. To this end, the narrative-events are organised to provide a framework of connections and interconnections which allow different individuals to be seen reacting to the same events in very different ways. But, as always, Edgar is at pains to show that it is not the individual psychology of the characters which determines these differences. A brief look at the way in which some of these chains are developed from the first scene will help to clarify this.

Destiny opens on Independence Day, in India, 15 August 1947. Three representatives of British rule in India prepare to move out. They are aided by Khera, who plays dumb, as is expected of him, but who knows far more than he shows (as Edgar demonstrates by his toasting of himself in Latin, 'Civis – Britannicus – Sum', at the end of the scene). Sergeant Turner enters, intent on getting all the paraphernalia and the loot of British rule that litters the set packed and off to England. Turner stands between Khera and the Colonel and Major who will enter shortly. These distinctions of rank are carefully stressed by Edgar from the outset, because, converted into class-terms, they will vitally affect the attitude of each character to subsequent events in

England. Over the activity of packing, the sounds of celebration can be heard; as they get louder, Turner eventually feels the need to comment to his 'native' helper:

> TURNER: Your people having a good time? (*Pause.*) I said, your people having a good time?
> KHERA (*stopping work*): Oh, yes. Having a super time. (*As if explaining to a child.*) Independence.
> TURNER: Oh, I wondered what it was. (*Pause.*) All right, get on. Now what's this here?
> KHERA (*helpfully*): Tiger. Stuffed.
> TURNER: You know, I just about worked that out for myself.
> KHERA: They shoot them, then they stuff them.
> TURNER *looks to heaven. . . . Enter a* COLONEL, *43 years old, upper class. . . .*
> TURNER: Sir!
> COLONEL: It's all right. (KHERA, *who has not responded . . . slowly and lackadaisically comes to attention. Pause.*) Oh, Lord, is this some more?
> TURNER: Yes sir.
> COLONEL (*to the tiger*): Ah. What have we here?
> KHERA: It's tiger sir. (TURNER *looking daggers.*) Stuffed.
> COLONEL (*smiling*). . . .

The Colonel is a 'civilised' man. He invites Khera to join them in a toast, not to Independence, but to the King and Mr Churchill. In the second scene he will introduce himself as having come home in 1948, and entered Parliament as a Tory of the old school. With his passing, the possibility of hanging onto his harmonious vision of English society will also pass:

Colonel Chandler, past his prime
Dignified. Worthy. Out of time.
Colonel Chandler, oyster-eyed
One fine summer morning died.

He will be succeeded as Conservative candidate by his
nephew, Peter Crosby, a new breed of Tory, 'bright,
high-flyer, all slim suits and unit trusts', as the Labour agent
will describe him. The Colonel's willingness to paper over
the divisions will be short-lived in the new England.

The attempt at the 'bridge party' in the first scene is
shattered by the arrival of Major Rolfe, who takes the
whisky-glass that Khera is holding and cuts straight through
any liberal pretence: 'Some bloody wog's whipped the
battery from the Land Rover.' He will come home in 1947,
and later stand unsuccessfully as candidate against Crosby
before moving rapidly towards the extreme-right position
that has seemed likely from his very first entrance. As he
makes clear in his monologue to the audience, the Major is
caught between a loathing for the 'spoon-feeding' of the
Welfare State, and a hatred for the public-school 'old boy'
network which will always keep him out of positions of
power in the Conservative Party:

The Major looks at England bemoans her tragic fate,
Condemns the mindless comforts of a flaccid,
   spongers' state,
Despairs of trendy idiocies repeated as a rote,
While the knot of old school tiredness is still tight
   round England's throat.

Unlike the Colonel or the Sergeant, he is not of either the
ruling or the working class. He is the representative of the

175

petit-bourgeoisie, whose potential for involvement preoccupies Edgar considerably in *Destiny*. When the Colonel quotes Kipling's 'White Man's Burden' at him, telling Rolfe that he had to learn it at preparatory school, Rolfe realises only too well that it is not necessary to remind him that he had not been to a preparatory school.

With the exception of the Colonel, a great deal of the play will be concerned with the future activities of these men, and the way in which their lives become ideologically interlinked. We next meet Turner in the fifth scene. In view of his activities in the first scene, there is a pointed irony in the fact that he is by now – 1970, as the pro-Conservative election-poster on his wall tells us – the owner of an antique-shop, making his living from the past. He is confronted in his shop by (further irony) a sharp, Cockney-accented Pakistani, who informs him that the entire block has been bought up for development by the Metropolitan Investment Trust, using a number of cover names and with the collusion of the local council. He serves an eviction-order on him, demonstrating his power to do so in two stages:

RAZAK: The rent is subject to a periodical review. Sunbeam, you have just been periodically reviewed. Direction: up.

TURNER: You can't do that.

RAZAK: Now there you're incorrect.

TURNER: I'll pay it. I'll refuse to go.

RAZAK: Oh, petal, please . . . I hate this bit. Tulip, I don't know if you've noticed, but among the merry navvies labouring next door, are several of our Caribbean cousins. Simple, cheery folk, all charmers to a man, but tending to the slapdash. Natural exuberance, you see. The kind of natural exuberance that pushes bits of scaffolding through windows, picking off the Georgian porcelain. (*Pause. He neatly stubs his cigar out on the table top*.)

TURNER: You bastard.

RAZAK: No, not bastard. Selsdon man.

Razak's reference to the conference at the Selsdon Hotel which produced the policies of the new Heath administration makes the point neatly. What Turner is confronted with is not something that arises, almost accidentally, from a localised set of circumstances, as he at first wishes to believe, but can be logically connected with the murkier workings of the capitalist system that his display of the Conservative election-poster declares him to be a supporter of. Razak argues strongly that he is being run out of business solely further to enrich the purchasing corporation: 'and you, the little man, the honest trader . . . you're suffering a gross deficiency of greed'.

Edgar's use of the Pakistani 'frightener' with his threat of West Indian intervention adds further levels of complexity to the situation. It is ironic that Turner should be so menaced, because he will next join the Tadley Patriotic League – Edgar's version of one of the many earlier extremist groups – and will chair the meeting at which affiliation to the 'Nation Forward' (the National Front) is agreed. At this meeting, paralleling the opening scene, three class-representatives speak of their dissatisfaction with the state of England. Their analyses of the malaise are actually mutually contradictory, each arguing from a conflicting class-perspective – as is demonstrated by the conclusions of the final speaker, an unhappy former Labour Party member and trade-unionist. Edgar allows him an angry but articulate outburst, even risking brief

laughter from the audience, before caution is abandoned
for an explicitly racist analysis:

> Come dinner-time there's that many turbans in the
> canteen, it looks like a field of bloody lilies. And smells
> like the Black Hole of Calcutta. And if one of 'em gets
> the push, they're all up in arms, shrieking about discrimi-
> nation. It's happening now . . . And it's not just at work. I
> got kids, and I'll be quite frank about the blacks. I hate
> 'em. And no-one's doing bugger all about it. That's what
> bothers me. Not the erosion of your bleeding middle-
> class values. Sooner or later, summat's got to be done.

The speeches are presented in a naturalistic form, but
Edgar deliberately makes no attempt to disguise the
schematic make-up of the scene. The worries of the
upper-middle, the lower-middle and the working classes are
displayed in their most potentially fascist form precisely so
that the Nation Forward speaker, Maxwell, can weld out of
them the conspiracy theory that is vital to the philosophy of
the extreme Right. As in the first scene, a working model of
an apparently reasonable, but demonstrably unreasonable,
conclusion is presented.

> Of course we disagree on many things. But more, much
> more, unites us than divides us. . . . You can change your
> class and your creed, but you can't change the blood in
> your veins. . . . Of course, it looks like many enemies – to
> the young lady it's the college reds, to Mr Attwood it's
> the multi-nationals, to Mrs Howard it's the banks who
> recklessly promote inflation and destroy her savings.
> And it's called by many things – names representing
> things we're taught to see as opposites – liberalism,

178

communism, finance capital. Things that, in fact aren't opposites at all.

This practical demonstration of the quasi-logic behind fascist ideology is extremely effective in the theatre. Far more so than the later, cruder dialogue between the two ex-schoolfriends, Tony (of Nation Forward) and Paul (left of the Labour Party), imprisoned in the same police cell after Nation Forward has broken up a picket-line. Here Edgar resorts to a less dramatically convincing assertion of the racist–class dichotomy: simply having them arguing, as Paul says, in mirror opposites. In the meeting, in contrast, Edgar allows his characters a full articulation of their worries, allowing for Maxwell's glib amalgamation of interests. But, by concentrating solely on the argument of this scene, vital though it is in attempting to understand the causal links that concern him, there is the danger of overlooking its stage-context. The characters speak within a framework which is studiedly shoddy, inefficient and muddled. There is scarcely anyone present, the Union Jack is hung upside down, the public-address system is on the blink, the first obsession is with collecting enough money to pay for the hall, and so on. What effect Maxwell's rhetoric might have is deliberately undercut. And through it all sits Turner, feeling his way in a new political arena, his role at present confined to introducing the speakers.

By the time we next sight Turner, plans for the by-election are well under way. Crosby has the Conservative candidature, and Paul has succeeded in getting his man, Clifton, in for Labour. Khera has become active in a newly formed union, representing the immigrant work-force, and a strike against discrimination is under way. Clifton has agreed publicly to support it, and the issue of racialism is placed centre-stage for the first time. Ultimately Crosby will yield to pressure from such as Platt, his agent and Khera's immediate boss, to present a modified version of Nation Forward's line to the electors. And it is in this context that Nation Forward enters the campaign, just as the National Front had been doing in selected constituencies since the late sixties.

Their candidate is Turner, still uneasy about his assumption of a public role, and in need of schooling:

CLEAVER: Turner, there's pressure from the Pakkies for a separate girls' school, religious grounds. Approve?

TURNER: All for it. As long as it's in Pakistan.

CLEAVER: No!

TURNER: Why not? It's funny.

CLEAVER: Flip. You say it shows the immigrants themselves can't integrate.

TURNER (*shrugs*): Ask me another.

Edgar uses this practice routine for a dual effect. First, and comically, it is a demonstration of the mechanical nature of Turner's argument; and in addition it allows Edgar to present the central contradiction of Nation Forward policy, a contradiction that will result shortly in Maxwell's eviction from the room and from the party. Turner has already complained that he finds much of Maxwell's populist talk in the speech he has written for him too left-wing, and it is left to Cleaver to articulate the dangers of the basic fascist heresy – the stress of 'socialism' over 'national' in National Socialism. Turner is assimilated by Cleaver into a move that will, by the end of the play, take Nation Forward into the bosom of the right-wing establishment – in a solidly anti-working-class stance – with money about to be released from the sort of large business-corporations that had previously supported the Conservative Party.

In the event, Nation Forward's intervention into the strike and the campaign proves decisive. They take votes off the Labour candidate and help elect a Tory MP. But, as Edgar points out, this is only a part of a move to make their movement respectable. At the end, negotiations are being opened about financial support. Turner is taken along to meet Rolfe, speaking on behalf of the potential money. Over the sherry, Turner, by now thoroughly converted to the Nation Forward position, discovers that Rolfe is the chairman of one of the interested sponsors, Metropolitan Investment Trust, the very organisation that had deprived him of his business and sent him into the world of the extreme Right in the first place. He ends the play completely confused, in the middle of asking Cleaver for an explanation as the lights fade.

I have dwelt on Turner's development throughout the play at some length because it helps to show just how and why Edgar has made a fundamental break with agit-prop. Whereas, in a conventional agit-prop play, Turner's role as emergent fascist would be at best peripheral, and at worst caricatured, Edgar develops him as one of the major characters – one on whose actions and their causes the audience will perforce spend a great amount of time thinking. There are a number of points in the play where Edgar does insist on a directly didactic approach – in the prison-cell scene, for instance – but generally he is less interested in peddling an anti-fascist line than in demonstrating to an audience how individuals might come to embrace fascism. Turner is of particular importance in this context because his social origins might, in other presentations of the development of such a man, lead us to expect a commitment to the supremacy of class over race as a tool of political analysis. Turner's is, if such an expression were appropriate to a play like *Destiny*, a potentially tragic situation: that of a man who has identified the disease and diagnosed a cure that will be demonstrated forcefully to him as wrong.

That he is not developed as a tragic character, but one whom the audience can stand back from, observe and learn from, is fundamental to Edgar's design. For certainly there could easily be, in a less carefully structured play, the risk of creating sympathy for a character whose views diametrically oppose those of Edgar. Indeed, several critics have argued that the best speeches are put into the mouths of the extreme Right. In one sense they have a point, but not for the reason implicit in such criticism, that somehow Edgar has made a mistake. His treatment of fascist philosophy is made the more convincing precisely because it never rests on the level of simple exposition, let alone the easy caricature of so much agit-prop. There are no easy villains; characters are allowed plausible explanations for their commitments.

One of the most dramatically daring examples of this comes at the end of Act II. Major Rolfe, whom we had earlier seen in India and then as unsuccessful Tory candidate – and who will in just one act puncture Turner's illusions – is alone on stage. He is in an army headquarters in Northern Ireland, having flown out to fetch the body of his soldier son, killed by the IRA. In a long and emotional speech he explains how he has more sympathy for the enemy who shot his son, and who had at least acted on what he took to be his own interests, than for an establishment that he sees as powerless to act on the rot that had started in Bombay all those years before. As he concludes, he raises a crumpled Union Jack, the reveillé sounds, and the lights fade down to signal the break.

Edgar works hard to elicit an emotional response which is, *in isolation*, at the very least, ambivalent towards Rolfe.

Without understanding the emotions that fire a Rolfe or a Turner, it is impossible to understand any urge towards fascism; and, without understanding, no real opposition strategy can be effective. What he offers is a momentary insight into the practical workings of extreme-right ideology. The audience is prevented from developing a sustained interest, and with it the dangers of identification with the views of such a character, however, both by the continual shifts in location, and by the need to place other less problematic examples of their behaviour alongside: Rolfe's indirect ruining of Turner, for instance, or the absurd obsession with disease displayed by Turner at the Tadley Patriotic League meeting. Thus each scene stands alone, and at the same time contributes to an overall structure which forces an audience to weigh what it has discovered in one scene against the contradictions of another.

I have concentrated on the fascist strands in the play because their treatment is what makes it so remarkable. The real impact of *Destiny* derives from its detailed examination of the dynamics of a political ideology that most of its audience would otherwise have approached only in terms of slogans. For Edgar, and for contemporary theatre generally, this was new ground. There is also considerable attention paid to opposition strategies, but there is never the same dramatic intensity. The presentation of the Labour candidate, Clifton, stays much closer to traditional agit-prop territory. Attempting to work within the Party and at the same time retain a socialist analysis, Clifton ends up with neither a parliamentary seat nor the satisfaction of having acted correctly. In one of the beautifully ironic conjunctions that abound in the play, he finally compromises on his support for the strikers whilst eating with his wife in an Indian Restaurant.

Although clearly Edgar intends *Destiny* to offer a positive line, the difference between his approach and that of too much earlier didactic theatre is well shown by the play's conclusion. Hitler, in an implied rebuff to Clifton's moderation, addresses the audience with an extract from his 1933 Nuremburg speech: 'Only one thing could have stopped our Movement. If our adversaries had understood its principles, and had smashed, with the utmost brutality, the nucleus of our new Movement. . . . Told you'. Anyone seeing in this only a call for direct action would do well to reconsider the totality of the play, and indeed Hitler's own words. The need is for action certainly, but before action comes the need to understand.

Edgar's interest in *Destiny* to present a more complicated account of political struggle is even more evident in the three plays that I mentioned as running simultaneously at the beginning of the chapter. Despite Edgar's stated desire to remove from the audience the possibility of psychological explanations, his interest in the relationship between politics and individual psychology has developed as he has increasingly grown in confidence as a writer. In *The Jail Diary of Albie Sachs* (1978), Peter McEnery gave a brilliant performance as the white South African lawyer imprisoned under the Ninety-Day Law for his anti-apartheid stance. Edgar did not attempt a full-scale epic account of the South African struggle, but chose instead to dramatise the experiences of one rather minimally involved participant. The effect is to suggest, by careful understatement, the full horror of the situation. Albie's attempts to while away the time, increasingly worried by the pointlessness of his unseen endurance under questioning, are punctuated by casual references to the more brutal aspects of apartheid that he as a white man is as yet protected from.

ALBIE: I have spent a day, for instance, going through the
states of America, alphabetically, geographically, and
related to major towns. . . .
(*Sound of a caning. Six strokes. A little male laughter.*)
So, alphabetically, there's Alaska, Arizona, Arkan-
sas . . .

Almost the entire play is set in a series of small
prison-cells, as Albie is first released then rearrested. The
diminishing of scale is accompanied by a heightening of
emotional intensity quite unlike anything Edgar had
achieved before. Edgar does not feel the need to present an
objective account of events; everything that happens is
monitored subjectively through the experience of the
prisoner. The audience is directly involved in the fate of
Albie. But that Edgar is, as always, concerned with a larger
political analysis than the concentration on a single imprisonment might suggest, is clear from the outset. Albie is
addressing a meeting before his imprisonment. He proposes a toast to Vorster for turning his injustice not only on
the blacks but on the white liberals:

It's good, that they're so scared, they're scared enough to
use it on the whites, on us, because it makes *us* choose
what side we're on, it tells us, and we didn't know, it tells
us what it's like. So thank you, Dr Vorster. You have told
us what it's like.

By reducing the scale of his play to the experiences of one
peripherally involved man, Edgar makes the point that
nothing this side of armed struggle is left; and he does so in
a way that no amount of heavy didacticism could achieve.
For what retains the interest of the audience is not the

presentation of a political analysis but its involvement with the man on the stage.

The Jail Diary does, however, differ from the other two plays in one important aspect. In an English context the issue of apartheid is not particularly contentious for most theatre-goers likely to be attracted to a play by a man who was established as the author of *Destiny*. There is, in the sense that Albie talks about above, only one side to be on. In *Mary Barnes* (1978) and *Teendreams* (1979) the situation is very different.

In these two plays, Edgar turns for the first time to aspects of counter-cultural movements dating from the sixties: in *Mary Barnes*, the new thinking on schizophrenia particularly associated with the work of Laing and Cooper; and in *Teendreams*, broadly, the women's-consciousness movement. However, by the use of narrative structures which bring the action from the late sixties to the present, Edgar is able to do more than simply present the events as enclosed histories. He is concerned rather with the way in which his characters can be shown as coming to terms, in the light of their later experiences in a changed world, with the ideas and attitudes expressed by them at the outset. Thus, although they are both, in a sense, 'issue' plays, the emphasis is on the effects of these issues on characters who are far more psychologically realised than in anything he had previously attempted. The plays seek neither to embrace nor to reject wholeheartedly the views articulated by these characters. No single 'correct line' is suggested, and, although both have politically encouraging endings of qualified optimism, there is no suggestion that these are the only possible endings. In short, they consolidate Edgar's move away from agit-prop to a new kind of political theatre – in which political behaviour is considered subjectively and not objectively.

Emphasis on the psychological aspects of human behaviour is clearly unavoidable in *Mary Barnes*, which is based on an account of the real Mary Barnes, diagnosed as schizophrenic by the medical establishment and 'recovered' by her relationship with a group of 'anti-psychiatrists'. The play opens in 1963, and is set almost entirely in an East End commune run by a group of therapists seeking an alternative to what they see as the butchery of conventional treatment. One of them, Hugo, offers a comic account of their objections:

A story. Backyard of a Glasgow bughouse. Jockie lies there, screaming, getaway ya buggers, getaway. To quieten him, the surgeon decides to perform a transorbital lobotomy. And it's a great success, for after it, old Jockie is heard screaming, Canna hear the buggas, canna hear the buggas no more.

It is not surprising that Edgar should have been attracted to the project, for the argument about the causes and treatment of schizophrenia raises questions that are crucial to his own developing interest in the politics of human psychology. Laing and Cooper had argued against the behaviourist analysis of schizophrenia, as an illness treatable with drugs and surgery. For them, it was a political condition, the product of a society whose conflicting pressures were such that schizophrenia could be seen as a perfectly sane response. They concentrated on the politics of the family, and it is this that chiefly concerns Edgar in the play. What his therapists attempt is the creation of a safe and tolerantly loving environment in which Mary can re-experience her growth from birth onwards, free of the sexual contradictions built into her real family life.

From the outset, Edgar stresses the contradictions. The

187

commune attempts to structure a world free of regulations: 'Rule one. There are no rules. Rule two. It is against the rules to question rule one. Rule three. It is against the rules to acknowledge the existence of rules one and two.' And, furthermore, it exists in isolation, in the middle of a working-class community which is deeply suspicious to the point of outright hostility of its activities. Inasmuch as they are to be successful in treating Mary, the success will necessarily be an individual one – offering neither a generally applicable political analysis, nor the possibility of a larger political mobilisation. Ironically, the whole Mary that eventually emerges is one whose commitment to the Catholic Church goes against all the commune's most cherished political beliefs.

What gives the play its strength is the quite extraordinary presentation of Mary's regrowth. Frequently comic, and more usually profoundly disturbing, the play is more concerned to demonstrate the way in which the individual can be destroyed by the political confusions of the family, than with suggesting directly political solutions. In one of the most dramatically daring scenes of the play, a newcomer, Eddie, is reluctantly drawn into acting out Mary's world with her. Mary, undergoing the experience of prebirth, wishes to be fed with a stomach-tube, as if directly to the foetus. Eddie tries to reason with her at first, but abandons this in favour of joining her in her world – drinking from a milk-bottle with childish glee, then inducing Mary to play the game with him:

> EDDIE *himself takes a drink of the bottle, and spits it over* MARY. MARY *looks astonished. Then* EDDIE *gives the bottle to* MARY, *who drinks and spits over* EDDIE. *She begins to chuckle.* EDDIE *drinks and spits.* MARY *drinks and spits. Laughs.* EDDIE *takes the bottle, drinks and swallows.*

EDDIE: Glug-ug-ug. (MARY *looks at him. He drinks again.*)
   Glug-ug-ug-ug.
MARY (*takes the bottle, drinks*): Glug-ug-ug-ug.
EDDIE (*takes the bottle, drinks*): Glug-ug-ug-ug.

It is impossible to recreate on paper the traumatic impact of this short scene on stage. In it, and in the relationship between Eddie and Mary which subsequently emerges, Edgar leaves behind the mechanics of political debate, in favour of an emotionally charged presentation of extreme interpersonal relationships.

Moreover, the larger historical perspective of the play, with its conclusion in 1978 in the now empty commune, gives further weight to Edgar's resolute refusal to present the isolated experiment as an overall solution. The commune, even in its time, had its failures and its rejects, and its present abandonment suggests strongly that its time has passed. Mary has been 'rescued', but her treatment cannot be simply appropriated for the malaises of the body politic.

Now, it might be argued that *Mary Barnes* is a one-off for Edgar, a special case, but a brief consideration of *Teendreams* will confirm Edgar's move towards a less mechanical view of political behaviour. *Teendreams* was commissioned by the feminist group Monstrous Regiment, and written in collaboration with one of its members, Susan Todd; where we might, however, anticipate a conventionally didactic piece of agit-prop, we are given instead a play that portrays a very complicated account of feminist struggle. As in *Mary Barnes*, Edgar is more concerned with examining the contradictions of his theme than with presenting a simplistic model which can somehow be superimposed onto the real world.

The play opens in 1975. Trisha, a girl of fifteen, is baby-sitting for her school-teacher, Frances. She plays her old records from the sixties and models the Laura Ashley dresses that she has discovered – all the time drinking Pernod and swallowing pills in what we shall later discover is an unsuccessful attempt at suicide. From this beginning, the play goes back in time, to the youth of the teacher, as a radical student in 1968 and her ensuing involvement with the women's movement, before finally bringing the narrative back to the build-up to the suicide attempt. The first scene, therefore, has a particularly important function: it waits, throughout the play, in need of explanation, an historical event shaped by, amongst other things, the attempts of one generation to intervene in the lives of the next.

> FRANCES: Blueprint. Change the world. In fact, a blueprint to escape the world. And me. And I've been on the run, from me, this seven years, and now at last I'm going to turn me in. It's quite simple. Thought we could change people. We were wrong.

Out of the experiences of Frances and her women friends in the events of 1968 there slowly emerges an awareness of the need for a specifically feminist perspective of revolution. As Ruth puts it, in the midst of the university-occupation, 'Everything is challenges, everything is new . . . So one does just wonder . . . Why the fuck we're still doing the typing and making the tea.' Much of the play is concerned with Frances's attempts to bring this developing analysis into her work as a teacher, surrounded by an essentially male dominated ideological structure; and, in particular, with her relationship with two of her pupils, Denise and Trisha – whose 'teendreams' give the play its title.

190

FRANCES: Denise, what did you mean . . . bout the way that boys talk. What d'you mean by that?

DENISE: Eh? (*She remembers.*) Oh. Oh, yuh. (*Pause.*) Well, just. Like, humping. Having. It, an'. Getting it. And slit. An' up your hole. And shouting, come on, show's your hangers. Shouting out, she got her rags on. Scrubbers. Slags. (*Slight pause.*) An all.

FRANCES: You needn't take all that.

DENISE: I don't.

FRANCES: But some girls do.

DENISE (*pause*): I don't.

FRANCES: You shouldn't.

DENISE (*pause . . . suspiciously*): Eh, Miss. You women's lib?

FRANCES: Well, yes. That's right. (*Pause.*) Because I think you shouldn't take all that. Because I think that that's a waste of you. I think you've got a better life, a life of your own.

What Edgar offers in such a dialogue is something that goes far beyond the conventional consciousness-raising of didactic theatre. Two completely distinct languages can be heard, supposedly communicating, but in reality speaking from unrelated social perspectives. It is not simply that Denise is less fluent than her teacher. Her re-creation of the brutality of male working-class language highlights the conditions of struggle for the girls, and provides the rationale for their escape into the phony commercial world of 'teendreams'. The situation for Frances is very different: she speaks the language of a woman who has been able, principally through her experiences in higher education, to attempt an analysis and a way forward which, whilst it will necessarily be conditioned by many of the social pressures which Denise will ultimately find intolerable, will allow her considerable freedom for personal development. The entry of feminists into the political debate did much to expose the contradictions inherent in a uniform, determinist view of political change, calling for a reassessment of the meaning of socialism for the individual.

But Frances's role as 'teacher' is a problematic one, offering for the two teenagers a new analysis of their lives in accordance with her, and not their, social experiences and possibilities. She is successful in puncturing their 'teen-dreams', but in so doing she removes the only stability that their lives possess. The point is carefully overarticulated by a male teacher, Brewer, a character who, as his name with its echoes of the male preserves of pubs and clubs suggests, has already been introduced as a deliberately unsympathetic representative of conventional chauvinist 'wisdom'. He tells Frances, 'you've transferred your agonies and insecurities and pain on to two schoolgirls, and what's happened is that you've destroyed them by your arrogant conviction that their choices, what they've chosen as their lives, their interests, their dreams, are worthy of contempt'. In Edgar's earlier plays, words from such a character would be introduced with the confident expectation of dismissal by the audience. Now, he is attempting something rather different. Brewer's is a long speech and, whilst there is no suggestion that we should accept the argument at face-value, it is there to be argued with. Brewer speaks some truth, but for the wrong reasons; he is not really concerned with the particular fate of these two girls, but with the use he can make of it as fuel in his understood larger argument against the feminist analysis with which Frances is desperately struggling.

Again, the stress is on the complications that ensue when the theoretical content of political debate is tested in the experience of the individual at large in a society in which change is as yet only a possibility, and not a deterministic certainty. The play ends three years on from where it started, in the present day. Frances has returned from work, still as a teacher but with a very different understanding of her role.

> FRANCES: Was on to using the conditional . . . And Indira Joshi said, 'I wish I *could* learn English very good, so I *could* get work in an office.' . . . And, of course, it started an almighty row. Some of them were scandalised, the older women specially. How terrible, disgrace, her husband would be so ashamed. But some supported her, the money, and the pride. I've never heard them get like that before. I left them to it, at it, still. It cheers you up. That kind of thing.

She has abandoned her role as bringer of instant enlightenment in favour of the practical use of her skills towards a measurable end – the teaching of English to immigrant women – but also operating as a small catalyst, who knows when to leave the room, in the cause of greater change.

The qualified optimism of the end of the play is achieved not by the unfurling of the fluttering banners of historical determinism, but by a presentation of the willingness of the individual to fight on, sadder and wiser, through all the contradictions of constructed reality. By *Teendreams* Edgar had come a long way from his heavily didactic origins as a writer, and there is every reason to suppose he will continue to develop in this direction. The earlier model of didactic theatre is at base one structured on the central importance of monologue, of a single correct voice – and that way, whether it be a monologue of the Left or the Right, lie the twin dangers of Stalinism and fascism. In his insistence on the need for dialogue, for argument, and for the articulation of the anguished debate without which no 'free' society of the future is possible, Edgar has moved political theatre into the role that best suits it – as the testing-ground of change.

7
On the Edge of the Eighties: Developments

JEREMY: Then just one question, Martin. How do you think they will react? The people who've been breast-fed on the milk of social kindness all these years? When the teat is pulled away? When the plateglass is put up between them and the goodies they've been promised as of right? I listen to the future and I'm hearing broken glass. I look into my crystal ball, and I see London burning.

MARTIN: I see. And so, what antidote do you prescribe?

TRELAWNEY: Well, in a word: Authority.

(Slightly misappropriated from David Edgar's *Maydays*, 1983)

Unlike the Conservative victory which proclaimed the end of the sixties, the success of Margaret Thatcher in May 1979 came as no surprise to anyone on the British left. Callaghan's attempts to muddle through after the resignation of Wilson failed to paper over the struggles within the Labour Party between the old right and centre hard-core, and the new 'grass-root' forces of the left, chiefly mobilised around the figure of Tony Benn – struggles which were seized upon with glee by the predominantly right-wing British press. In the face of such confusion, with a middle-of-the-road leader standing on a left-influenced manifesto with which he had little sympathy, and with an accompanyingly well-orchestrated media campaign in search of 'reds under the bed', the Labour defeat was inevitable. Thatcher's clearly articulated promise of a return to a simple model of strong government struck a chord in an electorate as disillusioned with the impotence of Parliament as it was uncertain about the implications of Britain's declining role, economically and politically, in the contemporary world.

What did come as a surprise, however, not least to many members of her own party, was her unswerving commitment to a full-blooded monetarist programme, the implications of which, if allowed to be fully realised, would bring about a change in the organisation of British society on a scale unparalleled since the days of the 1945 Labour administration.

In *A Short Sharp Shock for the Government*, Brenton returned (with Tony Howard) just one year after the General Election, to the territory he had explored in his response, in *Fruit*, to Edward Heath's victory ten years earlier. The play (originally entitled *Ditch the Bitch*, but renamed as a result of feminist objections) is a glorious romp through the excesses of Thatcher's first year in power. In one of the funniest scenes, 'Sir Keith Joseph meets the Alien', the audience is presented with a parody of monetarist philosophy, no less true for being conceived in comic terms. The Tory 'philosopher' agonises about the future, and as he does so the figure of the monetarist 'guru', Milton Friedman, bursts out of his chest:

KEITH: W-w-w-what must I do to be saved?

FRIEDMAN: Stop printing money on this planet.

KEITH: At last! A higher intelligence on Earth.

FRIEDMAN: You gotta let the rich get rich. Else the rich won't be rich . . . There is no short cut to economic recovery. Only one big cut.

KEITH: Cut?

FRIEDMAN: Like most of your country north of Euston Station.

KEITH: But Milton – people are living there. Or so I'm told.

FRIEDMAN: . . . I know the answers. You got a steel industry?

KEITH: Oh no.

FRIEDMAN: You got cotton?

KEITH: Lancashire, falling to bits. Or so I'm told.

FRIEDMAN: You got English cars?

KEITH: British Leyland. Poor Michael Edwardes. A bunny rabbit with blood in his mouth.

FRIEDMAN: No problem! Your cars and your cotton and your steel-plated teapots – and your people, above all your people – don't make money – so – close 'em down.

KEITH: So clear. So – (*a gesture*) stupid it's almost obvious. So – (*a gesture*) brutal it's almost kind . . . Monetarism. Something simple. Faceless, flashing in the sunlight. Numbers, rows of figures, bland.

A decade of parliamentary empiricism was over. Shorn of its rhetoric, what Thatcher's programme sought was even more far-reaching than that outlined by Brenton and Howard's 'Alien': nothing less than the essential dismantling of the implications of that 1945 socialist programme – with the running-down of the 'Welfare State', the privatisation of nationalised industries, and the creation of unemployment as a weapon against the trade unions in the service of an economic rationalisation in which profitability and feasibility were the only criteria. A new Tory Party had been forming throughout the 1970s, a new party with a scant regard for the 'old school' traditions and the political flexibilities of the liberal-conservative philosophy most recently exemplified by the man Thatcher had defeated for the leadership, Edward Heath.

The parliamentary Left was in no position to offer a strong alternative. Following Callaghan's failure to unite the Labour Party, he departed. The internal struggles were unsatisfactorily resolved with what was intended to be a temporary solution, the election not of Benn, but of Michael Foot, a man who had, since the early days of CND, represented the radical roots of the Labour Party – with, in particular, his commitment to unilateral disarmament – but whose political teeth had been cleverly pulled some years earlier by Wilson with an appointment to Cabinet responsibility over trade-union affairs. If it was seen as a temporary solution for the Party, this was not how Foot saw it, and his failure to give way in time for a more effective leadership to emerge in time for the 1983 Election was undoubtedly one of the causes of the Labour defeat.

In immediate terms, however, Foot's election appeared to offer a breathing-space. For the centre of the Party, it was an honour that could safely be accorded to a man in his last years of political life, before the crown could be placed on the head of one of Callaghan's obvious successors, Dennis Healey or Roy Hattersley. For the left it offered a small victory in itself, and the promise of a springboard for a properly socialist opposition to Thatcher's policies. For the right it was the final straw. Foot was elected leader in November 1980; by March 1981 the Social Democratic

Party had been formed. Its principal architects, the 'gang of four', set out to 'break the mould of British politics', offering an ill-defined umbrella for all who would join them, and finally forming an alliance with the Liberal Party in the hopes of becoming the non-socialist electoral alternative to the Conservative Party.

In the event, their chief contribution to the struggle to date has been to split the opposition vote. In the aftermath of Falkland Islands euphoria – skilfully milked by the Prime Minister with the willing collaboration of a tabloid press for whom the brief outburst of populist jingoism provided an excuse for the wildest excesses of enthusiasm – a General Election was called for June 1983. The disunified nature of the opposition, made more acute by the vote-splitting intervention of the SDP–Liberal Alliance, made the result a foregone conclusion. A campaign that concerned itself even less than usual with any discussion of political issues, resulted in the return of a government now fully determined to rewrite history; receiving a substantially reduced popular vote, but with a vastly increased parliamentary majority.

The implications of, first, the initial Conservative victory and, secondly and more disturbingly, Thatcher's re-election have brought about a redefinition of the political arena. Inevitably, attention has been increasingly less focused on extra-parliamentary political activity, with the realisation on all sides that the Conservative administration really does mean business, that it is prepared to question, and indeed directly to threaten, a whole series of assumptions about the structure of post-war Britain that both the major parties had previously, occasional tinkerings notwithstanding, thought best left alone.

The conditions would seem ripe for a revival of agit-prop theatre, but curiously there is very little evidence as yet to suggest that such a revival is under way. Although government legislation to restrict the freedom of the trade unions was temporarily abandoned in the run-in to the 1983 Election, plans are well in hand for a modified version of the previous administration's programme. The use of unemployment as a weapon against trade-union militancy may go some way towards explaining the failure to mobilise organised working-class opposition; and, without such mobilisation, agit-prop theatre has little to offer. With unemployment having risen by over 2 million since Thatcher first took power, and with the steady collapse of British manufacturing industry, the mood in the trade-union movement is gloomy, and even fatalistic, at present.

Furthermore, the generation of unemployed school-leavers thus created have remained so far largely inactive politically – struck perhaps by the same malaise of fatalism that has been Thatcher's chief contribution to political analysis. The government has increased, and proposes to increase yet further, the power of the police to deal with the rising crime-rate, and the possibility of urban disorder – a back-handed admission that there are potential problems, for the propertied and for the employed, in mass youth-unemployment. In the spring and summer of 1981 there were a series of riots in English cities, although they now seem to have been an isolated phenomenon. The following year Trevor Griffiths used these as the context for his play for Central TV, *Oi for England*, seeking both to analyse the unchannelled nature of the young rioters' aggression, and at the same time to offer a political 'reading' of it.

Oi for England is set in a cellar room in Moss Side, Manchester, scene of some of the most sustained rioting of the previous year. A group of skinheads are rehearsing a set for a potential gig. Their music is as deliberately crude musically as it is politically:

Sick of this, sick of all the shit,
Sick of them as stand while the other lot sit,
Sick of being treated like a useless tit,
Sick of being shoved, sick of being HIT!

Their aggression is generalised and unspecific – its roots are to be found in the Punk explosion dating from 1977, with the Sex Pistols' 'Anarchy UK' operating as an anti-Jubilee hymn; and it is also contained – both within the cellar cut off from the outside world, and by a commercial system which will, if they are successful, take their raw anger and turn it into a marketable product. The ugly emotion of their music carries much of the weight of the play, proclaiming as it does a refusal to be integrated into any notion of consensus politics.

They are joined by the fourth member of the group, Napper, an embryonic National Front supporter who has, we subsequently learn, raised the money to pay the rent by mugging an Asian worker. He introduces into their world the Man, who is prepared to consider offering them a booking at a huge free 'skinfest' that he is organising. Finn, who is significantly Irish rather than English, is suspicious from the outset, but they agree to play an audition-piece.

As the number ends, we hear the sounds of rioting coming in from the streets. The Man ignores them, speaking through his Citizens' Band radio, organising his activists to the optimum effect. Finn's suspicions are confirmed. The group, Ammunition (or White Ammunition as the Man wishes them to be), have been booked for a racist rally on the eve of the local elections:

THE MAN: MMI presents, see it? Movement Music Inc. Movement. (*One hand.*) Music. (*The other.*) Incorporated. (*The hands join*.) Concerts, music: politics by other means. All clear?

Through the intervention of the Man, and the fascist Movement he represents, the group are forced into a directly political decision. Previously, their involvement with the action that has been monitored through the walls of the cellar has been simply as a means of acquiring the expensive gear that their unemployed status would otherwise deny them. '*The floor is cluttered with miscellaneous goods looted during riots. The names and logos of principal Manchester stores (Lewis's, Lillywhite's, Safeway's, etc.) are prominent on boxes, containers and carrier bags.*' They eject Napper and decide not to accept the booking. The play ends with Finn preparing to join up with Gloria, the West Indian daughter of their landlord, on the streets. The immigrant community is, as she says, finally fighting back.

The group's stumblings towards a larger analysis are not, however, presented in terms of an agit-prop didactism. The qualified optimism of the ending has already been exposed by Finn's earlier dismissive parody of the titles of Anti-Nazi League group songs; ' "Black and white, unite unite" . . . "The Nazis are coming, they've been here before", "Adolf didn't do it, it's all a pack of lies", "There's a jackboot where my brain used to be" ' – and Finn's arming of himself and Gloria from the stock of looted sports-gear is presented in terms which invite the viewer to see that a self-conscious point is being made: '*they begin to prepare themselves as if ritually, yet with a faint sense of mockery at the conceit they're inventing*'.

Griffiths's interest in remaining within the territory of the skinheads, rather than appropriating their culture as a part of a convenient political allegory, was reinforced by the two touring productions of the play, presented to audiences of the young unemployed around London and in South Yorkshire. Live, Finn's final act of destruction on the group's instruments, before a tape comes up with an Irish Republican chorus, has an immediate dramatic impact that no amount of serious political debate could engender in such circumstances. For, what is destroyed is the only thing that might offer a chance of social betterment for many of the people in the audience. Music as a vehicle for social comment, and music as a possible passport to fame and fortune: it is on this knife-edge that the play rests.

Griffiths's conclusion with the Republican chorus serves a dual purpose. It renders the arguments of the Man about the need for retaining the purity of English blood palpably absurd; and, more importantly, it transfers the image of non-directed violence onto a specific political context. Elsewhere in the British Isles, a war which is only metaphorically conceived in the play is taking place in reality. Its slightly uneasy, almost sentimental, insertion at the end highlights a further anomaly.

The two Conservative administrations have continued, in broad terms, the policies of the Wilson and Callaghan governments in Northern Ireland. The continuation of the struggle, including sustained IRA bombing-campaigns in England in the mid-seventies and the 'H' Block strikes, against all British Army efforts to crush the IRA, have found little response in the political theatre.

Doubtless, the unhappy experiences of Portable in attempting to get *England's Ireland* staged provides part of the answer; and certainly the refusal of both BBC and ITV to allow anything of a remotely controversial nature about the Irish situation to be dramatised on radio or television has played its part. A peculiar conspiracy of silence has developed, as though it was all happening in another world, hundreds of miles away. In 1982, the Falkland Islands appeared closer than Northern Ireland on television.

Apart from the work of Arden and D'Arcy, political theatre has been little concerned with Britain's 'home war'; so that when, in 1980, Howard Brenton finally succeeded in accomplishing the task he had set himself from before the time of *The Churchill Play* – writing a full-scale epic about Northern Ireland's 'occupation' – the shock-waves throughout the media were as vast as they were predictable.

Although the obsession of the newspapers and Tory politicians with the play's simulated buggery – and the resultant unsuccessful private prosecution – helped to obscure Brenton's achievement, the chief surprises of *The Romans in Britain* were other than sexual. As the play's title suggests, Brenton does not begin in contemporary Ireland. Instead, he opts for a grand epic sweep from, in Part I, England on the brink of Roman invasion in 54 BC, to, in Part II, England on the brink of Saxon invasion in 515 AD. My problematic use of the term 'England' helps to emphasise his central preoccupation. The modern state confidently labelled as 'English' is actually the product of a series of colonial occupations. *The Romans* offers its audience a succession of images of this colonialisation, with all its resultant brutality, as a way of approaching, at a tangent, the particular problems caused by the English occupation of Ireland.

So, by setting Part I at the beginning of the Roman invasion, and Part II in a period of imminent invasion when the previous activities of the Romans have already retreated into the stuff of myths and story-telling, Brenton seeks first of all to suggest a degree of identification between the Roman invaders of England and the English invaders of Ireland. And to do so, furthermore, in a context in which the sole representative of the race that will give the country its name, the Anglo-Saxons, is a dying soldier who speaks in a language as unintelligible to the villagers on stage as it is to the audience in the theatre. Brenton's use of language makes the relationship between past and present always problematic. He makes no attempt whatever to invent appropriate forms of discourse for the different periods of colonisation, as is quickly established from the outset. As the play opens, two criminals appear on stage. Ironically, they are from Ireland, a country that has achieved a name before England.

CONLAG: Where the fuck are we? By the sea? Daui?
DAUI: Day in, day out. Lying in a boat with salt round the back of my eyeballs. In a river up to my neck. Marshes with leeches. Moors with birds of prey. Rocks with wild cats. In sun, in rain, in snow – I have heard you ask where the fuck we are.
CONLAG: Well. Where are we?
DAUI: How do I know?

The play is then set both in and out of 'history'. The familiarity of the language allows Brenton to make connections economically. So, when the Romans stumble upon the Celts, they naturally address them as 'wogs'. The terms of colonial abuse can be as easily applied by Romans to Britain, as they will be at the end of Part I – when Caesar and his soldiers suddenly re-enter, to the sound of helicopters, in the uniform of the modern British Army – by English to Irish: 'fucking bogshitting mick', as the soldier refers to one. Or again, at the beginning of Part II, Major Chichester, hiding in an Irish field for a meet with the IRA, complains that he hasn't 'talked to an Anglo-Saxon for three bloody months'; telling the British soldiers who discover him that, if King Arthur were to walk out of the trees, he would look to them like 'one more murdering mick'.

The structure of the play reinforces this paralleling of experience. Virtually the whole of Part I is concerned with the effects of the Roman invasion; concluding with the final deliberately jarring leap into contemporary Ireland. Brenton has worked carefully for his effect. What is most disturbing about his Romans is that they are not presented as the bringers of enlightenment and civilisation. The chief occupation of Brenton's soldiers is digging field-latrines, and the major concern of their leader, Julius Caesar, is with settling old scores and falsifying his personal memoirs. The Cook's account of them in Part II may well be as reliable as any. 'I don't believe there ever were Romans. Or the children's story is right. The Romans were giant, stone snails. The roads are the slime they left behind.' By implication, the English occupation of Ireland becomes a longer history of brutalisation and conquest; not the glorious quest that is conventionally associated with the Roman invasion.

The jump from past to present, now established, is used to greater effect in Part II. The invasion by the Anglo-Saxons is seen only in terms of its effects. There are no fights or skirmishes, simply images of confusion, distrust and disease. Inhabiting a present whose past is already shrouded in mystery, the natives face fearfully a future of yet further disruption and death. The one remaining link with the past is a Roman matron, abandoned and left to die of the plague by her servants. This, and the 'slime they left behind', are the sole mementoes of Roman 'civilisation'.

Running in and out of these scenes of occupation, Brenton gives us glimpses of contemporary Northern Ireland. Part II opens with Major Chichester hiding in a

206

field, initially with the intent of killing an IRA leader, but more latterly in the hope of explaining the past and its connections with the present.

> CHICHESTER: I keep on seeing the dead. A field in Ireland, a field in England. And faces like wood. Charred wood, set in the ground. Staring at me. The faces of our forefathers. Their eyes are sockets of rain-water, flickering with gnats. They stare at me in terror. Because in my hand there's a Roman spear. A Saxon axe. A British Army machine-gun. The weapons of Rome, invaders, Empire.

His attempts, towards the end of the play, thus to explain the connection, are rightly mocked by the woman on whose land he has been hiding. Shorn of its rhetoric, what Chichester is attempting, in the words of the IRA leader he has been awaiting, is to 'deny your Imperial heritage'. The woman's connection between Roman Britain and English Ireland bring together all the interlinking images in the play that has preceded it.

> What right does he have to stand in a field in Ireland and talk of the horrors of war? What nation ever learnt from the sufferings it inflicted on others? What did the Roman Empire give to the people it enslaved? Concrete. What did the British Empire give to its colonies? Tribal wars . . . Ireland's troubles are not a tragedy. They are the crimes his country has done mine.

Brenton's refusal to allow a humanist rationale of the 'troubles' – 'Ireland's troubles are *not* a tragedy' – is underlined by the shooting of Chichester that follows. Chichester's historical links are fatalistically conceived, offering no way out. In the short final scene the efforts of the sixth-century natives to struggle on (mocking any humanistic rereading of history) are punctuated by the discovery of Chichester's dead body – as out of place in Ireland as that of the Roman matron in Anglo-Saxon England. But already the cook who had earlier doubted the existence of the Romans has turned poet, offering yet another version of the past to take its place alongside the myths created by men to gloss over the harsh political realities of conquest.

His story echoes the end of Brecht's *Caucasian Chalk Circle*, where the Singer describes Asdak's brief rule as judge as a 'Golden Age that was almost just'. It is an appropriate echo in a play which clearly owes much to Brenton's more recent work on the epic theatre.

> FIRST COOK: Actually, he was a king who never was. His Government was the people of Britain. His peace was as common as rain or sun. His law was as natural as grass, growing in a meadow. And there never was a Government, or a peace, or a law like that. . . . And when he was dead, the King who never was and the Government that never was – were mourned. And remembered. Bitterly. And thought of as a golden age, lost and yet to come. . . . What was his name?
>
> SECOND COOK: . . . Er – any old name. Arthur? Arthur?

His 'fairy-story' has already been used by Chichester. Just as past history can, and has been, rewritten to serve the needs of the invader, so, too, can and will the present: poetic tales to cover brutal reality, dramatic lies in the service of a supposedly larger 'truth'. Brenton's ultimate achievement in *The Romans in Britain* is his working demonstration of the manipulation of myth in the cause of power. In stature, it stands alongside Edward Bond's *Lear* (1971) and *The Woman* (1978), the second of which, with its exciting re-examination of Greek myth, clearly influenced Brenton directly. All three plays demand of a contemporary audience the need to requestion past cultural models as an essential prerequisite for any analysis of the present. History, in political theatre of this kind, is no longer static and settled; past and present co-exist in a troubled but irresistible discourse.

In part, this sense of discourse becomes possible in political theatre precisely because the playwrights now have a settled body of work from which to draw. There is by now a 'tradition' with established sets of conventions, each with its own history, and each demanding re-examination in the light of changing contemporary history. David Hare's only stage-play of the eighties to date, *A Map of the World* (produced first in Australia in 1982, and then at the National in 1983), is a case in point. In it, Hare re-explores much of the territory of his plays prior to *Fanshen*. *A Map of the World* is inhabited by articulate beings such as are to be found in *The Great Exhibition* or *Knuckle*; but, whereas in the earlier plays Hare used their articulation to pinpoint the despair of a specifically English world, limited both geographically and socially, by 1982 he felt the need to transpose these characters into a territory that is in no sense their own. The play is set in the Third World, and the main narrative thread is concerned with the activities of delegates and news-reporters involved in a UNESCO conference on world poverty.

This displacement of characters to location allows Hare to bring from his earlier work an analysis of social thought that is demonstrably absurd in its Bombay context. The absurdity is stressed from the outset. The opening scene, and indeed most of the play, is set in a European-style

209

hotel, and most of the early *Angst* is concerned with the impossibility of obtaining drinks from the Indian waiters. Stephen, a youngish journalist, is disturbed by the incongruity, and is in turn ridiculed by Mehta, a famous but Europeanised writer who is due to speak at the Conference:

MEHTA: It is hard to help the poor. Young men like you, who have left the universities, find this sort of talk easy, just as any woman may make a group of men feel guilty with feminist ideas – how easy it is, at dinner tables, to make all the men feel bad, how we do not do our share, how we do not care for their cunts, how their orgasms are not of the right kind, how this, how that, this piece of neglect, this wrong thinking or that – so it is with you, you young men of Europe. You make us all uncomfortable by saying 'The poor! The poor!' But the poor are a convenience only, a prop you use to express your own discontent. Which is with yourself.

Stephen's attempts to counter Mehta's argument will eventually lead to them competing in debate for the sexual favours of an American woman musician – thus combining the worlds of the public and the private in ways which are prefigured by Mehta's speech. But, having established this dialogue of confrontation, Hare immediately breaks the terms of its conventions. The lights change, a director calls 'CUT!' and we are left observing a film being shot in a film studio.

What is being filmed, it transpires, is a screen-version of a novel by the real Mehta based on events at an actual conference. The 'real' characters argue that the account being presented by the film is distorted and inaccurate; a theme which parallels the refusal of the 'real' Mehta to preface his Conference speech with a statement about the essential dishonesty of all fiction – a demand made by various Marxist delegates who disapprove of Mehta's politics. Through this tangled maze of relationships, Hare offers a critique both of easy Western solutions to the problems of the Third World – suggesting in particular that no formal separation of worlds is possible – and of the reliable objectivity of this, or any other, analysis. The account of social reality offered by the political theatre is, Hare strongly intimates, as compellingly in need of questioning by its audience as any other account.

This stress on the need for a complexity of analysis is not new in the theatre, but it is something that has only slowly evolved in the kind of theatre discussed in this book. For many playwrights whose work dates from the late sixties, complexity and, worse still, ambiguity were readily identifiable with a mainstream bourgeois-humanist tradition. Better to say anything strongly and definitively than to risk embroilment in the webs of potential mystification. Political theatre generally has come to recognise the need now for a more open-ended presentation of the struggle for change. To argue that this is evidence simply of a greater maturity within the new drama is to miss the point. It is more importantly a recognition of the changed political world confronted by the playwright. The need for hard work, agonised debate and, even, compromise have been lessons not comfortably learned during the seventies; but evidence of their assimilation is everywhere to be found in political theatre in the eighties.

One of the most obvious manifestations of this development is the movement away from, and the questioning of, essentially millennial politics, both past and present. There has been, particularly since the Thatcher victory of 1979, a new readiness to examine political debate within the broad umbrella of the Labour Party – a readiness that was in part prompted by the agonised debate, and in-fighting, characterising the Party since the mid seventies. In *Thirteenth Night* (1981), Brenton used the model of *Macbeth* to present a 'dream play' in which a Stalinist Labour leader successfully mounts a coup on a socialist administration. As the play was being produced, he was acutely aware that critics might mistakenly associate the Macbeth figure, Jack Beaty, with that of Tony Benn, the figure-head of the grass-roots left movement.

The theoretical nature of its narrative is stressed by its opening. Characters appear on stage after a constituency meeting. Their talk is about as non-millennial as could be imagined, full of petty bickerings and the minutiae of political relationships. A fight breaks out with some fascist thugs immediately after the Duncan figure, Dunn, has asked in exasperation, 'If a socialist party really came together in Britain, not Labour Party, real Socialist Party – what would it face?' In the fight, Beaty is knocked unconscious, and the 'dream play' begins with his nightmare response to the question.

> I still get a nightmare. I am a concert pianist, in black tails, white bow-ties, shiny black dress shoes. Hands manicured and flexed I walk from my dressing-room alone, along the corridor. I listen to my breath. Then I'm on the platform. Wham! The audience a mountainside of humanity, raging for music. The orchestra a band of brilliant men and women, disciplined and honed. . . . And on the conductor's podium, his baton one mile long – why, Karl Marx. . . . The orchestra crashes in, the great chords ascend – intolerable excitement – my ribcage burns – Karl nods to me – my entrance – I raise my hands

like hawks to bring them down, and – I remember. I can't
play the piano.

Beaty's doubts about his ability to play to an agreed
political score give the rest of the play its shape. Like
Macbeth, Beaty is tempted into direct violence, but this
time in an attempt to create out of the Labour administration a socialist Britain in one stroke.

> All the slogans coming home to roost. Black crows on the
> chimneys of the Grand Hotel, in a northern English
> town. Do it now. After all the agendas, party conferences
> – it comes down to this. Boot in a hotel door at night. Kill
> a drunken man. Simple. Brutal. The politics is in the
> consequences.

In this light, the 'dream play' serves as a warning, a possible
future to be avoided – all the more tempting for its setting
within the inevitable frustrations of working within a
system that simply will not give ground. By the time it was
produced, with Thatcher's administration securely in control of a rightward change, the warning seemed, for the
time being, not too urgent. The roots of the play lay in a
slightly earlier situation.

Howard Barker, who had in plays such as *Claw* and
Stripwell (1975) presented exciting spectacles of the interrelationship of public and private corruption, had, by 1978,
already become very uncertain about what, if anything, had
been achieved by the shock tactics of the new theatre on the
old:

> I think the end products of the sixties and seventies have
> been negligible. I don't think the prevailing values of our
> generation are fundamentally any different from the

prevailing values of the previous generation – the intellectuals are broadly left, the masses are broadly right. (Quoted in Itzin, *Stages in the Revolution*)

More recently, Barker, whilst retaining his interest in the switching of dramatic styles and his commitment to a powerful rhetorical dialogue, has moved more towards discussing events within the political mainstream.

That Good Between Us (1977) used a narrative background of a left-wing army coup to question the efforts of the Labour Party to muddle through, as Callaghan currently was, on the traditional mixture of compromise and expediency. It is a theme he returned to the following year, in *The Hang of the Gaol*, where an investigation into the burning-down of a prison is used to demonstrate the failure of the organised Left – represented in various forms on the investigating committee – to make inroads on a right wing securely in charge of all organisations of control, including the ultimate institution, the prison itself.

In his most recent play, however, the action is moved directly into the debate within the Labour Party subsequent to the 1979 Tory victory. *A Passion in Six Days* was produced in Sheffield to coincide with the 1983 Labour Party Conference. The narrative is exclusively concerned with events at the previous year's Conference, though including the probable election to leadership of a man clearly modelled on Neil Kinnock, who actually succeeded Foot in 1983. Not, however, that Barker is primarily interested in reconstructing the Conference in any naturalistic manner. Although Michael Boyd's production followed the text in allowing for a ready identification between characters on stage and their counterparts in the Party leadership – notably Foot and Kinnock – the emphasis was, as the title suggests, on the passion that is

214

engendered by political struggle. It was a passion inter-
preted by Barker in many different ways.

There are problems in creating an apparent identification between the stage characters and their public counterparts, but the overall effect was to suggest the existence of
private lives behind the public façade. At the beginning of
the second act, for instance, the Benn figure, Stephen
Fenton, addresses Conference. He tells them, in a device
that is reminiscent of Beaty's concert story in *Thirteenth
Night*, what it is that haunts him:

> My nightmare. My nightmare is as follows. It is dawn in
> Downing Street. Very early, and vaguely wet. And I find,
> when I call for my servant, I am alone in the house. What
> is more, the thing that has awoken me is repeated. This is
> the scream of a low-flying jet, whose shadow passes
> menacingly down the street.

He notices that there is no constable on the step, and goes
to the Cabinet room, where he considers a gun given him by
Castro. Then, noticing that the traffic has returned to the
streets, he makes his way to the Commons, but, despite
repeating that he is Prime Minister, is at first denied
entrance because he is wearing his dressing-gown. Finally,
he takes his seat, only to hear the Queen announcing the
dissolution of the socialist government.

The overall effect of such a speech is peculiar. Although
it transpires that Fenton is presenting his nightmare to
Conference in order to draw conclusions from it as an
allegory, the audience is left also with a possible insight,
through the particular paranoia, into a link between the
psychological and the political. The fact of the conclusion
to the nightmare cannot rob an audience of its first thought
– that it was, unusually, tuned directly into the mind of the

politician, rather than listening to yet another rhetorical exercise.

One of the main threads of the narrative follows the attempts of various of the delegates to relate their personal relationships to their political ones. In contrast to the antics of the drunken MP Harry Gaukroger, under threat of losing his seat if automatic reselection is passed, and for whom the annual Conference offers the opportunity to renew his liaison with his landlady, other delegates seek to open up the sense in which socialist struggle is to be understood. John Axt speaks to their motion:

> I want to see a party committed to the freedom of people – not primarily, who owns the means of production, but what are the means of production for? Who for? Love, family, parenthood, marriage, are the primary experiences of the human animal; it is there that socialism must work its transformations if changes in our economic life are to have any meaning . . . the Labour Party forgets it is the party of personal liberty, and that means sexual liberty, and we must free ourselves from our own capitalism, the capitalism in our own hearts.

The response of the Chairman, 'The blue light is on, brother', only interested in the length of the speech and not its content, takes us to the heart of what Barker is attempting in the play. He rejects both the stultifying bureaucracy of the Party and the efforts of its more extreme *entristes* – his version of Militant Tendency is a well-rehearsed group of hecklers calling themselves Absolute Faction – to replace reason as compromise with reason as the doomed following of a rigidly 'correct line'. His characters are confused, but the more sympathetically drawn ones are struggling towards an analysis which will unite the public and the private.

Passion in Six Days is a romantic play. It is easy to see why its enactment of the link between the passion of politics and the passion of sexuality should have offended invited representatives of the Labour council, and caused them to walk out. But its romanticism carries with it a demand for re-examination of the very nature of socialism. What is significant is not only the details of the argument, but the fact that a playwright who ten years earlier would have lumped together politicians of Left and Right as equally ineffective and corrupt should now regard it as essential to take the argument back within the diffuse ranks of the Labour Party.

Two particular moments in the play stay in the memory. One is at the very end, when Emily Drum, who had earlier seconded John Axt's motion and who is subsequently to offer him sexual support, is left alone on stage, the Conference over. Quietly proud, she counts up the number of hours, 160 in all, that she has spent attending branch-meetings, executive-committee meetings, and the like – the end result of which is that her motion will now be written into the Party Manifesto. It is a small, a tentative move towards a possible redefinition, and it has been achieved through conventional Party channels.

The second is more formally presented. The old peace-campaigner, Lord Isted – based loosely on Fenner Brockway – has made a couple of crucial interventions in the play. A convinced pacifist, he tells the technicians setting up the lights about his experiences at the hands of three soldiers in a prison-cell in 1916:

And they struck me, jeering at my great size, that such a hugely built man would not protect himself, but sub-

mitted to be bled and bruised by men smaller than
himself, which was a kind of miracle to them ... And
later, as I shivered, the third soldier returned and flung
me a blanket, saying I must be Christ, and he wouldn't
beat Christ. To which I said that every man was Christ,
and he laughed, finding it impossible that Christ was in
him too ...

The passion of his 'passion' leads him later to make his
annual appeal to the Party-leader to move a disarmament
motion. When this is refused, Isted speaks directly to the
Conference. In one of the most moving speeches I have
ever heard in a theatre, the old man succeeds in capturing
the attention of the audience in a way that briefly takes
them out of watching a play into experiencing the passion
on which his entire political life has been based. He opens
quietly: 'You've got no right to be alive.' There is a long
pause. 'Nor has this building any right to stand. Nor the
cathedrals. Nor the tower blocks. Nor the beech trees down
the rich man's avenue. No right.' His speech combines a
history of the struggle through history for freedom with a
stress on facing a situation which, if allowed to go
unchecked, will make all this history meaningless. It is the
fruit of a passion which, Barker argues, was and should be
again at the base of any real socialism. He concludes,

> We must disarm now. Every minute is a gift. Is a piece of
> luck. Every second an unearned gem. We must disarm
> NOW. (*Pause.*) Move to the doors quietly, and disarm,
> NOW. Do this before some false step sets the rockets off.
> Remember, you have no right to be here any more.

This remarkable speech, from this strangely rich play,
brings us inevitably into the single most pressing concern of

218

recent political theatre. One effect of Common Market entry has been a redefinition of Britain's placement in the political geography of the world. If it has yet further opened up the possibilities of multinational capitalism, this has in many ways, especially given the general world and European recession, proved less important than the new access offered to European radical and socialist movements. The national Campaign for Nuclear Disarmament has grown enormously in strength by its association with European Nuclear Disarmament; and international boundaries have assumed less importance in the face of a European Ecology movement, the activities of Greenpeace, and so on.

This has had obvious effects in more generally public attitudes also, and in particular with respect to Britain's relationship with NATO and with the United States. And all this has taken place in the context of a rapid escalation of the arms-race with Russia, dating from Reagan's election as President in 1980. The anti-nuclear debate has become the single most important feature of political life in Britain, and throughout Western Europe. Protest at the imminent deployment of Cruise and Pershing missiles has grown monthly, symbolised by the continuing activities of the Women's Peace Camp first instituted outside Greenham Common airforce-base in 1981. For the first time ever, public-opinion polls indicate that a majority of the population are against a reliance on the nuclear deterrent. Both Edgar (in *Maydays*, 1983) and Brenton (*The Genius*, 1983) end their most recent plays outside Greenham Common: Edgar with the lights from the missile-carrying planes dazzling the audience, and Brenton with the stage-lights blacking on the protesters as they climb the wire.

In *The Genius*, Brenton picks up the theme, developed in Brecht's *Galileo*, of the responsibility of the scientist to his society (the working title of the play was *Galileo's Goose*, whose un-golden egg is modern nuclear theory). A brilliant American professor, refusing to allow his discovery of a new mathematical theorum to be used by the military authorities, accepts 'exile' in an English Midlands university. Here, continually stoned as an escape from his *Angst*, he discovers a first-year female undergraduate who has accidentally stumbled on the groundwork of the same discovery. Together they attempt to prevent their work from being used to create a further generation of death-weapons.

The Professor, Leo Lehrer, discovers no more peace in the supposed security of his exile than had Brecht's Galileo in his. The University is no place of pure research. Even the chief undergraduate dissident is revealed, in Brenton's world, as a planted spy. The machinery of control, with the educational establishment placed as just one of the cogs in the larger system, is presented sketchily in the play, however, for it is not what mainly preoccupies Brenton. Writing in the nuclear world, which was just accessible to Brecht (who indeed made changes to the original text of *Galileo* in reaction to the testing of the first atomic bomb), Brenton has turned the earlier writer's conclusion on its head. The crime of Brecht's scientist was his recantation in the face of the Inquisition, thus denying science the possibility of public access. That of Lehrer is to have looked in the first place.

Brenton's scientist of the eighties takes issue with Brecht's, arguing that a latterday pope would do right to destroy the new knowledge.

I have come to the conclusion that all the investigations into the atom, discoveries, calculations, formulations, nearer and nearer to the description of the force of nature – the scientific quest of the century – is fundamentally malign. All the technology that has flowed from it, atomic fission, power stations to bombs, the actual material – is malign. Get your head round this one, philosopher. What if the most unnatural thing our species can do, is to understand nature itself? Malignity! In the ideas, in the idea of the ideas. If I were religious – and thank the fuck I'm not – I'd start talking about evil.

Lehrer and his brilliant student, Gilly, are easily manipulated pawns in the political machinations that emerge in the second half of the play; and Gilly's gesture in posting the information that the Western establishment has taken from them through the letter-box of the Russian Embassy has about it a sense of romantic futility. Unlike the escapist Lehrer, she has acted directly, but the question that the play leaves as, in effect, unanswerable is that of what ultimately can be done. Lehrer joins Gilly at the Peace Camp, and the audience is left with an ambiguous blackout, the protesters caught on the wires. Visually, the final image works in two directions: are Brenton's characters attempting to break into the missile-base, or are they attempting the act, first contemplated in *The Churchill Play*, of breaking out from the prison? Brenton remains as resolute in his desire to find answers, as he is in his refusal to provide glib solutions.

Edgar's route to Greenham Common in *Maydays* is very different. The play is a vast sweep through a post-war socialist history of Europe. A variant of epic in structure, one scene develops from another, as lights cross-fade, and trucks are moved in and out. The effect is to suggest a continuity of action that plays against the historical and geographical jumps made by the narrative. It is thus formally less broken than *Destiny*, which was much nearer the basic Brechtian model. It suggests a need for the

221

audience to make connections between the various parts of
the play, something that is further stressed by Edgar's now
familiar use of interrelated plots and character-groups.

Edgar's landmarks are all public ones: May Day 1945
(though significantly opening not with the Labour victory,
but with a Communist rally); Hungary in 1956; the
beginnings of CND in 1962; events between the spring of
1968 and the Vietcong victory of 1974; and then a
sequence that moves from the immediate lead-in to the
1979 Election to the present day and Greenham Common.
But, if the progress of the narrative is to be traced by
reference to public events in the socialist calendar, Edgar is
far more concerned with the thinking behind individual
choices and actions than in any of his previous adaptations
of the epic.

Although there is an appropriately large cast, the action
is chiefly centred on the reactions of three individuals, from
different generations, to this socialist history, parts of
which they have each entered at various times, and out of
which they will each move, towards versions of a right-wing
stance. The dominant concern of *Maydays* is with defection, and with an analysis of the reasons for these individual
defections from Left to Right.

The young man addressing the Communist rally at the
beginning is Jeremy Crowther. Through the play he will
move from leaving the Party in the aftermath of Hungary
(the direct experience of which will start the second man,
Pavel Lermentov, a dedicated Russian Party-member, on
the road to his own defection); drifting into teaching in a
public school, whilst still regretful that he was too young to
fight in Spain (the school where the third man, Martin
Glass, is first radicalised by his opposition to nuclear
warfare); into the academic life in 1968 (where Glass is
beginning his move towards a revolutionary position); and

finally into a hard-right stance as a part of a caucus intent on consolidating an anti-socialist future for Britain (in which he will be joined by Glass, now disillusioned with revolutionary politics, and safely ensconced on *The Sunday Times*; though not by Lermentov, who has left Russia after many years in labour camps but who will not give his support to their movement).

However, although Edgar's use of the three central protagonists allows him to cover a vast amount of ground, there can be little doubt where the real interest of the play lies. Glass is the most developed character, and it is his experiences, radicalised after 1968, that come closest to those of Edgar and the other playwrights discussed in this book. *Maydays*, as its title suggests, is both a chronicle of the history of all those May Days, and an International Distress Call. It questions, always disturbingly, and frequently in a wickedly funny way only perhaps possible with the benefit of hindsight, what happened to the revolutionary urges of an entire generation of the disaffiliated Left. In the final scene, Glass meets up with an old comrade and lover, Amanda, at the Peace Camp. Ironically, flushed with money and success, he has just repurchased his old family-home, a vicarage where his father had led protest to the first generation of nuclear weapons, immediately adjacent to the base and now in use as part of the Peace Camp.

MARTIN: So what's your present bag, then? Apart, that is, from Battered Lesbians against the Bomb?
AMANDA: I'm running a resources centre.
MARTIN: Well, well, well. I run a XJ12.
AMANDA: There's gold in them thar Tory think-tanks, then?

MARTIN: Well, silver, certainly . . .

AMANDA: We produce a kind of newspaper. Do have a copy.

MARTIN: Thanks. Well, this is all quite clear. 'Facilities'. 'Advice Bureaux'. The Women's Movement. Peace Groups. 'Black Defence Campaigns'. From whom does who wish to 'reclaim the night'? What in the name of all that's holy is 'alternative technology'?

AMANDA: Oh, you know, finding ways of making things that people actually need. Like, ploughshares, as opposed to swords.

But Edgar's starting-point with communism, and its betrayal into Stalinism, is far from peripheral. Edgar's is no local parish history of the British Left. The international connections are always there to be made, and parallels between the move of communism from revolutionary party to bureaucratic orthodoxy, and the tension in modern British socialism between the desire for individual spontaneity and the need for collective organisation, are stressed frequently. Glass is, indeed, attacked by both Trotskyites and anarchists on his inability to accept leadership, by leaders and by all respectively. It is a point made by the leader of Socialist Vanguard, to which Glass was briefly aligned. Addressing a univerity protest-meeting in 1968, James Grain comments on the slogan on a banner, 'The Revolution is the Festival of the Oppressed', noting that it is from Lenin, but that it is only half the quotation:

Revolutions are festivals of the oppressed and exploited . . . At such times the people are capable of performing miracles. But we shall be traitors and betrayers of the revolution, if we do not use the festive energy of the masses to wage a ruthless and self-sacrificing struggle for the direct and decisive path.

Edgar's move away from an agit-prop form, which, as he said, had effectively attempted to do without psychologically conceived characters, towards a political drama in which free play is given to the individual, is largely a response to his growing awareness of the problems raised by the two halves of Lenin's quotation. Without organisation, *Maydays* suggests, any hopes for a socialist future are futile; but without the, frequently unseen, struggles of individuals for freedom, the struggle will not be worth attempting. So, this remarkable play ends, not with the bang of nuclear war or the whimper of unheeded Western protest, but back in Moscow. Two men on bicycles had earlier arranged to meet at night so that one might take the manifesto published by the other for his unofficial trade-union to the West.

> KOROLENKO: Well, then?
> PUGACHEV: How long?
> KOROLENKO: How long?
> PUGACHEV: Do you think you'll last? A week, a month, a year?
> KOROLENKO: Maybe. Who knows? 'May Days'.

That this play, concerned exclusively with a meticulous examination of the state of socialism, should find a home in the new Barbican Theatre in London – and that it should furthermore do so only to the surprise of the right-wing critical mafia – is a measure of how far political theatre has developed in Britain since 1968. And, whilst it is not true to say that political theatre dominates the major subsidised theatres, it is certainly a major presence; and it is accompanied by an alternative-theatre circuit that is better organised and in a more healthy condition than it has ever been. That this has been accompanied by a move towards the right in public political circles, gives rise to the question with which I started. Is this evidence of genuine cultural penetration, or of containment? It is a question that preoccupies all the writers I have discussed, but I sense no let-up in the struggle.

By a curious coincidence, this last chapter was completed the day before the screening of David Hare's film *Saigon: Year of the Cat* – curious coincidence because, although the script for the play was completed some four years ago, it has been a long time in the making; and its belated appearance, with its echoes of the anti-war struggles of 1968, leading to the American withdrawal from Saigon in 1974, create a strange link between the beginning and the end of the period I have been considering.

Hare's play deals with the last days in the American occupation of Saigon. The North Vietnamese are expected daily, plane-tickets to America are at a premium, and the administration belatedly makes efforts to get rid of all the evidence that will connect the South Vietnamese collaborators with it. But the American Ambassador refuses to accept the inevitability of defeat, and, as the last helicopter leaves, the central character, Chesneau, a CIA agent, remembers too late that he has not destroyed the list of South Vietnamese agents; that he has unwittingly committed the final act of betrayal on the people that the United States has pledged itself to help.

> *Inside the helicopter the group has settled, cheerful . . .*
>   *Suddenly he remembers*
> CHESNEAU: Shit.
> JUDD: What?
> CHESNEAU: I've remembered . . .
> JUDD: What?

CHESNEAU (*looks down, appalled, disturbed; avoids the question*): Something.

JUDD (*a joke*): Do you want to go back?

CHESNEAU (*turns, looks back, the truth dawning on him of what he has done.*)

CHESNEAU (*under his breath*): God forgive us.

PILOT: Hey, you guys. We're all going home!

Fast fade.

In the wake of Grenada, with the war posture of the US in Lebanon and the promise of further intervention by Reagan in Central America, and with the first Cruise missiles already installed at Greenham Common, there is a certain grim irony in the timing of this film. In the midst of a still-collapsing economy, this offshore island is going through some rapid rethinking about international politics as well as domestic. One speech in *Thirteenth Night*, from Jack Beaty's dream of addressing the audience at Westminster Hall – a play that was broadcast for the first time on the radio this week, to complete the coincidence – keeps coming into my consciousness:

Abandon nuclear weapons and we leave the Western world. And the Western world leaves us. I mean, of course, American money. But since half our country is owned by America we would be left a bleeding corpse on the shore of Northern Europe. Right! The only course, nationalise American assets. And get poorer. For the cost of international sanity will be poverty. Which can only be made tolerable by a new equity. A new social justice – the policies we have all striven for. With new friends abroad. For socialism in this country will, like it or not, drive us to our only moral place in the world.

227

Britain must join the Third World. New friends. And a new enemy. America.

But then, *Thirteenth Night* is only a dream, and it is only a play.

Notes

Only Chapters 1 and 4 have numbered notes. In the other chapters, shortened references are given in parentheses, and full details can be found in the bibliographies for the individual playwrights, or in the general bibliography. In the parenthesised references and below, the following abbreviations are used:

P & P   Plays and Players
TQ   Theatre Quarterly.

In Chapter 2, all unlocated quotations are from unpublished interviews of Howard Brenton by the author.

Place of publication London unless otherwise stated.

1. 1968 and All That: Agit-Prop or 'Avant-Garde'

1. Jonathan Hammond, at the Society for Anglo-Chinese Understanding conference 'The Politics of Culture – China and Britain', held at the Roundhouse, London, 1972; quoted in *Time Out*, June 1972.

2. Alain Touraine, *The May Movement: Revolt and Reform*, trs. L. F. Mayhew (New York: Random House, 1971) p. 64.

3. David Edgar, 'Political Theatre', published in two parts in

Socialist Review, 1 April and 2 May 1978; later republished as 'Ten Years of Political Theatre, 1968–78', in *TQ*, VIII, no. 32 (1979).

4. Stuart Hall, Raymond Williams and Edward Thompson (eds), *New Left May Day Manifesto* (1967; rept. Penguin, 1968) p. 1.

5. Ibid.

6. Catherine Itzin, *Stages in the Revolution: Political Theatre in Britain since 1968* (Methuen, 1980) p. 1.

7. Cf. *Ten Days that Shook the University* (Situationist International); also Raoul Vaneigem, *The Totality for Kids*, trs. Christopher Gray and Philipe Vissac (Internationale Situationiste).

8. Peter Stansill and David Mairowitz (eds), *Bamm: Outlaw Manifestos and Ephemera 1965–70* (Harmondsworth: Penguin, 1971) p. 131.

9. Published in Bordeaux, Apr 1968, and reproduced ibid.

10. Edgar, 'Ten Years of Political Theatre', *TQ*, VIII, no. 32.

11. Sylvia Harvey, *May '68 and Film Culture* (British Film Institute, 1980) p. 12.

12. Howard Brenton, 'Petrol Bombs Through the Proscenium Arch', *TQ*, V, no. 17 (1975) p. 20.

13. Peter Ansorge, *Disrupting the Spectacle: Five Years of Experimental and Fringe Theatre in Britain* (Pitman, 1975) pp. 1–2.

14. David Hare, 'Humanity and Compassion Don't Count', *P & P*, Feb 1972, p. 20.

15. John McGrath, 'Better a Bad Night in Bootle . . .', *TQ*, V, no. 19 (1975) p. 54.

16. Brenton, 'Petrol Bombs', *TQ*, V, no. 17, p. 7.

17. Hare, 'Humanity and Compassion Don't Count', *P & P*, Feb 1972, p. 18.

18. McGrath, 'Better a Bad Night in Bootle', *TQ*, V, no. 19, p. 54.

19. From an unpublished interview with Catherine Itzin, quoted in *Stages in the Revolution*, p. 139.

20. David Edgar, 'Towards a Theatre of Dynamic Ambiguities', *TQ*, IX, no. 33 (1979) p. 4.

21. McGrath, 'Better a Bad Night in Bootle', *TQ*, V, no. 19, pp. 48–9.

22. John McGrath, *A Good Night Out. Popular Theatre: Audience, Class and Form* (Methuen, 1981).

23. Edgar, 'Ten Years of Political Theatre', *TQ*, VIII, no. 32.

24. Edgar, 'Towards a Theatre of Dynamic Ambiguities', *TQ*, IX, no. 33, p. 13.

25. Ibid., p. 10.

4. Coming to Terms with the Seventies: Fusions

1. Clive Barker, 'From Fringe to Alternative Theatre', paper delivered at the Conference on British Drama and Theatre in the Sixties and Seventies, Wilhelm Pieck University, Rostock, Sep 1976; published in *Zeitschrift für Anglistick und Amerikanistik*, vol. 26, no. 1 (1978) p. 62.

2. Itzin, *Stages in the Revolution*, p. 158.

3. *Guardian*, 12 July 1978.

4. 'The Man behind the Lyttelton's New Play', *The Times*, 10 July 1976.

5. Brenton, 'Petrol Bombs', *TQ*, V, no. 17, p. 12.

6. Sandy Craig, 'Unmasking the Lie: Political Theatre', in Craig (ed.), *Dreams and Deconstructions: Alternative Theatre in Britain* (Amber Lane, 1980) pp. 30–1.

7. McGrath, *A Good Night Out*, pp. 98–9.

8. Richard Seyd, 'The Theatre of Red Ladder', *New Edinburgh Review*, Aug 1975.

9. *P & P*, Dec 1972, p. 32.

10. Edgar, 'Ten Years of Political Theatre', *TQ*, VIII, no. 32, p. 29.

11. Louis Althusser, *Lenin and Philosophy and Other Essays*, trs. Ben Brewster (New Left, 1971) p. 204.

12. Brenton, 'Petrol Bombs', *TQ*, V, no. 17, p. 14.

13. Howard Brenton, 'Messages First', *Gambit*, VI, no. 23 (1973) p. 26.

14. John Arden, *To Present the Pretence: Essays on the Theatre and its Public* (Methuen, 1977) p. 158.

15. Edgar, 'Towards a Theatre of Dynamic Ambiguities', *TQ*, IX, no. 33, p. 8.

Bibliography

Place of publication London, unless otherwise stated. For abbreviations, see Notes.

HOWARD BRENTON

Published Plays

All published by Eyre Methuen, unless otherwise stated.

Revenge (1970).
Plays for the Poor Theatre (*The Saliva Milk-Shake*, *Christie in Love*, *Gum and Goo*, *Heads*, *The Education of Skinny Spew*) (1980).
Lay-By, collaboration with Brian Clark, Trevor Griffiths, David Hare, Steven Poliakoff, Hugh Stoddart and Snoo Wilson (Calder & Boyars, 1971).
Plays for Public Places (including *Scott of the Antarctic* and *Wesley*) (1970).
Hitler Dances (1982).
Magnificence (1973).
Brassneck, collaboration with David Hare (1973).
The Churchill Play (1974).

232

Bibliography

Weapons of Happiness (1976).
Epsom Downs (1977).
Deeds, collaboration with Ken Campbell, Trevor Griffiths and David Hare, in *P & P*, May 1978.
Sore Throats (1979).
Trs. of Bertolt Brecht, *The Life of Galileo* (1981).
The Romans in Britain (1980).
Thirteenth Night and *A Short Sharp Shock* (1981).
Trs. of Georg Büchner, *Danton's Death* (1981).
The Genius (1983).

Articles and Interviews

Brenton, David Hare and Snoo Wilson, 'Getting the Carp out of the Mud' (on *Lay-By*), *P & P*, Nov 1971.
Peter Ansorge, 'Underground Explorations: Portable Playwrights', *P & P*, Feb 1972.
'Disrupt the Spectacle, the Obscene Parade: Bring it to a Halt', *Time Out*, 22 June 1973.
'Disrupting the Spectacle', *P & P*, July 1973.
'Messages First', *Gambit*, VI, no. 23 (1973).
'Interview', *Guardian*, 9 May 1974.
'Petrol Bombs through the Proscenium Arch', *TQ*, V, no. 17 (1975).
'The Man Behind the Lyttelton's First New Play', *The Times*, 10 July 1976.
Interview with Ronald Hayman, *New Review*, 1976.
'Meet the Wild Bunch', *The Sunday Times*, 11 July 1976.
'How a Bitch was Ditched in the Name of Satire', *Guardian*, 20 June 1980.
Philip Roberts, 'Howard Brenton's Romans', *Modern Drama*, XXIII, no. 3 (1981).

DAVID HARE

Published Plays

All published by Faber & Faber. (See also Howard Brenton.)

Slag (1970).

New British Political Dramatists

The Great Exhibition (1972).
Knuckle (1974).
Teeth 'n' Smiles (1975).
Fanshen (1976).
Plenty (1978).
Licking Hitler (1978).
Dreams of Leaving (1980).
A Map of the World (1983).
Saigon: Year of the Cat (1983).

Articles and Interviews

'Humanity and Compassion Don't Count', *P & P*, Feb 1972.
'Current Concerns', *P & P*, July 1974.
'From Portable Theatre to Joint Stock ... via Shaftesbury Avenue', *TQ*, v, no. 20 (1975).
'Turning over a New Life', *P & P*, June 1975.
Peter Ansorge, 'David Hare: A War on Two Fronts', *P & P*, Apr 1978.
'A Lecture given at King's College, Cambridge' (1978), in *Licking Hitler*.
Radio Times, 12 Jan 1980.
'After *Fanshen*: A Discussion', in David Bradey, Louis James and Bernard Sharratt (eds), *Performance and Politics in Popular Drama* (Cambridge: Cambridge University Press, 1980).
'Ah! Mischief: The Role of Public Broadcasting', in Frank Pike (ed.), *Ah! Mischief: The Writer and Television* (London: Faber & Faber, 1982).

TREVOR GRIFFITHS

Published Plays

All published by Faber & Faber, unless otherwise stated. (See also Howard Brenton.)

Sam, Sam, in *P & P*, Apr 1972.
Occupations and *The Big House* (Calder & Boyars, 1972).
The Party (1974).
Apricots and *Thermidor* (Pluto, 1979).

234

Bibliography

All Good Men and *Absolute Beginners* (1977).
Through the Night and *Such Impossibilities* (1977).
Comedians (1976).
Trs. of Anton Chekhov, *The Cherry Orchard* (1978).
Country (1981).
Oi! for England (1982).
Adapt. *Sons and Lovers* (Nottingham: Spokesman, 1982).

Articles and Interviews

'A Play Postscript', *P & P*, Apr 1972.
Kenneth Tynan, 'Party Piece', *The Sunday Times*, 16 Dec 1973.
Peter Ansorge, 'Current Concerns', *P & P*, July 1974.
Albert Hunt, 'A Theatre of Ideas', *New Society*, 16 Jan 1973.
'Transforming the Husk of Capitalism', *TQ*, VI, no. 22 (1976).
'From Home to House', *Times Educational Supplement*, 25 June 1976.
Interview with Pat Silburn, *Gambit*, VIII, no. 29 (1976).
'Interview', *Leveller*, Nov 1976.
'Interview with Raymond Williams', *Leveller*, Mar 1979.
Leonard Goldstein, 'Trevor Griffiths' *The Party* and the Left Radical Critique of Bourgeois Society', in *Political Developments on the British Stage in the Sixties and Seventies* (Rostock: Wilhelm-Pieck-Universitat, 1976).
'On *Sons and Lovers*', *Socialist Worker*, 23 Jan 1981.
'A Novel Lawrence', *Radio Times*, 10 Jan 1981.
'*Reds*, White and Blue: The Politics of Colour', *New Musical Express*, 17 Apr 1982.
'Enabling Perception to Occur', *Liberal Education*, no. 45 (Spring 1982).

DAVID EDGAR

Published Plays

Two Kinds of Angel, in *The London Fringe Theatre* (Burnham House) (1975).
Dick Deterred (*Monthly Review Press*, New York, 1974).
Wreckers (Eyre Methuen, 1977).
Destiny (Eyre Methuen, 1977).
Ball Boys (Pluto, 1978).

New British Political Dramatists

The Jail Diary of Albie Sachs (Rex Collings, 1978).
Mary Barnes (Eyre Methuen, 1979).
Teendreams (Eyre Methuen, 1979).
Nicholas Nickleby, Parts I and II (Dramatists' Play Services Inc., 1982).
Maydays (Eyre Methuen, 1983).

Articles and Interviews

'Green Room: Against the General Will', *P & P*, May 1973.
'Residence Permits', *P & P*, July 1975.
'Theatre, Politics and the Working Class', *Tribune*, 22 Apr 1977.
'Exit Fascism, Stage Right', *Leveller*, June 1977.
Racism, Fascism, and the Politics of the National Front (Institute of Race Relations, 1977); repr. from *Race and Class*, XIX, no. 2 (1977).
'Political Theatre, Part I and Part II', *Socialist Review*, 1 Apr and 2 May 1978; repr. as 'Ten Years of Political Theatre', *TQ*, VIII, no. 32 (1979).
'Towards a Theatre of Dynamic Ambiguities', *TQ*, IX, no. 33 (1979).

GENERAL BIBLIOGRAPHY

Books

Ansorge, Peter, *Disrupting the Spectacle: Five Years of Experimental and Fringe Theatre in Britain* (Pitman, 1975).
Arden, John, *To Present the Pretence: Essays on the Theatre and its Public* (Eyre Methuen, 1977).
Bigsby, C. W., *Contemporary English Drama*, Stratford-upon-Avon Studies 19 (Arnold, 1981).
Bock, Hedwig, and Wertheim, Albert, *Essays on Contemporary British Drama* (Munich: Max Hueber Verlag, 1981).
Chambers, Colin, *Other Spaces: New Theatre and the RSC* (Eyre Methuen, 1980).
Craig, Sandy, *Dreams and Deconstructions: Alternative Theatre in Britain* (Amber Lane, 1980).
Elam, Keir, *The Semiotics of Theatre and Drama* (Eyre Methuen, 1980).

Bibliography

Goorney, Howard, *The Theatre Workshop Story* (Eyre Methuen, 1981).

Harvey, Sylvia, *May '68 and Film Culture* (British Film Institute, 1980).

Hunt, Albert, *Hopes for Great Happenings* (Eyre Methuen, 1976).

——, *The Language of Television* (Eyre Methuen, 1981).

Itzin, Catherine, *Stages in the Revolution: Political Theatre in Britain since 1968* (Eyre Methuen, 1980).

Kerensky, Olga, *The New British Drama* (Hamilton, 1977).

Lambert, J. W., *Drama in Britain 1964–1973* (British Council, 1974).

McConville, Maureen, and Seale, Patrick, *French Revolution 1968* (Harmondsworth: Penguin, 1968).

McGrath, John, *A Good Night Out: Popular Theatre: Audience, Class and Form* (Eyre Methuen, 1981).

Mairowitz, D. Z., and Stansill, Peter, *Bamm: Outlaw Manifestos and Ephemera, 1965–70* (Harmondsworth: Penguin, 1971).

Marowitz, Charles, *Confessions of a Counterfeit Critic* (Eyre Methuen, 1973).

Pike, Frank (ed.), *Ah! Mischief: The Writer and Television* (Faber & Faber, 1982). (With contributions from Edgar, Griffiths and Hare.)

Taylor, J. R., *The Second Wave: British Drama of the Sixties* (Eyre Methuen, 1978).

Touraine, Alain, *The May Movement: Revolt and Reform*, trs. L. F. Mayhew (New York: Random House, 1971).

Trussler, Simon (ed.), *New Theatre Voices of the Seventies* (Eyre Methuen, 1981).

Wandor, Micheline, *Understudies: Theatre and Sexual Politics* (Eyre Methuen, 1981).

Articles etc.

Barker, Clive, 'From Fringe to Alternative Theatre', *Zeitschrift für Anglistick und Amerikanistick*, xxvi, no. 1 (1978).

Barker, Howard, 'Energy – and the Small Discovery of Dignity', *TQ*, x, no. 40 (1981).

Bigsby, C. W., 'The Politics of Anxiety: Contemporary Socialist Theatre in England', *Modern Drama*, xxiv, no. 4 (1981).

New British Political Dramatists

Birchall, Bruce, 'Down with Illusion', *Socialist Review*, 1978. (A reply to Edgar's 'Political Theatre'.)

Campos, Christophe, 'Paris after the Revolution', *TQ*, I, no. 3 (1971).

Cohn, Ruby, 'Modest Proposals of Modern Socialists', *Modern Drama*, XXV, no. 4 (1982).

'Grant Aid and Political Theatre: 1968–77, Part I and II', *Wedge*, I (Summer 1977) and II (Spring 1978).

Grillo, John, 'An Excess of Nightmare', *Gambit*, VI, no. 23 (1973).

Hammond, Jonathan, 'A Potted History of the Fringe', *TQ*, III, no. 12 (1973).

Hennessy, Brendan, 'London's Theatre of the Fringe', *Gambit*, IV, no. 16 (1973).

Holme, Horst, 'Political Analysis, Theatrical Form and Popular Language &c', in *Political Developments on the British Stage in the Sixties and Seventies* (Rostock: Wilhelm-Pieck-Universitat, 1976).

Klotz, Gunther, 'Alternatives in Recent British Drama', in *Political Developments on the British Stage in the Sixties and Seventies* (Rostock: Wilhelm-Pieck-Universitat, 1976).

McGrath, John, 'The Theory and Practice of Political Theatre', *TQ*, IX, no. 35 (1979).

'Political Theatre for the Eighties: Debate in Progress', *TQ*, IX, no. 36 (1980).

'Political Theatre', *Gambit*, VIII, no. 31 (1976).

Shank, Theodore, 'Political Theatre in England', *Performing Arts Journal*, Winter 1978.

'The State of the Nation's Theatre', symposium in *TQ*, III, nos 11 and 12 (1973).

'Theatre Survey no. 1: Guide to Underground Theatre', *TQ*, I, no. 1 (1971).

Williams, Heathcote, 'Corrugated Iron in the Soul: The Community Plays of Rough Theatre', *TQ*, VIII, no. 29 (1978).

Wilson, Snoo, 'A Theatre of Light, Space, and Time', *TQ*, X, no. 37 (1980).

'The Year of the Cheviot', *P & P*, Feb 1974.

238

Index

Index

Index

Index

Index

Index